Big Picture Economics

Big Picture Economics

*How to Navigate the
New Global Economy*

Joel Naroff
Ron Scherer

WILEY

Cover design: Michael J. Freeland
Cover image: © Photodisc / Jupiter Images

For Cindy
     —Joel

For Kathy
     —Ron

Contents

Preface

At times, the economy may seem like a washing machine with economic news sloshing all over the place. Consumer spending is up; the stock market is down. The Federal Reserve is lowering interest rates; Congress is cutting spending. Sometimes it may seem hard to believe anything ties it all together.

In *Big Picture Economics: How to Navigate the New Global Economy*, we show that there is one thread that holds it all together: Context.

Every sector of the economy—the consumer, business, the Federal Reserve, and Congress—all need to look at what's going on around them when they make critical decisions buying new products, building new factories, hiking or lowering interest rates, or setting budget goals.

To help us reach that conclusion, we talked to real people. A truck driver explains how he sees the economy firsthand as he barrels down the highway and how it affects his financial decisions. The manager of a Tex-Mex restaurant chain describes the economics of making tacos and enchiladas in the middle of a recession. An administrative assistant, who had been furloughed, shares her budget-cutting secrets as she watches her paycheck shrink. A former president of the Dallas Fed describes how the central bank makes decisions. And an ex-staffer of a key congressional committee talks about how our politicians make decisions that affect us all.

At the same time as we are talking to real people in *Big Picture Economics*, we are trying to give a deeper perspective on economics, sometimes known as the Dismal Science. We look at the factors that make up the business cycle, as well as discuss global issues and taxation. We discuss whether a balanced budget is good, bad, or irrelevant. We delve into monetary policy, examining why the Federal Reserve has kept interest rates low for a long time. And we try to give some historical perspective on how we got to where we are.

To illustrate that we are all economists, we talked to the mayor of Tampa, Florida, about how he copes with running a city during a time when tax revenues are falling. One of his economic indicators: Are young people out walking their dogs? Yes, he sees it as part of context—an indication more people are living downtown.

The president of Arizona State University considers himself an education architect, redesigning the learning landscape at one of the nation's largest universities. But he also tells us how he had to don an economist's hat once the state legislature made a major cut to his funding.

Indeed, many of the people we talked to opened up about how the Great Recession—the one that began in 2007—influenced them. Yes, there were a lot of belts being tightened, but we also found that tough times stimulate a fair amount of creativity. A restaurant manager decided that he would offer patrons specials they couldn't refuse so people would get used to eating out even when the economy was tanking. A president of the university started online courses that quickly brought in $100 million. A mayor tried to figure out ways to attract the type of business that would keep his daughter from moving away in search of rewarding work.

To better understand context and the corporate mind-set, we explore the inner workings of a huge new semiconductor factory to find out what economic factors made the owner of the factory decide to invest billions of dollars in the middle of the recession. In the same chapter, we also talk to a merger master, who helps corporations decide whether it's a good time to buy or sell assets.

At times, Congress may seem to ignore what is happening in the economy. To get a deeper understanding of how Congress does or does not use context, we talked to a former staffer who worked on a key budget committee. He explained the context around some curious political decisions. In *Big Picture Economics*, we also look more closely at one of the largest parts of the federal budget—health care. It may sound counterintuitive, but we find that the rate of growth of health care spending is slowing. But a doctor who treats overweight patients every day warns that the drop may be only temporary unless we start to control what we eat.

In the last chapter of the book, we try to look into the future. We opine that one thing is certain: the rate of change is accelerating. In that chapter is a short discussion about the possible future of flying robots. Perhaps they could be used by farmers to examine their crops more closely, said one of their creators. After the chapter was written in late 2013, Jeff Bezos, the chief executive of Amazon.com, told the CBS show *60 Minutes*, that he could envision the online retailer making deliveries to customers using what Amazon calls octocopters. Yes, very similar to the flying robots at Hearst. Getting government approval to use them could be a few years away—if it ever comes. But who knows—books may get delivered to your doorstep by an octocopter in the future.

All of this came together for us in a relatively short period of time. One of us is an economist and the other a journalist. In November 2012, over lunch at a mall in suburban Pennsylvania, we started to fill a legal pad with ideas, which eventually became chapters. That set us off on the adventure of writing a book. We can't promise exotic locales, but we found that places such as Saratoga Springs, New York, and Bayonne, New Jersey, offered plenty of surprises in the world of economics. We hope you take the trip with us to discover why context matters in *Big Picture Economics*.

Acknowledgments

Writing this book was a collaboration—and not just between Joel and Ron, but also between the authors and all the people who helped make this book happen. A community effort, if you will.

For Joel, this book has been a long time in the making. For several years, a number of fellow faculty members at the Pennsylvania Bankers Association Advanced School of Banking, including Jim Clarke, Lyle Sussman, and Lance Kessler, suggested that I write a book. They were part of my e-mail list for my economic commentaries. The thought at the time was to make a collection of those notes since they were usually short, funny, irreverent, and to the point.

It was an interesting idea to essentially write a book that used my signature commentary called "In a Nutshell." However, I never really wanted to write a book. I never thought I had the staying power to do all that it takes to complete such an undertaking. Indeed, I often refer to myself as the ADD economist since I constantly wander around when I give talks or do research.

Out of the blue, Bill Falloon of John Wiley called and asked if I was interested in writing a book. Like a fool, I said yes. We agreed to a contract and off I went. And did very little. Bill was extremely patient, but events caused me to push back the writing. Without his willingness to create new deadlines and his understanding of the issues that were causing the delays, this book would have been scrapped a long time ago.

Eventually, my wife, Cindy, in cahoots with my son, Adam, both of whom had been extraordinarily supportive of my efforts, decided I needed some real pushing and nagging. Cindy gave me a deadline, at which point I either had to get it done or give it up. That is when I decided I couldn't do this alone. So I called Ron, who had been interviewing me for years about economic issues when he was at *The Christian Science Monitor*. Though Ron was usually on deadline, we not only talked about the issue at hand but we had many fascinating conversations about all sorts of economic problems. I knew we could work together, so I told him about the book and asked if he wanted to be a co-author. We met, discussed how it would work, and Ron's enthusiasm rekindled mine. In less than a year, the book was written.

In coming up with and refining the ideas in this book, over the years there were many friends, colleagues, and business reporters, including but clearly not limited to David Kotok, Rick Lang, Marty Crutsinger, Steve Liesman, Tim Mullaney, Paul Davidson, Rex Nutting, Brian Toolan, Danielle Kurtzleben, Bob Moon, Joe Liro, Mike Connor, Mark Zinman, Joe Besecker, Gary Pulcini, Don George, and Mark Fox, who knowingly or unwittingly helped me hone my thinking on so many of the issues discussed. They were guinea pigs for my thoughts, but thankfully they didn't recognize how crazy I was. They bear no responsibility for anything that is written and would probably demand that I say so.

But, ultimately, it was Cindy's confidence that I could actually write a book that made this possible.

In Ron's case, as a journalist with over 40 years of experience, he has amassed a significant list of people whom he called on for help in finding people to interview, potential sources of information, and suggestions for ways to illustrate economic concepts.

When looking for information, one of the best places to start is with a librarian. Ron is particularly grateful for the help provided by long-time friend Leigh Montgomery, who is the librarian at *The Christian Science Monitor*. Even though Ron had retired from the

Monitor in 2013, Leigh continued to help with suggestions and potential sources.

Another librarian, Ben Gocker, at the Brooklyn Public Library, was also helpful when Ron wanted to find the location of Flatbush National Bank, where the first bank-issued credit card was issued. Ben pulled out hard copies of 1940s magazines that included ads from the bank. The simple ads got Ron headed in the right direction to find the bank, which had become a furniture store.

A former journalist-colleague at the *Monitor*, Alexandra Marks, fielded Ron's panicked phone calls, always offering useful suggestions. Alex was particularly helpful on the issue of the fracking of natural gas, which she wrote about for a cover story for the *Monitor*'s weekly magazine in April 2012.

In 2012, Mayor Bob Buckhorn of Tampa came to New York to talk about how the Republican convention would help his city. He handed Ron his card and said to call at any time. Thanks to Bob's administrative assistant, Bridgett McCormick, who made that happen, finding time for Ron to talk to her busy boss.

At a holiday party in 2012, Ron ran into Chris Owens, the executive director of the National Employment Law Project. She offered to help with the book, which she did. But she also got some of her colleagues to pitch in, and Ron is grateful to both Mike Evangelist, who provided the data showing that most of the jobs since the end of the recession have gone to seniors, and Mitch Hirsch, who helped locate Griffin "Griff" Coxey, who brought to life the difficulties of being over 55 and looking for a better job.

Over the years, the firm Development Counsellors International (DCI) has introduced Ron to scores of mayors, businessmen, and local or regional economic development entities. For this book, Susan Brake and Brooke Carrillo came through with some key interviews with people who gave him perspective on Northeast Indiana, a region Ron would have overlooked otherwise.

One of DCI's former clients was the Saratoga Economic Development Corporation, which put Ron in touch with Travis Bullard, who could explain in layman's terms how his firm, GLOBALFOUNDRIES, makes semiconductor chips. The Saratoga folks, Shelby Schneider, former director of marketing, and Dennis

Brobston, president of SEDC, came to New York for coffee, where they put into context where Bullard's company fit into the scheme of things.

Ron also wants to thank a whole flotilla of public relations people who normally ask media types, "When is the interview going to run?" In this case, many of them had to line up clients under the premise that the book would be out in the spring of 2014. In other words, there would be no instant gratification.

Early in the book, Norita Taylor of the Owner-Operator Independent Drivers Association helped Ron find truck driver Scott Grenerth, who moves large coils of steel from the steel mill to the users. Scott turned out to be a real gem, even calling Ron when he was trying to maneuver his rig through a lake-effect snowstorm in Indiana.

Ron would also like to thank Jeff Crilley, a Dallas-based public relations blizzard who through the years has helped Ron. He corralled Scott Nordon of the Tex-Mex restaurant Posados.

Thanks also to Virgil Renzulli of Arizona State University, who helped track down the very busy president of ASU, Dr. Michael Crow, ASU economist Dennis Hoffman, and Jenny Kampp, who was full of ways she saved money during hard times.

For years, Carrol Van Stone of Van Stone Publicity in Shepherdstown, West Virginia, has called Ron right around the holidays to pitch some of her retailing clients. But when she called about a client who could talk about mergers and acquisitions, the connection did not gel—at least until the book, when Ron realized Carrol could help with her client David Braun.

Many journalists have turned to the Brookings Institution in Washington for perspective. Ron is no exception and wishes to thank his old friend DJ Nordquist as well as Rachel Harvey, who helped locate the very busy Elizabeth Kneebone.

Another important Washington source for journalists is Roberton "Bob" Williams, a fellow at the Tax Policy Center, a joint venture between Brookings and the Urban Institute, who helped to give some perspective on changes in the tax law. Thanks also to the Urban Institute's Stuart Kantor.

Ron is also grateful to other PR types, including Jim Engelhardt of the Manufacturers Alliance for Productivity and Innovation; Molly

Battles of the Rosen Group; Lara Wade of the University of South Florida; Andrea Hurst, who represented research firm CoreLogic; and Catherine "Caytie" Daniell of the National Center for Policy Analysis, who helped Ron get some time with Bob McTeer, former president of the Federal Reserve Bank of Dallas. Many thanks also to Jeff Lenard of the National Association of Convenience Stores, who helped Ron find Greg Parker; and thanks to Aaron Ellis, who worked with Ron on port issues related to trade. Thanks to other people on the docks, particularly John Pope in Long Beach, California, and Patricia Cardenas in Corpus Christi, Texas.

Ron and Joel also wish to thank Wiley senior development editor Meg Freeborn, who helped the duo navigate around the shoals encountered by the authors in their first book.

There are likely scores of other people Ron and Joel have missed who made suggestions for the book. Thanks to all for the help.

Chapter 1

Introduction to the Economics of Context

Economic thinking, whether we recognize it or not, is an essential part of household, business, government, and Federal Reserve decision making. But how do we use economic information to make intelligent decisions so we can make our lives or businesses better? The answer is not complex, but it does require a certain logic that is too often missing in most economics books.

When it comes to using economics to help make decisions, what matters most is context. While economists like to argue that theory is the truth, theory only gets you so far. Economics and economic policies don't operate independent of the way people think and react. Economics is all about taking human reactions and creating a way to understand how those decisions are made. Those reactions will differ under a variety of economic circumstances. Thus, you need to know where you have been and where you are so you make a correct decision about how you can go forward.

If real people or real businesspeople want to manage their lives or their companies in a way that actually takes into account the economic factors in which they are operating, they need to know why the growth, decline, or stagnation they are experiencing is occurring. That is because we haven't repealed the business cycle.

It is all about where you are in the business cycles and how outside factors, such as the world economic activity as well as human perceptions, combine to create the economy we must deal with. And, most important, it needs to be recognized that conditions change and any business decision must be made in the context that what currently exists may not be the case going forward.

We will look at examples from two different industries—trucking and hospitality—to see what context means in the real world.

Adapting to the Economy—View from the Cab of a Truck

In the trucking business, the difference between a down time in the economy and a buoyant economy can be felt in the pocketbook.

During dry times, truckers sit around waiting for loads to haul. Competition for the few available loads is fierce. To save money, truckers put off buying new equipment.

But when the good times are rolling, truckers rock. They can pick and choose where they want to go and when they want to go there. They can buy vital fuel-efficient equipment that can save them money in the long run or just make the rig look good. Trucker Scott Grenerth, who has been driving since 2002, has seen it all. Here's how the business cycle matters to him.

When Grenerth pilots his powerful tractor-trailer down the highway, he sees more than the road ahead—he sees the economy. He has that unique view because most of the time he's moving large coils of steel that are used to make vehicles.

In a typical day, Grenerth, who owns and operates his own rig, picks up a coil of steel at a mill in a place such as Burns Harbor, Indiana, and then drives it 463 miles to a steel service center in La Vergne, Tennessee, near where a Nissan plant turns out vehicles.

As he makes his run, he gets a rough idea of what's going on— or not going on—at the auto plants by looking at the lots where they store cars until they get an order from a dealer to ship them.

Is the lot full? Is it empty?

On a day when the lake-effect snow was slowing traffic as he arrived at a steel plant to pick up a load, he talked on his bluetooth phone about his experience when the economy was at its lowest point in the recession.

"Anytime I drove past any of the auto plants, whether Detroit-based companies or Japanese-based, or the BMW plant down in South Carolina, any of the plants—and I see them pretty good from the cab of the truck—you could tell the number of vehicles sitting in their lots ready to ship out," he recalls. "I mean I am going 65 miles per hour, and you can see there are 20 of them sitting there. You can easily estimate it and that is not normal."

And, of course, Grenerth could also tell how bad the economy was by what was happening to him. After delivering a load, he would pull into a truck stop and sit there with other truck drivers waiting for a dispatcher to offer him an assignment.

"If I arrived first thing in the morning, I would not get a load to pick up until the next day," he says. "So I would miss an entire day's work to make some income."

Bottom of the Recession

He remembers what turned it around for him: the Cash for Clunkers program started in 2009 by President Obama. The federal government, in an effort to stimulate the economy and help the auto industry, gave individuals cash to trade in gas guzzlers for new cars. The plan, which cost Uncle Sam over $2.8 billion, resulted in about 700,000 trade-ins, according to the Department of Transportation, which managed the program.[1]

In addition, under the American Recovery and Reinvestment Act (ARRA) of 2009, the Obama administration gave extra tax breaks for small business.[2]

According to the IRS, the ARRA allowed small businesses the option to expense up to $250,000 of the cost of certain equipment and property. And the IRS, on its web site, said many small businesses that had expenses exceeding their income for 2008 could carry back their losses for up to five years instead of the normal two years.[3]

However, Grenerth says that he did not get any help from any of the government programs. "My truck was already paid off by then," says Grenerth. "To the best of my knowledge, there was nothing substantial in the way of government programs that I used."

From the Bush Economic Stimulus Act of 2008, Grenerth and his wife did get a rebate check, which would have been about $1,200. "I have no clue what happened to that money," says Grenerth. "It went in the checking account and got spent."

As Detroit recovered, Grenerth's business started to improve as well. In fact, by January 2013, the economy had improved so much that his dispatcher at Fikes Truck Line, Inc. in Hope, Arkansas, which leases his rig, was offering him loads 24 hours in advance.

What the Business Cycle Meant to the Business

But there is also no question that the downcast economy affected his business and his life. For a trucker, one of the major factors in whether they make any money is how much they spend on fuel. Fuel is critical since they put so many miles on their trucks: Grenerth estimates he logs 120,000 miles a year. In early 2013, his 2002 International 9200 had over 1,120,000 miles on the odometer. So his big white truck has burned a lot of diesel.

One way to cut down on fuel consumption is to install what are called "low rolling resistance" tires. He describes the tires as made of compounds that lower the rolling resistance of the tire. "It takes less effort to get down the road," says the trucker.

Grenerth had wanted to switch to the tires before the recession, but they were an expensive purchase. Once things slowed down, so did the idea of getting the new tires.

"When you are not making as much profit as you were before, you are more likely to say, 'Put that on the backburner,'" he says. And, indeed, they went on the backburner until 2012.

At the same time, as things slowed down, Grenerth became a lot less picky about his jobs. For example, when times are good, he'll ask his dispatcher to try to find a load at the end of the week that will get him relatively close to his home in Arlington, Ohio, which is about an hour south of Toledo. But as he waited for work, he told the dispatcher, "I'll take whatever and wherever you've got. I need to go where loads are available."

Like a lot of truckers, the 44-year-old Grenerth gets to experience the ups and downs of the economy firsthand—in fact almost before most people because he hauls semiprocessed material that is used to make other things.

The closest to the economic action are the truckers who move goods to retailers, says Grenerth. When consumers pull back, merchants stop ordering. Goods back up at the warehouse. "People who are hauling goods to the retailers are feeling it pretty close to the economy when it slows down," he says.

But, eventually, the company buying the goods stops ordering as well. And that's when Grenerth feels it. "I know if it slows down for me, it's eventually going to slow down for everybody else," he says.

Of course, Grenerth was correct.

During the recession, at the same time Grenerth was waiting at truck stops for work, the restaurant business was struggling to fill tables, which leads us to the next example.

The Service Sector—The Enchilada Stops Here

The restaurant industry is particularly tied to the business cycle and consumer confidence. When times are good, Americans go out to eat. And, for the most part, times have been good and the restaurant industry has grown.

According to the National Restaurant Association, industry sales in current dollars have increased from $239 billion in 1990 to a projected $660.5 billion in 2013, an increase of 176 percent.[4] The Restaurant Association says the industry share of the food dollar has grown from 25 percent in 1955 to an estimated 47 percent in 2013.[5]

However, there have been some minor downturns in sales during economic sniffles in 1974, 1980, and 1991. By far the worst fall-off in dining out was in 2008 and 2009 when the economy caught a really bad cold. According to Restaurant Association data, inflation-adjusted sales fell 1.2 percent in 2008 and 2.9 percent in 2009.[6]

Although sales dropped, many consumers just scaled back where they ate, says Mary Tabacchi, an associate professor of food and beverage management at the Cornell School of Hotel Administration.

"If they were eating at a better restaurant, they might have just scaled down to T.G.I. Friday's," says Ms. Tabacchi. "If they had been eating at T.G.I. Friday's they might have scaled down to something cheaper. The consumer does not stop going to restaurants."

The belt tightening in the most recent recession caught Posados Restaurants, based in Tyler, Texas, by surprise. Here's how the changing economy affected this growing regional chain and what they did to adapt to the shifting context around them.

Texans love their spicy beef and bean chimichangas, burritos stuffed with ground beef, diced tomatoes, and shredded lettuce, and fried chalupas, which are crispy on the outside and filled with chicken and beans on the inside. More cheese on everything, thank you.

Restaurant entrepreneur Andy Gugar understood this craze for spicy food, and in 1987 he decided to build a full-service Tex-Mex restaurant in Tyler, Texas, in the eastern part of the Lone Star State.

With only $50,000 in his pocket, he opened up Mercados. For his first two years he and his wife worked 20 hours a day building up the restaurant customer by customer. He started expanding the full-service casual-dining concept into a chain called Posados.

At first it seemed too easy.

"There have been years like 2004 to 2006 when all you had to do was show up to make money," recalls Scott Nordon, the chief operating officer, who started working for Posados in 2001.

"It gave you a false sense of security. We'd say, 'Let's put up more stores, expand the overhead.'"

Expansion was relatively easy. GE Capital was providing loans at what seemed like a good rate to the company. With sales growing and money available, expansion seemed to make sense.

Posados grew from East Texas to Dallas and into Louisiana. By 2007, right before the recession, there were 14 Posados. For the managers, it seemed like the good times would not end.

Before the recession, on a Saturday night—the busiest night of the week—Nordon says there could be a 30- to 45-minute wait for a table. The average location could ring up about $12,000 to $14,000 in sales.

Helping to drive sales is the upbeat mood in the restaurant. Background music helps give the restaurants a festive feeling. The beat of the music picks up through the day until by dinner the restaurant is throbbing with hip Latin music.

"The goal is that we want people to think they are on vacation in Mexico," says Nordon.

The Cash Register Stops Singing

But, on the down cycles of the economy, things are different. In 2009, the operative word for Nordon was "slower." Customers coming into the restaurants did not have to wait for tables. The buzz that comes from a full restaurant was missing. Instead of growing at a normal 2 percent to 3 percent per year, sales plunged 8 percent to 10 percent.

"It was shocking. It was a real eye-opener," says Nordon. He recalls the management at Posados having to spend extra time doing morale building for the staff.

"We kept telling them this is a temporary thing, we're going to come out of this even stronger on the other side," he says.

The downturn forced the Tex-Mex restaurant to look deeply at its own business practices.

"We had to ask ourselves what can we do without and what do we really need," says Nordon.

There were layoffs. The company decided to outsource purchasing, information technology (IT), and human resources. The goal was to cut corporate overhead but not diminish the dining experience by reducing wait staff or cutting back on the quality of the food.

"We did not want to sacrifice the guest experience," recalls Nordon.

Managers were told to let customers know how much they appreciated their business.

"When those guests come in, wrap your arms around them, thank them for coming in," Nordon told his managers. "You have to make sure they are getting the best possible product, the best food and service because there are so many dining options out there."

The economic downturn also forced Posados to go after customers it would have turned down when times were good.

"I know there were catering orders where the customer would say we only have $5 or $6 per person to spend on the event," he says. "Before, we would have shied away from it, but now we were saying, 'Someone is taking that money—why not let it be us?'"

During the downturn, Posados found that customers became very price conscious. Instead of ordering two margaritas, they only ordered one. They looked for specials. Nordon refers to it as "managing the bill."

Observing this, the restaurant decided to use it to their advantage. It offered a promotion every day of the week of $6.99 for any two items such as one taco and one enchilada, or one chimichanga and one burrito. Rice and beans were included. Nordon bought advertising on television and ran banners in the restaurants to let potential customers know what they were doing.

"Our customers went crazy," he recalls. "People who had been coming in maybe once a month or once every 21 days started coming in once a week," he says.

Posados became more creative. With the purchase of an adult entrée, they offered customers a "kids eat free on Mondays and Tuesdays" promotion.

"When we tried to take it away, the customers became real vocal about it, so we said why not go ahead and leave it in place," says Nordon.

While Posados was adapting to the changing economic landscape, U.S. government efforts to stimulate the economy had a very limited effect on Posados. After some people received rebate recovery credit in 2009, Nordon says they saw a spurt of new business for a few weeks. "Customers were actually talking about it—'hey, I got a stimulus payment and I'm coming out to eat.' That lasted about two or three weeks."

As a small business, Posados got no help from Uncle Sam. "We just had to suck it up," he recalls. One of the lessons of the downturn, Nordon says, is not to get too excited about the good times.

Celebrate for 15 Minutes

"What we've learned is to celebrate the good times but not for too long," he says. "We tell the managers when they have a good month, it's their 15 minutes of fame and then go focus on next month."

The downturn also made the company look more closely at its own expansion. It became much more conservative in its approach, which may also say something about why the post-recession economic expansion in the nation has been so slow.

Any new Posados are more modest in size—6,000 square feet instead of 12,000 square feet—a typical size for a prerecession location.

The new restaurants are also paid for with cash flow instead of bank borrowing. In fact, in 2013 Posados was close to paying off all its debt from GE Capital. "We don't want to deal with the banks—we want to be our own bank," he says.

Instead, Nordon envisions the company growing only as fast as its free cash flow. "If we follow that model and don't chase a rabbit down the trail we'll never go out of business," he says.

As both Grenerth and Nordon illustrate, it's vital to adapt to the business cycle.

What Does Economics Teach Us about Context?

Economics is sometimes called the Dismal Science. For many, that saying brings a shake of the head and a "you got that right" response. Whether it was the simple fact that the worst teachers we had were our economics teachers or the totally incomprehensible presentations we saw on television or at a luncheon, listening to an economist talk was the equivalent of mental torture.

The economics discipline is viewed as dense, confusing, and maybe most damning, having very little to do with the real world we all live in. Economists are seen as having been put on this earth to make weather forecasters look good since their prognostications are not thought to be very accurate, especially with all the caveats attached to them. Compound those criticisms with the unfortunate use of jargon, more often than not to confuse or make pronouncements sound more important than they really are and you understand why few people like to sit down and read about the economy. That is just wrong.

But the real problem with economics and economists is that the so-called economic gurus and popular writers too often provide information that is of little value to those who need the information to make critical decisions—households, businesspeople, and even those in government. For far too many, economics is really nothing more than the black arts, where mad economists put numbers into a black box and cryptically tell us the state of the economy and forecast where it is going.

While all that may be true, the term *Dismal Science* actually did not derive from our boring experiences in school or even the head scratching that the columnists or talking heads create. Its origin was the writings of economist Thomas Malthus, who theorized in his *Essay on the Principle of Population* (1798) that population would inevitably out-pace food production, and that would lead to starvation.[7]

If it wasn't bad enough that Malthus predicted famines would rule the world, he followed that up with a set of solutions that were even more depressing. Some of his suggestions included a greater death rate and limits on the birth rate. Basically, a distressing forecast about the world's inability to feed itself was coupled with solutions few would ever want to see come to pass.

Thankfully, Malthus was wrong. Indeed, he turned out to be, unwittingly, a classic example of a leading economist who failed to see that numbers and logical theories by themselves do not present a full or even accurate picture of the way the economic world could or would work. Theories and models by which economists, including Malthus, understand how the economy operates do provide critical insights into the real world. They are just not the be-all and end-all of analysis.

What Malthus failed to see was that the technology that was used in farming was already changing in ways that would reshape the way the agricultural sector would operate. The budding industrial revolution would allow land that was farmable but not reachable to be brought into productive use. Critically, it would also dramatically increase the supply of food by turning land that was for a variety of reasons previously unusable for planting crops into property that could be farmed very profitably.

The whole agricultural system would benefit from what we all now know simply as technological innovation. Tractors would replace oxen, and plantings would be done by machinery producing greater crop yields. Harvesting would use machines reducing crop loss, thus raising output. The new technology of agriculture would lead to rapidly rising production on the land already being tilled as well as on the new lands, increasing world food supply and staving off the famines that once seemed inevitable.

But Malthus was not totally wrong. His ideas had value, but only in a limited sense and in certain locations—another important lesson. Even in today's world, there still are countries where birth rates exceed the improvement in food production. Technology and its use is not evenly spread throughout the world. Those countries or regions where the ability to bring new farm land into productive use was limited or where the access to technology was restricted continue to this day to face problems meeting the food needs of their population. But the Malthusian theory had little relevance for much of the world where farmland could expand and machinery was available.

There was one last change that wasn't foreseen but flows directly from the changing agricultural technology: Agricultural supplies are no longer viewed as being limited to what any one nation can produce but what the entire world can create. The ability to feed everyone is not simply a national issue but a global matter. That is an example of how changes seem to pop up as the needs arise. Conditions change and it is the circumstances under which the theory is applied and the data are analyzed that makes all the difference.

The lesson from the Malthusian misreading of the changes that were already under way, not the ones that were not foreseeable, is that a theory that may sound logical on the surface can make for potentially really bad policy. By assuming that farmers could not feed the world, Malthus had to look toward controlling population. That is, if the problem is that food supply could not expand fast enough, reduce the demand for food! But population growth was not the issue: It was the way farmers operated that had to be restructured, including what crops should be planted, what sizes farms should be, and what technology should be employed to create the greatest amount of food.

In other words, Malthus wound up blaming the victim instead of getting at the root cause of the problem. Sound familiar? We seem to do that all the time. Inflation too high? Put in wage and price controls! Deficits too large? Raise taxes; no, lower taxes; no, increase spending; no, cut spending! When it comes to policies, sometimes keeping it simple is simply stupid, but we do that because it is too hard for many to recognize that the right thing to do depends on the circumstances in which the economy is operating.

Economic Theory and Fiscal and Monetary Policy

To bring this back to the real world of today, consider the issue of budget deficits. When the economy is weak, a rising budget deficit would be normal. Indeed, during slowdown it may even be good policy to have it increase. Falling business activity reduces employment and that leads to lowered business and income tax revenues. At the same time, spending on social programs such as unemployment insurance and food stamps soar. Is the rising government spending, much of which kicks in automatically, bad? Hardly, as they sustain families and maintain at least some level of spending. That is why they kick in automatically.

In contrast, when the economy is booming, you would expect tax revenues to rise and social spending to fall. That should automatically create a narrower budget deficit. Is that good? Well, if the budget deficit increases when the economy is booming, not decreases as expected, that could actually create more inflation, which is hardly a good thing.

If you come to the conclusion that the budget deficit should be reduced, what should be done about it? If you hike taxes to raise more money, the economy is supposed to slow and the deficit rise, right? Not necessarily. After President Clinton raised taxes in 1993, the economy went on the longest expansion in history, and six years later there was a budget surplus. But that doesn't mean it is good to raise taxes. In 2009, when the budget deficit was soaring because of the Great Recession, the last thing the economy could afford was a tax increase that would have reduced demand even further.

Will tax cuts raise or lower the deficit? Many believe strongly that lowering taxes would increase spending, accelerating growth and ultimately generating more revenues. But while President Reagan cut taxes dramatically and the economy boomed, the deficit also widened sharply. Similarly, when President George W. Bush reduced taxes in 2001 and 2003, growth picked up, but the deficit expanded as well. As those examples show, there is no such thing as a free tax cut, which pays for itself.

The reason for this confusion about the impact of the same policy—in this case, a tax increase—is that consumers and businesspeople react differently to tax changes when their economic circumstances differ. Lowering taxes when the economy is booming would likely mean more spending, but that could create real problems by adding to inflation. But lowering taxes when the economy is collapsing, such as in the spring of 2009, may not cause the economy to grow very much or at all. Households and firms might be more interested in hoarding money, so they have a cushion just in case their jobs are lost or their businesses falter, than in spending it. Under those circumstances, a tax cut could do little for the economy.

What is true for tax cuts is just as true for spending. When is the right time to cut government spending: when the economy is good, when it is bad, when the deficit is high, or when the deficit is rising? Do you really want to cut spending when the economy is in recession? Do you really want to increase spending when the economy is growing rapidly? Where you are in the business cycle—in other words, context—determines the answer, as there is no single approach that works all the time.

That need to understand the context in which policy is being made is true not just for our political leaders, who control taxes and spending, but also for the nation's central banker, the Federal Reserve. The Fed members look at not only where the economy currently stands when they make decisions on the proper level of interest rates, but also where it is going. A weak economy may require more stimulus, but not all the time. It could be the right move when there is a recession, but if inflation is out of control after many years of strong growth, lowering rates could be absolutely the wrong thing to do.

Finally, there is the issue of investing and the stock markets. Small investor timing of the equity markets is classic example of the failure to recognize context. It is frequently said that small investors get in at the top and sell at the bottom. They wait until prices have run up and then simply cannot pass up a "good deal." Prices always continue to go up, right? Unfortunately, wrong. After buying at the top when the economy is about to turn, they then wait until prices have bottomed before they sell. What goes up doesn't have to come down significantly, but it happens in a lot of cases. Understanding the context of the rise and fall of stock prices, not just that prices have gone up or down, is the difference between having a secure retirement and working until you are 80.

The point of all this is that economic logic can provide crucial information for decisions that are being made by every part of the economy such as businesses like Posados and small businessmen like trucker Grenerth. And while they have to figure out ways to cope with the business cycle, Washington institutions such as the Federal Reserve and the White House have sometimes had to find their way as well.

Notes

1. National Highway Traffic Safety Administration. Press release, August 26, 2009. www.nhtsa.gov/About+NHTSA/Press+Releases/2009/Cash+for+C lunkers+Wraps+up+with+Nearly+700,000+car+sales+and+increased+fue l+efficiency,+U.S.+Transportation+Secretary+LaHood+declares+program +%E2%80%9Cwildly+successful%E2%80%9D.

2. American Recovery and Reinvestment Act of 2009. Information Center Update, May 21, 2013. www.irs.gov/uac/The-American-Recovery-and-Reinvestment-Act-of-2009:-Information-Center.

3. IRS: Net Operating Loss Carryback, Sec. 179 Deduction and Other ARRA Business Provisions. www.irs.gov/uac/Net-Operating-Loss-Carryback,-Sec.-179-Deduction-and-Other-ARRA-Business-Provisions.

4. National Restaurant Association. Facts at a Glance." www.restaurant.org/News-Research/Research/Facts-at-a-Glance, February 6, 2013.

5. Ibid.

6. www.restaurant.org/Pressroom/Press-Releases/Restaurant-Industry-Outlook-Brightens-in-2010-as-S, February 6, 2013.

7. Essay on the Principle of Population. Printed for J. Johnson, in St. Paul's Church-Yard, 1798.

Chapter 2

The Federal Reserve, Congress, and the Use of Context in Economic Policy*

T his chapter discusses where context is currently used, such as Federal Reserve policy, and where context isn't used or, worse, is misused, such as in formulating tax policy and producing budgets.

In the previous chapter, we made the case that neither individuals nor executives look at the world the same way under all sets of economic circumstances. That we had to argue that context matters when

---

*All quotations not attributed to published sources are from personal interviews conducted by the authors.

it comes to the economic decisions of the average person is also a commentary on the way the world of economics sometimes works. It is just as odd that there are some who believe businesspeople think the same way whether their companies are booming or collapsing. But that is the way it is. We know, though, that context does matter to households and businesses.

But the reality that decisions have to be different given the context in which they are made is not limited to individuals and executives. Context is probably the most important concept in all aspects of the economy, especially public policy. That includes fiscal policy, which is the result of the many strange ways that Congress and the president come to an agreement on spending and taxing levels, as well as monetary policy, which is made by the Federal Reserve.

Public Policy Spreads a Wide Ripple

The importance of public policy is that it has a major impact on businesses and households. A healthy, vibrant private sector makes the U.S. economy hum, which even the most government-oriented person has to admit. Businesses create the jobs and the wealth in the economy.

But public policy has a major effect on how corporations operate. Whether it is through regulation, spending, and tax policies or the management of interest rates, the manner in which the government and Federal Reserve operate influences the ability of companies to grow and thus create the economic conditions where unemployment will be low and income and wealth gains strong.

Unfortunately, not every decision made by our elected officials or monetary authorities have the outcome that is desired. Indeed, fiscal and monetary policy sometimes winds up doing more harm than good. Whether they were implemented with good intentions or to impose a political or economic point of view does not matter: bad policy still creates real problems.

The reason that some policies, even those that appear sensible on the surface, miss the mark usually stems from a failure to develop and implement them in the context of where the economy is and where it is going. That is not to say we don't want the government or the

Federal Reserve to try to help. We do. But if context is secondary to economic or political philosophy it may be better for our policy makers to just stand there and do nothing.

Consider the debates and disagreements about the budget deficit that have been going on for decades. These have not been trivial arguments over whether the government should or should not spend more than it takes in. They are discussions about the priorities of government policy.

More recently, the political parties have gone to war over the need or desirability or necessity of "balancing the budget" or reducing the deficit. Some members of Congress have simply refused to vote for any budget that does not contain a reduction in the deficit. Others argue that deficit reduction should be done over time and fight for every penny of spending.

But the effectiveness of any decision on budget policy will depend on the shape of the economy at that time. Nothing shows that more clearly than a debate on February 26 and 27, 2013, between Federal Reserve Chairman Ben Bernanke and members of Congress when the Fed chairman testified before Congress as part of the semiannual Humphrey-Hawkins hearings to discuss monetary and economic policy.

The Fed chairman's testimony preceded the March 1 implementation of automatic budget cuts because Congress and the White House could not agree on ways to reduce the federal budget deficit. As a result of the impasse, $85 billion in cuts—known in Washington as *sequestration*—were scheduled to take place at the Department of Defense as well as such agencies as the Federal Aviation Administration (air traffic controllers), Department of Agriculture (meat inspectors), and the Commerce Department (National Oceanic and Atmospheric Administration and economic statistics), among other government agencies.

Since most entitlement programs and pension plans were excluded from the reductions, the impacts on the remaining programs were significant.

Bernanke, in his prepared remarks, thought the timing of the automatic spending cuts (which took place) was bad. Instead, he told lawmakers that they should consider replacing the near-term cuts with polices that reduce the federal deficit more gradually in the near term, but more substantially in the longer run.[1]

"Such an approach could lessen the near-term fiscal headwinds facing the recovery—while more effectively addressing the longer-term imbalances in the federal budget," explained Bernanke.

Earlier in his testimony, he pointed out what seems logical, cutting spending and reducing the deficit, might not turn out to be the case in the real world: ". . . besides having adverse effects on jobs and incomes, a slower recovery would lead to less actual deficit reduction in the short run."

But some fiscally conservative Republican members of the congressional committees pushed back irrespective of whether the timing of the cuts was good or bad.

At the Senate hearing, several senators took issue with whether there was a problem with cutting spending and whether the sequestration would hurt the economy. They argued that the cuts were necessary as a signal that Congress would deal with the budget deficit. That could help growth, if markets and businesspeople wanted cuts right now rather than over time.

Senator Toomey felt that even if the spending restrictions were implemented, nothing significant would happen to economic growth.

In the House, some of the representatives were also skeptical of the Fed chairman's comments.

Rep. Randy Neugebauer of Texas told Bernanke, "I found it was kind of interesting when you said that we need to take a slower approach to deficit reduction and that the economy, you know, couldn't withstand a major reduction in government spending. Don't you find that a little disconcerting that we have let the government become so much of the economy that cutting our deficit so that we don't mortgage the future of our children and grandchildren—should be even a consideration in deficit reduction?"[2] The Fed chairman's advice met with an even larger outcry from Republican Rep. Sean Duffy of Wisconsin who worried about rising interest rates once the Fed stopped being so accommodative. This could cause the federal budget to rise as interest payments climbed.

"So, we'd have an additional $200 billion to $300 billion of additional dollars going to service our current debt. Fair to say?" asked Duffy.

"That's right," replied Bernanke.

Suddenly, Duffy, with a hand going around and around, said he could see lights going off, sirens blaring over the prospect of additional trillions of dollars needed over 10 years to service the nation's debt as interest rates rise.

"And I'm almost setting a proverbial can on my counter and you're kicking it, saying, 'Listen, don't worry about $85 billion in cuts; do it a different day.'"

Pointing to his own chest, Duffy concluded, "I listened to what you are saying and I think you are giving cover to a set of policies that aren't responsible and we are all going to pay the price for the fiscal irresponsibility. And instead of encouraging responsibility, you come in and say, 'Listen, to cut 2 percent of our budget, you can't do it; it's going to have a great impact on our economy. Mr. Chairman, that doesn't make sense to me.'"

Bernanke replied that the cuts taking place in the spring of 2013, at a time when the economy was growing slowly, would cost a lot of jobs. The Congressional Budget Office (CBO) predicted sequestration could result in the loss of about 750,000 positions.

The prospect of fewer jobs did not seem to faze Duffy very much. Instead, he told Bernanke he thought there was already too much fat in the budget.

"And so on that point, how many jobs are lost if we cut the $27 million that go to Moroccan pottery classes? Or the $2.2 billion in free cell phones? We pay $700 billion (sic) to see how long shrimp can run on a treadmill. I believe we pay for the travel expenses for the watermelon queen in Alabama. There is fat in the budget."[3]

Of course, one man's fat is another man's job, and the effectiveness of any decision on budget policy will depend on the shape of the economy at any given time.

Clearly, government spending and taxing decisions, which economists call fiscal policy, cannot be made in an economic vacuum. Yet many still argue that all you have to do to balance the budget is to either cut taxes or raise taxes.

The problem is that there exists a disconnect between spending and taxing decisions and the impact on general economic activity.

We are acutely aware that tax policies affect how much money we have left in our paychecks at the end of the month. Households also clearly recognize that government spending decisions determine whether the roads are paved or filled with potholes. But the next step, relating the paycheck problems and the building of the park up the block to the rate of growth of the economy, is just not there.

So how do Congress and the administration actually figure out the budget?

The View from the Hill

In Congress, the budget process usually starts in late fall and early winter when the individual departments draw up their budgets and receive guidance from the Office of Management and Budget, which is responsible for devising and submitting the president's annual budget proposal.

By mid-January, the nonpartisan CBO has locked in its economic forecast for both the fiscal and calendar years, and by the first week of February the president's budget usually is revealed.

On the Senate side of Congress, the Senate Finance Committee has jurisdiction over tax, trade, and social welfare. The Senate Budget Committee's budget resolution sets the broad parameters for existing and proposed legislation.

On the House side, the Constitution requires all tax legislation to originate with the Ways and Means Committee, which also handles trade, health, and social welfare legislation. The House Budget Committee also tackles broad questions of federal spending and taxation.

In Washington, scores of congressional staff members work to try to make sure the various committees meet their deadlines and adhere to the law, but a joint budget resolution has not passed Congress since April 29, 2009, and congressional leaders have often bypassed committees.

One former staffer who follows Congress for Wall Street is Pete Davis, who first started working on the Joint Committee on Taxation in 1974 only two years out of the University of Rochester where he received a BA in economics. In 1981, he shifted over to the Senate Budget Committee for three years.

When Davis started working on Capitol Hill, he had no expertise in the federal budget. But his knowledge of computers led to his hiring to run the U.S. Treasury income tax model.

Becoming a staffer on the Joint Committee on Taxation put Davis into the center of the budget process.

Congress established the committee in 1921 when the lawmakers realized they needed some expertise to handle the implementation of the modern income tax, which had been created in 1913. At first, the income tax affected only a few very rich people but gradually it started applying to business and then to a larger segment of the population.

The committee, says Davis, became a repository of tax lawyers and economists who did nothing but work on tax bills.

But, Davis says Congress, in its wisdom, was also concerned that there might be some political favoritism in the way the tax laws were applied and some taxpayers might be getting some large refunds that they did not deserve. So, early on, Congress gave the committee the authority to audit any tax refund over a certain amount—an effort that continues to this day.

Congress's concern about budgeting came to the fore soon after Davis joined the committee.

In 1973, President Richard Nixon became upset with what he perceived as Congress's spendthrift ways. He refused to spend money in appropriations bills he had signed. Congress challenged this "impoundment" and eventually reached a compromise with Nixon. The end result was the 1974 Budget and Impoundment Act, which established the modern-day budget process.

To try to avoid making the economic forecast and cost estimates a political tool, the new law established the nonpartisan CBO to support the budget process.

"They have a really good group of outside economic advisers, top economists from Wall Street, and top economists from academia, who meet with them quarterly, and these are some of the least covered news events in Washington," says Davis. "But they matter because it is the beginning of the budget process."

Why the Economic Forecast Matters

The economic forecast is critical because it sets the starting line for the congressional budget process. Based on its economic assumptions, the CBO estimates what is termed the *baseline*, which is basically the amount of spending and revenue current law will produce over the next 10-year period.

A weak economy may mean tax receipts will be lower. In theory, lower tax receipts might be a constraint on spending. An economic forecast showing the economy with more zip might allow more spending or perhaps a tax cut.

"Once you've decided on the economic assumptions and the baseline that goes with those assumptions, you have effectively made most of the policy decisions," he explains. "And that's why these things are so hotly debated, which is why on occasion the committees will adopt their own modified economics and not the CBO's."

How can Congress or the administration make economic assumptions that affect the budget?

"When I was on the budget committee and we needed some more money to balance the budget, maybe we decide we're going to have a good year in corporate profits even if the economy is not doing too well," he recalls. "And, if you have more corporate profits, you have more corporate income tax."

In 1981, newly elected President Ronald Reagan assumed the economy would boom because of his record-breaking tax cuts, but interest rates would remain low. This became known as the "Rosy Scenario."

"No macro economist would agree you would have low interest rates with that much growth," says Davis. "With strong growth you get higher interest rates because there is greater demand for funds."

But, with low interest rates, Reagan could put together a budget with a low public debt component. This made it easier to argue that the budget was closer to balanced.

Economic Assumptions Matter: The Rosy Scenario

In hindsight, the Rosy Scenario did not play out as advertised. The budget deficit soared, rising from $78 billion in FY1981 to $127 billion the following fiscal year and $207 billion in FY1983.

Comics joked that Rosy Scenario was the highest-ranking woman in the Reagan administration. However, rankled conservatives maintained that the forecasts were simply different from those of the CBO and perhaps not that much different in terms of economic gimmickry than later presidents.[4]

Davis thinks the battle over Rosy Scenario marked the first time there was serious policy debate over economic assumptions in Washington. "And the media was pretty much of the opinion that Rosy Scenario was a fabrication," he says. "And, they were right but I can't prove it even though I was on the inside of it."

Rosy Scenario may have led to a loss of trust in the economic projections, says Davis. "So, thereafter, economic assumptions became a matter of partisan politics."

In some ways, Davis believes the debate over the economy is skewed in the administration's favor because the various departments are the main source of economic information to Congress. Although few people think the data are politically slanted, the interpretation of the data has a political effect.

For example, major data such as the Labor Department's monthly unemployment statistics and the Commerce Department's releases on the gross domestic product are delivered to the White House the night before they are released to the public. The Council of Economic Advisers quickly writes a summary of the data and an analysis.

"So the administration is the first one to put their spin on the economic numbers," says Davis. Of course, the opposition political party is quick to respond, issuing their own press releases.

But the importance in terms of economic context is that the economic view of members of Congress is up for grabs. "It's now a debate," says Davis.

"Prior to 1981 (Rosy Scenario) when the numbers came out, they came out. And the administration would basically put their spin on it, but you didn't get too much debate over the numbers or the economics or what the policy was."

From his 11 years working on budgets and even more watching the Hill for Wall Street clients, he thinks most members of Congress have a desire to show a balanced budget, which was last done in 2001 under President Clinton. "I can't count the number of times we put out balanced budget resolutions, after which we didn't actually get anywhere near balance, and in fact we went in the opposite direction."

Despite the members' desire to spend more than the United States collects, Davis says they generally understand economics.

"First of all, they are all lawyers," he explains. "And these are all smart people, but they have learned from hard political experience that if they accept the basic laws of economics, it will get them unelected. I can't count the number of times when very intelligent people have looked at me as if I were crazy when I told them something I thought was the most plain vanilla, nonpartisan, technically accurate statement you could make about the economy in one way or the other."

In late 1992, Davis began his own consulting firm, Davis Capital Investment Ideas, which advises clients on what goes on at his old stomping ground. From his perspective of being a part of or watching Washington, he thinks the battle over interpreting economic information—critical to understanding the context of the economy— has become far more intense in recent years.

"Now everything is debated and there is always a lot of spin over what caused any change in employment or economic growth or whatever," he says.

Does One Policy Fit All?

One of the biggest reasons there is confusion on the part of the public about fiscal policy is that too many of our elected officials have proposed and implemented policies that sound good when put into sound bites but don't stand the test of logic or economic analysis.

If there is one thing that encapsulates the whole absurdity of government policy, it is the view that one policy fits all. On one side you have a whole political point of view that has managed to simplify the world by saying there is a solution to our problems, and it is to simply cut taxes or cut spending. Got a problem with growth, cut taxes. Got a problem with the budget deficit being too large, cut spending. Got a problem with the economy not operating as efficiently as you would like it, cut taxes. Having a bad hair day? Cut taxes. Okay, the last one is pushing it a bit, but you get the point.

In contrast, there is a whole political strategy that takes the exact opposite approach to cutting taxes. Got a problem with growth, spend more. Got a problem with the budget deficit, raise taxes, especially on the wealthy. Got a problem with efficiency, reform the tax code by raising taxes, especially on the wealthy or special interests. Having a bad hair day . . . forget that one.

As we all know, the United States is a consumer nation, and we have built our economy on a thriving middle class that likes to spend money. So the logic is that a tax cut, which gives people more money, translates into more spending. But cutting taxes and having those tax cuts generate large increases in economic activity are two different things.

What we saw after the tax cuts in 2001 and 2009 was that reductions in taxes don't necessarily generate a whole lot more spending. The reason is obvious: While people or businesses may have more funds to work with, when they are worried about the future, they save instead of spend. Especially in 2009, while we were in the middle of the worst recession since the Great Depression, there were not many individuals or business managers who thought that taking the additional funds and going out and buying goods or investing or hiring made a whole lot of sense. Survival, not growth, was the operating plan. Consequently, the money was squirreled away, and the tax cuts did little to increase growth.

The lesson that should have been learned is that tax cuts that are implemented when households and businesses are uncertain about their future have limited capacity to move the economy. However, when the economy is getting better, it is likely that much of the newfound money in the paychecks or the corporate tills will wind up being spent on lots of new things. You have to pick and choose when to cut taxes, and that means context is critical.

The point is that when the our elected officials look at policy, they rarely look at it from the point of view of what will work best given the economic circumstances. Instead, they take a very limited view that their policies always make sense. Can you really argue that cutting taxes doesn't add to growth? Doesn't it make total sense that if you don't have enough money to pay your bills, you need to get more money and the best way to do that is to raise taxes? Well, the answer is "not necessarily," and that is not something that policy makers like to hear.

The misused concept that tax cuts increase growth has caused some unfortunate decisions on the part of our political leadership. Take the nugget that if you want to reduce the budget deficit, reduce taxes. The logic: Tax reductions get the economy growing faster and increase tax revenues. Using simplistic economic analysis, that actually seems to make sense.

What is wrong with that thinking? Well, it does not take context into account. Even if household purchases and business investment rise, there is no certainty that the added growth will make up for the loss of revenue that result from a tax cut.

What is forgotten is that everyone receives the tax break but not everyone spends more. Yes, growth may improve, but it may not do so by enough to compensate for the lower tax rates. The result would be rising budget deficits, not narrowing shortfalls. Indeed, economic studies have shown that at least over a period of two or three years, just about all tax cuts have led to lower tax revenues.

After the massive tax cuts in 2001 and 2003, projected budget surpluses turned into huge and rising budget deficits. Essentially, the economy did not respond strongly enough to the tax breaks to offset the loss of revenue from lower rates and special tax deals.

The reality is that there is no such thing as a free tax cut. You have to take the good parts, the reduction in taxes taken out of the private sector and the resulting higher spending, with the bad—the loss of revenues—which means you have to balance the two. And the extent of the loss of public-sector revenues and private-sector spending increases will be determined by the decisions of businesses and households, and that will depend on the context of the changes.

Similar discussions can be made about tax increases, spending cuts, and spending increases. While on the surface you would expect a tax increase to slow growth and thus cause deficits to rise, that just may not be the reality. Who gets taxed and how they react to those increases is what matters.

For example, the tax increase on individuals with family income over $450,000 may lead to relatively modest cutbacks in their spending. In contrast, the ending of the payroll tax holiday, which increased taxes on everyone, was a worry. When you raise taxes on lower-income households who don't have the savings to offset the higher taxes, something has to give. Usually, that is spending.

Similarly, spending increases don't necessarily cause the economy to surge. Clearly, there will be more growth as the government buys more goods or services or hires more people. But once the additional government spending ends, there may not be any new private-sector activity that is created to pick up the slack.

The total impact of the spending increases also depends on how the money is spent and what is done with the money by those firms who benefit from the new spending. Do firms hire more people, or do they simply work the employees already on their payrolls more. Companies that are still concerned about the future and that have employees who are underemployed because of a weak economy will not hire lots of additional workers, so the impact on growth will be limited. Finally, if goods and services are purchased from companies that outsource their production to foreign countries, the additional labor growth will occur outside the United States.

As for spending cuts, you need to know what spending is cut before you can even make the first statement about their impacts. A reduction in foreign aid assistance or subsidies for firms might lead to limited cuts in demand for U.S. products. Yet it is also very possible that a tax increase, spending increase, or spending cut could cause large changes in the economy, but that will happen only when conditions warrant it.

While fiscal policy has become a hostage of political theory, where context frequently gets trumped by philosophy, the other side of government action, monetary policy, has generally gone the opposite route—but not all the time.

The direction and impact of monetary policy—the setting of interest rates—is as dependent on the condition of the economy as is fiscal policy. In most cases, the Fed's decision on what to do about interest rates has been entirely a consequence of the monetary authorities' reading of the economic tea leaves.

Examples abound as to how monetary policy has not been held a prisoner of theory, but instead uses theory in a contextual manner. The actions of the Fed in fostering growth once the Great Recession ended and in taming the threat of high inflation in the early 1980s illustrate that monetary policy can be quite flexible.

A Bank Loaded with Economists

How does the Federal Reserve use context to set policy? Economist Bob McTeer got to experience the process firsthand when he became president of the Federal Reserve Bank of Dallas in February 1991.

When McTeer arrived at the Dallas Fed that winter, the U.S. economy was just barely recovering from a recession that was partially caused by the Fed's raising interest rates because of inflation worries and an oil price that had jacked up after Iraq invaded Kuwait in the summer of 1990.

On top of all that, savings-and-loan (S&L) associations that specialized in making home mortgages had cratered, which was particularly affecting the Lone Star State. "In the aftermath of the S&L banking crisis, Texas was undergoing what some people called a credit crunch," recalls McTeer. "And the officers and directors of the Dallas Fed seemed to be much more aware of that than the rest of the country, and so the Dallas Fed was sort of a leader in the system in being concerned about that and talking about it at system-wide Fed forums."

McTeer's initial experience at the Dallas Fed illustrates one important way the Fed keeps track of the economy: it uses its 12 district banks and their branches as windows on the national economy.

"At each meeting of the Reserve Banks and each meeting of the branches' board of directors, the directors talk about what they see in their communities," says McTeer, who guided the Dallas Fed for 14 years and had a total of 36 years working for the Fed.

"It's sort of like the canary in the coal mines; eventually, all this stuff will become part of the statistical apparatus, but before it has a chance to do that, it is sort of like an early warning system."

The Importance of the Beige Book

At the same time, each district reserve bank has a research staff that eight times a year calls local area businesses to ask about business conditions.

"This is an ongoing dialogue, not just choosing a different business every time," explains McTeer. "Research assistants in the research department will have 10 to 15 businesses that they regularly call and ask questions like: Are you adding workers, or are you shedding workers? Are your sales rising or falling? Are your inventories in line with where you want them to be?"

The information from all the calls ends up in a research product called the Beige Book (for the color of its cover), which typically runs about three pages per district. A typical Beige Book covers everything from ticket sales for Broadway plays to the level of the Mississippi River, important for shipping.

Although some economists consider the Beige Book to be of marginal value since it is anecdotal, McTeer says its importance is that the Beige Book sometimes captures early turning points in the economy before the statistical data catches up.

Some of the anecdotal information will also flow to the Federal Open Market Committee (FOMC), which decides interest rate policy and formally meets eight times per year. Each of the district presidents attends the FOMC meetings, but most only get to vote every third year.

Going into the meetings, the Fed's staff puts together a Green Book, which McTeer describes as a summary of what's going on in the economy, and a Blue Book, which outlines policy options. Those books are put together by one of the largest repositories of economists in the world.

According to the Federal Reserve Board web site, as of March 2013 there were over 300 PhD economists. They write about arcane issues such as the Anderson-Moore Algorithm, which the Fed's Web page describes as "a fast and reliable method for solving linear saddle point models" (basically a mathematical way to solve large computational models of the economy) to understandable surveys of small business.

From Beige to Blue and Green

The main discussions at the Fed's meetings are over the direction and intensity of the economy, particularly in how it relates to inflation and the rate of job growth.

"Traditionally, central banks are there to keep inflation down and to protect the value of the currency," says McTeer. But he notes that the Employment Act of 1946 made it a government responsibility to stimulate employment to hold unemployment down. Eventually, it became a dual mandate for the Fed to keep unemployment down and hold inflation in check.

As far as inflation is concerned, McTeer says the Fed prefers to use the Personal Consumption Expenditure price index, which is put together by the Bureau of Economic Analysis, a division of the Commerce Department. "Apparently, that is considered less distorted by housing than a couple of the others," says McTeer. "But you also watch things that you believe cause inflation like excessive money growth, excessive expansion of bank credit, and so forth," he says.

At the same time, the Fed monitors the employment situation. Although the Fed under chairman Ben Bernanke has set a target of reducing the unemployment rate to 6.5 percent, McTeer says the Fed usually monitors how many net new jobs are created each month as opposed to the unemployment rate.

"The Fed always believes the employment numbers are more sensitive to economic activity than the unemployment numbers," says McTeer, who in recent years has become a blogger and a distinguished fellow at the National Center for Policy Analysis, a Dallas think tank that has a free market orientation.

Slow growth in job creation is one of the reasons that the Fed has acted differently than it might have in normal times.

Fed Policy

The economy grew consistently after June 2009, the end of the downturn. Normally, one would have expected that monetary policy would have turned from aiding the economy through keeping interest rates low to watching out for inflation and raising interest rates. That was the normal course of action, and interest rates tended to rise not that long after growth reappeared. But that didn't happen. Instead, the monetary authorities determined that there were special circumstances that arose from the collapse of the housing and financial sectors that were holding back the economy from reaching its potential. Therefore, more help than normal was needed.

In essence, the Federal Reserve treated the Great Recession as a special situation, and uncharacteristic economic environments require nontypical monetary policy responses. In this case, it was determined that keeping interest rates extraordinarily low for an extraordinarily long period of time was the best course of action in order to insure a full economic recovery.

When it comes to interest rates, the Fed did the opposite in the early 1980s. After an extended period of high and rising inflation during the 1970s, Fed Chairman Paul Volcker decided there was no choice but to raise interest rates sharply if the inflationary cycle of higher wages and rising prices would ever be tamed. Monetary policy had to become extreme if inflation was to be tamed. He used what was ultimately nicknamed the "nuclear option" and drove short-term rates up to levels never seen before or since in this country.

The Fed policy worked and inflation was slowed in the early 1980s, setting the stage for better growth by the middle of the decade. It succeeded because Mr. Volcker recognized that circumstances, not theory, should drive policy. That is, it was not a matter of just raising rates enough to slow the economy, but maybe you had to burn down the economy in order to save it. He may have caused a recession, but he also created the conditions for better growth in the future.

Obviously, there is no such thing as normal monetary policy. Yet not all monetary policies make sense. The Federal Reserve under Alan Greenspan came to the conclusion that it could not or should not do anything about an economic bubble. When tech stocks soared in the 1990s and housing costs skyrocketed in the 2000s, the monetary authorities did little to slow the rises. The assumption was that restraining economic growth would cost the economy too much; it was not clear if the policy would succeed or that it was even possible to recognize a bubble until it actually burst.

The philosophy that the market knew best and the Fed should not interfere with it cost us dearly. It is fair to argue that the Great Recession was in no small part a consequence of the Federal Reserve blundering about home price increases and the effects of a housing bubble on the economy.

From Bubbles to Fed Meetings

McTeer recalls that Greenspan used to say that real estate is a lot of local markets instead of one national market. And while Greenspan might agree that there was some froth in some of those markets, McTeer recalls Greenspan "once humorously defined froth as little itty bitty bubbles."

McTeer thinks the reason the Fed misunderstood what was taking place in the economy in 2007 was that it did not understand how loans being made to people with less than stellar credit, termed *subprime loans*, could bring the entire economy down.

Many of these loans were collected together in packages and resold to global investors who wanted to beef up the return to their port-folios with the high interest rates being paid by subprime borrowers. Investors bought securities that were backed by assets—mortgages made to subprime borrowers. In theory, if the borrower defaulted, the home could be sold to cover the loan. However, no one figured that the default rates would drag home prices down by over 50 percent in some markets.

Some members of the FOMC certainly underestimated what was taking place in the economy, which was entering a steep reces-sion. According to the transcript of the September 18, 2007, meetings, released in 2013, some Fed district bank presidents were more con-cerned that the Fed was not adhering to its short-term interest rate target of 5.25 percent.

"I think allowing the fed funds rate to be so low for so long away from our target really creates a credibility problem for this committee," said Dr. Charles Plosser, the president of the Philadelphia Fed. "It puts us in an awkward position now because, in effect, it hasn't gone unno-ticed by the investment community."

Plosser was not alone. Gary Stern, president of the Minneapolis Fed, added his view that "when we establish a target, we have an obli-gation to achieve the target."

In addition, the Fed underestimated what the impact of the collapse in the markets would be on the banking system. According to the tran-scripts from that September FOMC meeting, Bill Dudley, then the Fed's manager of open market activities but soon to be the president of the Federal Reserve Bank of New York, told the members that the banks could have a potential earnings problem because of the disruption in their ability to syndicate loans.

However, Dudley told the committee, "I think the uncertainty about it will probably turn out to be more of a problem than the actual reality, but it's going to take time for us to find out what the actual reality is.

The Fed Goofs

As it turned out, the actual reality was far worse than anticipated. By October 2008, Congress had to authorize a $700 billion fund called the Troubled Asset Relief Program (TARP), which added capital to the banking system, helped prevent the collapse of the auto industry, and had to invest in the giant insurer AIG.

"From my perspective, one of the reasons people didn't get what was going to happen is that they never connected very well in their minds the subprime loans that were being made to securitization," says McTeer.

McTeer confesses he did not understand what was happening. "I remember in the early 1990s occasionally somebody would say banks are making loans that they know can't be repaid. And I remember thinking, 'Well, why would they do that?' I did not fully understand . . . that they would sell these loans as part of the securitization process. They just moved the risk to someone else."

McTeer says people in the Fed did in fact worry that there was a real estate bubble. But he says the view was that "what goes up can go back down, and there was no reason to expect it to be so catastrophic."

But the Fed may have also failed to judge the housing market in the context of the broader economy. What the Fed failed to recognize is that while it might be good when housing or stock prices rise sharply just after a major economic slowdown, it is not necessarily good when that happens after the economy has been expanding strongly for an extended period. That is, it was not a threat that home values finally started to jump in 2012, as it allowed the long recovery in the housing market to continue.

But in 2007, those home price gains were occurring after the housing market had reached record levels and the economy had been expanding solidly for an extended period. Then, the price surge represented a level of exuberance and irrational expectations that could not be sustained. The price bubble was a threat that had to be dealt with but wasn't. The context of price changes matters, and it should have made a difference on how monetary policy was conducted. Unfortunately, it didn't, and the bubble burst and the Great Recession followed.

The public policy disasters that have resulted from the failure to recognize context are legend. The huge budget deficits in the 1980s and 2000s were in no small part the result of the thinking that tax cuts can cure all. The Great Recession was set in motion by the Federal Reserve's misreading the economic landscape and trusting markets to work without the necessary oversight. The sluggish growth at the end of the Great Recession was at least in part a result of muddled thinking about what a stimulus bill should look like. In all those cases and so many more, simplistic thinking failed to recognize that policies work only when they are implemented in the context that makes sense.

Public policy failures usually result from not recognizing that the consumer and business reactions to the same policies differ according to their perceptions about current and future conditions. As we will see in the next chapter, people shape their actions based on the economy as they see it.

Notes

1. Federal Reserve Board transcript of Bernanke testimony.
2. www.gpo.gov/fdsys/pkg/CHRG-113hhrg80869/html/CHRG-113hhrg80869.htm, January 9, 2014.
3. Ibid, January 9, 2014.
4. For example, on April 4, 2011, Kevin Hassett, director of Economic Policy Studies at the American Enterprise Institute, argued that Reagan's forecasts were ridiculed because they were unconventional, not wrong.

Chapter 3

We Are All Economists and Don't Know It

We all have to make decisions that are shaped by the economy as we see it at the time: Can I afford a new bedroom set? Should I expand my business or cut back on my employees' hours? Should I buy a sirloin steak or ground chuck?

In this chapter, we look at how context determines not only what we buy but where we buy it. When we feel good about the future, it's off to the malls and the department stores. But even if we have the same income, when we are worried about losing our jobs, we may want to buy as carefully as possible. Under that set of circumstances, discount stores may become the location of choice. These are the trade-offs we make as we substitute one product or shopping location for another, and that is what economics is all about.

There is nothing quite like a recession to make people focus on their choices. In Arizona, we find a household trying to make adjustments as a member of the family gets furloughed. In Tampa, the mayor tries to cope with shrinking revenues. The president of one of America's largest universities has to adjust to fewer state dollars for higher education. And a businessman fears the worst but decides to expand anyway.

Context Tells Us What We Can Afford

During the 1992 election campaign, in order to keep his frequently out-of-control candidate Bill Clinton from veering wildly from message, James Carville placed a sign in the campaign headquarters that said: "The economy, stupid." Over time, that saying morphed into the more recognizable "it's the economy, stupid." The message worked, and Clinton was elected president.[1]

But if the key to winning the presidency was focusing on the state of the economy and how to make it better, there also had to be a strong belief that the average person would understand what made the economy weak and what policies would bring stronger growth to the country. Though not directly discussed, there was a real faith that voters were better economists than anyone gave them credit for.

The reality is that we are all economists; we just don't realize that we use economics all the time in our daily activities and our workplaces. We make clear economic decisions when we go to the supermarket, buy houses or SUVs, accept job offers, or determine which restaurant to eat at or what kind of vacation to take. If we are small-business owners or a cog in a huge corporation, our actions have economic implications. And if we run small towns or large universities, it's the economy, and we would be stupid if we didn't recognize it.

Think about your trip to the supermarket. It would be nice if all we had to do was fill up the cart with whatever we wanted and pay for it. But most of us cannot do that. We have limited resources. It would be wonderful to eat the finest cuts of meat or the highest-quality seafood every night, but that is just not possible. We don't have the money!

The most basic concept in economics is that there is a limited amount of resources. Indeed, economists talk all the time about the "allocation of scarce resources between competing uses." Sounds complicated, right? Hardly. We all do that every day.

Let's go back into the supermarket. Since we don't have all the money in the world, or at least enough to not be worried about what to buy and what not to buy, we have to make hard decisions of what goods to put into our carts. Even if we don't budget exactly by setting a limit on what we can spend, we don't go up and down the aisles tossing just anything into the cart.

Instead, we decide how much we can afford to spend on meals. We allocate our money between breakfast, lunch, and dinner; proteins and vegetables; snacks and desserts, frozen and fresh products; healthy foods and junk foods; cleaning items and paper goods; pet products and light bulbs.

The list of decisions we have to make every shopping trip goes on and on but every one requires us to be an economist. Yes, we have to limit our total cost at the checkout counter, but we must do that in a way that also maximizes our health and enjoyment of life. Do we buy the Oreos or buy a roast? Do we buy the two-liter soda or the six-pack? Is it hamburger today or boneless chicken breasts? Pasta or steak? Name brand or store brand?

The mixture of goods that wind up in the shopping cart adds up to a lot of money but a lot of enjoyment as well. And, frequently, no two trips look anything like each other. We have different needs and desires at different times. We like variety, and we can satisfy a sweet tooth by buying cookies, ice cream, cakes, or candy. There are infinite choices, but we have to make them.

Critically, for shoppers, context matters. Every adviser tells you not to go shopping on an empty stomach. We all know the results of that. Our basket is filled with what we want now, and we wind up spending more than we probably would if we didn't have eating on our minds.

But the state of the economy also matters. When times are goods, it is easy to splurge. We feel comfortable about the future, and that makes it easier to spend more money. We buy the better cut of meat and the name brand product and treat ourselves to desserts and snacks. But when the economy is in recession and we worry about our jobs, store brands and hamburger look pretty good.

The changeover from high quality to lower—or perceived lower—quality and priced products is what economists call the *substitution effect*. When prices rise or incomes fall, we substitute goods we can afford for goods that are no longer affordable. That is precisely what happened during the Great Recession when many households started buying increased amounts of store brand products and other, lower-cost meats, poultry, and fish. As the economy recovered, shoppers started to "up-buy" or once again purchase the more expensive name brands and higher-quality goods.

Frugal in Arizona

In Phoenix, Arizona, Jenny Kampp knows all about economic trade-offs. Jenny, the mother of toddler Chloe, and her husband, Jon, fit the category of America's middle class. They live in a three-bedroom house with their Bichon Frise, Fozzy. Jon is in retailing; Jenny works as an executive assistant.

Before the recession hit, Jenny and Jon enjoyed going to local bars for happy hour with friends. But when the economic downturn started, Jenny says they noticed "things were sort of going downhill" even though both still had jobs. One of the first things they cut out were some of those happy hours. If they did go out with friends, they tried to make it on a night when drinks were two-for-the-price-of-one.

Then, as their perception of the economy darkened, they started to cut out going to restaurants and instead ate at home. Because they were eating in more, Jenny became far more price conscious. She started subscribing to the Sunday papers in order to get more coupons and look at the advertisements. She joined Groupon, a deal-of-the-day web site that sends vouchers for the specials that she signed up for.

As she got deeper into the frugality mind-set, Jenny also started to make even tougher economic decisions in the grocery store. Instead of buying brand-name products, she started to buy store brands of the same product. For example, she found she could buy the grocery store version of Wheat Thins. "They taste a little bit different," she says, but they save $1 to $2 a box.

As the Kampp family started to eat at home more, Jenny's mom gave them a subscription to a meal-planning service called the Six O'Clock Scramble. Each week the service e-mails her five dinners and a list of everything she will need for cooking. Aside from reducing the stress of worrying about what to make at night, it helped to cut down on impulse purchases.

"It's kind of like going to the grocery store on an empty stomach," she says. "It's a bad idea because everything looks delicious. But with the meal planning you know what you need, you have your shopping list, and then you are not as prone to deviate from the list."

Of course, they did not cut out restaurants entirely. But since Jenny is a vegetarian, they tend to eat at Mexican or Italian restaurants that have lots of vegetarian options in the menu. And one of their favorite restaurants, Buca di Beppo, often has coupons in the papers or online.

"Sometimes we will go do that and I know the servings are so huge that we will also have leftovers that we can eat another night of the week," she says.

The Economy Gets Worse

As the economy worsened, Jenny temporarily had her hours cut through a company-mandated furlough. "It definitely impacted me," she recalls. "I was like 'I need to cut out anything that I don't really need.'"

The family eliminated the movie channels on their cable network to save $30 a month. They cut their electric bill by agreeing not to use certain appliances, such as the dishwasher and the washer and dryer, during the peak hours of 3 P.M. to 6 P.M.

Luxuries became fewer and fewer. For example, Jenny cut trips to the beauty salon. "I previously would go to the salon and get a facial," she says. "I try to do that at home—you know, an at-home spa treatment because I can save so much more money," she says.

Jenny also started to look for any free things she could do with her daughter but still be stimulating. They found they could take Chloe to the park or to a lake to feed the ducks.

A membership in the Phoenix Zoo saved a lot of money compared to the cost of paying for each trip. "It's pretty expensive for a family of three to go to the zoo here, so a membership saved us a ton of money," says Jenny. To save even more money when they go to look at the cheetahs and zebras, Jenny packs a picnic lunch so they don't overspend at the concessions.

The downturn in real estate has also affected their outlook. Jon and Jenny purchased their house in 2008, when real estate prices had started to decline. But Jenny thinks it's likely that their home continued to decline in value, partly because two of their neighbors walked away from their homes.

The foreclosed homes were ultimately purchased and spruced up. But, Jenny says they have come to the realization that they will likely be in the house for another ten years. "We are not going to be able to turn around and sell it for as much profit until then," she says.

There was one economic trade-off Jenny and Jon decided not to make: cutting spending on day care for their daughter. "There were other places we could have gone that were maybe half the cost per week," she says. "But, you know, you get what you pay for, and I wasn't willing to do that. It's expensive, but it's worth it to me."

Public Officials as Economic Forecasters

If you think it is hard enough dealing with the crazies that populate government at all levels, imagine what it must be like when you also have to create a strong, vibrant economy while also balancing the needs of competing economic interests. That is what public officials do all the time, and the successful ones are not just good politicians but good economists as well.

A governing official is faced with a myriad of concerns. First and foremost is the budget. Budgets may sound like just a balancing act between revenues and expenditures, but it is not that simple. What is required is a forecast of what those two major items will be over the coming year.

Basically, if a budget is to be balanced—and at the state and local government level, that is a legal requirement—a mayor or governor has to be an economic forecaster. They have to make determinations about how fast the local economy will grow and what that means for jobs and income business activity.

What are the factors that matter most to the local political leader as economist? First, you have to know how you are doing. That is actually becoming easier than it had been. The information revolution has made data available in ways never before known. The housing market has information down to block levels. Data on tax revenues can be sliced and diced to understand what types of firms are growing or slowing.

Numbers are nice, but as an economist who has done forecasting for an extended period of time, a "feel" for what is happening is sometimes more important than the data. Indeed, there have been many times that I have written that the numbers just don't look right because they run contrary to normal trends or other data sources.

You have to augment the data with real-world experiences if you are going to understand how rapidly the economy is growing. Government officials who "take the pulse" of the electorate are also getting a feel for the unknowns in forecasting. If people feel uncertain, those negative views may not be seen in the data for months, but they matter when you are making a budget forecast. A cautious electorate might be pointing to a slowdown, and the worst thing you can do is overestimate growth and therefore revenues.

When it gets down to actually doing a forecast, it is critical to understand the basic structure of the local economy. While the national economy may determine overall growth rates, the devil is always in the details for forecasters. In the case of local economic analysis, the details are the key industries and sectors of the economy.

It is usually the case that a given area will grow at a different pace than the nation. Phoenix, Miami, and Las Vegas boomed in the mid-2000s because they were the center of the housing market surge. Energy price spikes have allowed places like Texas, Alaska, or, more recently, North Dakota to post growth rates that dwarf the national rates.

There are also special factors. In times of war, areas with major defense facilities spurt ahead, but when peace blossoms, they undergo huge adjustment problems. Areas with great tourist facilities tend to do really well but can suffer greatly in times of economic slowdowns. They may have more volatile economies. In contrast, retirement communities that are less dependent on job growth might rarely show higher than national growth rates but manage to do a lot better during the downturns. They have more stable economies.

Thus, the first thing state or local politicians must do is take stock of their strengths and weaknesses and how national trends interact with them in order to make a local economic forecast. That provides the basics for the revenue estimates any governor or mayor must make.

If budgeting is job one, building a stronger economy is job two. Every politician wants to look toward the future and create a better economy. That requires a longer-term forecast than with the budgeting process. Governing officials have to then recognize what the emerging economic trends are, and how those resulting changes will impact the local economy. It makes no sense to base a budget on a growing industry if the firms in those industries are being left behind.

When you think about it, a politician needs to be able to do both short-term and longer-term economic forecasting. For the budgeting process, understanding the next 12 to 24 months is usually good enough. But to build a better economic base, the next decade is crucial. It is doubtful that if you scratch a politician, you will find a person who views himself or herself as an economist. But it takes a good economic sense to be a successful political leader; just ask Bob Buckhorn, mayor of Tampa, Florida.

A Mayor as Economist

Economists like to consider themselves observers of human behavior. Are people optimistic? Are they buying new cars or used cars? Are they remodeling their homes or looking to trade up?

If economists are people watchers, consider Bob Buckhorn, the mayor of Tampa, Florida, an economist. Buckhorn says he can sense how his city is doing economically by walking and driving around Florida's third-largest city. Every day he tries to talk to as many people as he can: the drivers of the solid waste trucks, people out picking up groceries, merchants opening up their storefronts. He drives through upscale neighborhoods and areas of town that he describes as "teetering on the brink of some serious issues." And he keeps an eye on the bulldozers and dump trucks: are developers confident enough to build "spec" houses, or are they just doing remodeling?

"Well, I think for me, the prism through which I always think about economics and the economy and how it affects the city is through the eyes of my neighbors, friends, and constituents," says Buckhorn. "It's hard for me to separate my job from my personal opinion because as a mayor we feel the downturns as much as any elected official potentially could because it's our citizens that are affected most directly, whether it's by increased opportunities or unemployment or everything in between."

In terms of the economy, the nation's mayors often observe some of the subtle movements first. When a big employer in the city is even thinking about laying off workers, the mayor hears the scuttlebutt. And when a firm is thinking of expanding, the mayor usually wants to know what he can do to help.

In the case of Tampa, Mayor Buckhorn keeps an eagle eye on permit activity. From about 2008 to 2010, developers pulled back and permits declined. In 2011 and also in 2012, permit activity started to rise again.[2] "So that tells me people are moving dirt and throwing up steel again, which obviously translates into tax revenues for local government," he says.

But the mayor also has another more unusual way he gauges his local economy: he watches to see how many people are walking their dogs on the streets.

Yes, dog walkers.

"To me that is an indication that people are living downtown," explains Buckhorn. "Part of our mission is to stop the brain drain leaving Florida, which has been a one-way street, and to attract that creative class, those bright young professionals to downtown Tampa, specifically. So that's sort of my unofficial polling I do every day as I am driving around the city—how many young people I see walking dogs in the downtown corridor."

Tampa's Faulty Economic Model

Halting the brain drain is just one of Buckhorn's economic challenges. In 2011, his first year in office, he faced a $34.5 million deficit.[3]

To balance his budget, he eliminated 146 jobs. The following year, the budget gap shrank to $24 million and the city eliminated 30 positions. In FY2014, Buckhorn estimated a preliminary budget gap of $19.2 million, which he proposed bridging with increased property tax revenue and department reductions as well as some other changes.[4]

One of the major reasons for the red ink is that Florida has no personal income tax and instead relies on property taxes. "And, property taxes are cyclical, obviously, and very much tied to construction and the increase in valuation in people's houses," says Buckhorn. In Tampa, after rising steadily, property values peaked in 2009 and then began falling. According to Buckhorn's budget documents, property values had fallen 23 percent from their peak to 2014. Property tax revenue tumbled from $163.6 million in 2008 to an estimated $123 million in 2014.[5]

The shortfall in property taxes is just part of the problem, says the mayor. He thinks Florida relies on what he terms a *faulty economic model*, which he describes as a three-legged stool. One leg of the stool is agriculture, such as citrus groves and vegetable farms. Another leg of the stool is tourism, mainly people fleeing the winter in Canada and the northeastern states or taking their children to attractions such as Disney World. Finally, the state relies on developers putting up new subdivisions and advertising to retirees to "come on down to the Sunshine state." He thinks the real estate leg of the stool has been the most problematic.

In the mid-2000s, speculators started snapping up homes and condos in the expectation that the value of the house would rise. The buyers hoped to "flip" the house by selling it quickly to someone else. When the real estate bubble burst in 2009, banks foreclosed on thousands of homes in Florida that had been purchased by speculators who could not sell the properties and could not make the mortgage payments. "You can't build subdivisions for people that don't exist," says Buckhorn.

His solution to Tampa's problem is to try to change what he terms the city's "economic DNA."

Changing the Economic DNA

To change Tampa, he wants to start to add more "value-added clusters of jobs" that will allow Tampa to keep its educated young people from leaving. "My daughters and that intellectual capital, that creative class, is not coming to Tampa for a call center job," he says. Instead, Buckhorn wants to build on existing strengths, such as education, that he thinks can provide sustainable jobs.

Tampa is home to the University of South Florida, which has 47,000 students at its three institutions in Tampa, St. Petersburg, and Sarasota-Manatee. Importantly, USF, considered a major research university, gets about $400 million a year in applied research grants, mostly from the federal government and private partnerships.

"So the key for us is to find how to move it out of the halls of academia and the Petri dishes and into the marketplace to create jobs, to create companies and new technologies," says Buckhorn.

Tampa already has a model for this: it has worked with USF to help locate the Center for Advanced Medical Learning and Simulation (CAMLS) in downtown Tampa and away from its campus. CAMLS is a training center for simulation in robotics for doctors and surgeons from all over the world.

Buckhorn says the CAMLS center is expected to generate about 15,000 room nights a year in downtown Tampa. Tampa is also actively trying to get equipment manufacturers to set up in the city.

In November 2012, Buckhorn and the dean of the USF medical school went to Israel to try get companies there to "establish a footprint" in Tampa.

"This is the type of industry that will create lots of opportunities around it," he says. "Not only is it doctors and PhDs, MPHs [masters in public health], it is also technicians who need to operate and service the equipment. Those are real jobs, real opportunities, real wealth, and it's in the downtown core, which heretofore hasn't had that type of technology."

One might think the shift away from real estate development would put Buckhorn in the crosshairs of the real estate developers. Not necessarily, he says. "They realize if you don't have the jobs here with sustainable incomes, no one is going to be buying the houses. So, in a perverse way, they are all-in with me because they know they can't build for people who don't exist or don't have an income."

For a mayor who terms himself the "cheerleader-in-chief," this thrust into economics may seem like a far cry from fixing potholes and shaking hands at the shopping center. Not so, says Buckhorn. "Mayors tend to be ambidextrous, very pragmatic, far less wedded to an ideology and far more concerned with getting results," he explains. "If I had to paint myself, I am pretty much of a pro-business centrist Democrat. But as a mayor, there is no Republican or Democratic way to fill a pothole. We just get the job done."

While Buckhorn manages a city, Dr. Michael Crow, the president of Arizona State University in Tempe, Arizona, guides a center of learning. But, like Tampa, ASU has to adjust to the ups and downs of the economy, forcing Dr. Crow, who is not trained as an economist, to act like one. And just like the consumer in the grocery store, he has had to make decisions on how to make his budget stretch and stretch.

How an Educator Put on an Economist's Hat

Dr. Crow's passion is designing new systems to help people learn. Ever since he arrived at ASU in 2002, he has frequently rethought how to educate his growing student body. He has termed ASU "the New American University," an inclusive educational institution that focuses on student access and a quality learning experience. He has brought in world-class professors but made it clear that ASU did not have a goal of being the equivalent of a Harvard of the Southwest.[6]

But once the recession rocked his state, economic circumstances became a major driver of Dr. Crow's penchant for reconfiguring the learning landscape at ASU, one of the nation's largest universities.

As he donned an economist's hat, Dr. Crow asked such basic questions as:

Can a department be merged with another department to give the students a broader education but save money at the same time?

Since some students prefer shorter semesters for some courses, can they be shortened but still get the job done and possibly give the students a chance to save money by taking more courses? And can the university itself be transformed from the mind-set of a state agency into a series of enterprises that work with each other to solve societal problems and give everyone an incentive to work harder?

Asking these types of questions is not unusual for Dr. Crow, who calls himself "an architect of knowledge enterprises." But in 2009, the

questions were not rhetorical. Arizona was hemorrhaging money—
an unusual situation in recent years. In the past, Arizona outpaced
the national economy. Between 1963 and 2011 Arizona grew at non-
inflation-adjusted 8.9 percent per year compared to 6.9 percent for the
United States over the same period.[7]

Behind the growth was a burgeoning population, which grew
by an annual average rate of 3.07 percent per annum over the past
48 years compared to an annual average rate of 1.05 percent nation-
wide, according to the Bureau of Economic Analysis.[8] People became
attracted to Arizona because of its sunny weather, relatively low cost of
living, and plentiful jobs.

The state's growth took off after World War II, when a significant
number of veterans returned and remembered a stint they had in the
state before being sent to fight, says Dr. Dennis Hoffman, an economics
professor at ASU's W. P. Carey School of Business. "They remembered
the climate and scenery of Arizona, so they moved back to the state
after the war," says Dr. Hoffman.

At about the same time in the postwar years, Arizona began to
attract an increasing number of defense companies, helped in part by
a congressional delegation that worked hard to keep contractors in the
state, says Dr. Hoffman. "Our congressional delegation—very unlike
today, I might add—was very keen on seizing opportunities for federal
investments of all types in the state of Arizona," he says.

Eventually, semiconductor companies, such as Motorola and Intel,
started to build large chip-producing factories in the Phoenix area. The
region's economy grew even more as financial services companies set
up an increasing number of call service centers and data centers.

All this growth helped to support a vibrant construction industry.
"If people want to move here and stay, you become a population mag-
net, you will invariably be reliant on construction," says Dr. Hoffman.

A Fiscal Grand Canyon

But in the mid-2000s, developers in Arizona, much like those in Las
Vegas, Florida, and parts of California, suddenly started to build and
build. Speculators purchased homes hoping to flip them for large profits.

"The national pro-real estate crowd would come in—kind of the cheer-leader type—and they would say things like 'We know housing starts are three times higher than a normal period, but housing will sustain itself because Phoenix is where the jobs are,'" recalls Dr. Hoffman. "There was this failure to think through that many of the jobs were in this real estate construction engine such as sales, financing, and contracting."

When the housing boom imploded in 2007, Arizona was one of the worst-hit states. One indication of how bad the housing market had gotten is called negative equity, where the value of a home is worth less than the balance on the mortgage. In Arizona in the last quarter of 2009—one of the worst quarters in the real estate crunch—nearly 54 percent of mortgages in the state had a negative equity, more than double the 25.7 percent national rate, according to CoreLogic, a real estate data and analytics firm.

As the real estate sector tumbled, unemployment in the state soared from 3.5 percent in 2007 to 10.8 percent in January of 2010.[9] With fewer people working, the state's revenues, which mainly come from income taxes and sales taxes, fell 21.9 percent in January of 2009 compared to the prior year. In an effort to get revenue, the state sold a significant part of its Capitol complex, including the House and Senate chambers, and then leased them back.

As the state scrambled, it cut spending. By FY2009, the impact on ASU's budget was dramatic. "In a 15-month period, we lost 40 percent of state revenue as a result of the recession," says Crow. In dollar terms, Crow says it amounted to about $200 million in lost revenue. What made the losses even more dramatic is that $100 million of the cuts came in the last three months of the university's fiscal year after most of the money had already been spent.

"So that was a tremendously complex thing we had to go through and they combined that with another $100 million reduction in the next cycle," says Crow. The economist part of his life kicked into high gear.

Crow Solutions

To start with, ASU had to immediately tighten its belt. Dr. Crow instituted a furlough program, where everyone from senior administrators, such as himself, and deans to secretaries took some form of pay cut. Some 500 staff and 200 faculty associates—people who may have taught one course, for example, lost their jobs. Travel was reduced or eliminated.

But Dr. Crow also realized he needed to make more fundamental changes: the university would need to find new sources of revenue by locating partners in the private and nonprofit sectors. Dr. Crow targeted an area where he was trying to make ASU into a leader: green energy. In sunny Arizona—296 days of sun or partial sun in Phoenix—solar energy made sense.[10]

ASU embarked on a program of partnering with such companies as Arizona Public Service, Salt River Project, another large utility, and a host of smaller companies to provide solar energy. For the most part, the companies built the solar facilities and ASU became the consumer. Dr. Crow estimates that, as of the beginning of 2013, the private solar investment was approaching $200 million. "It's an elaborate way in which we can secure our energy price, lower our carbon footprint and have no capital outlay," says Dr. Crow.

ASU and Dr. Crow had experience with partnerships even before the recession hit. In 2006, the city of Phoenix wondered if ASU would be interested in moving some of its colleges from Tempe to downtown Phoenix. Indeed, Dr. Crow was interested. After an agreement by Phoenix to invest $300 million, the university moved its nursing school; its School of Public Programs, which had a lot of urban-oriented classes; the School of Arts and Letters (for people who had not yet declared a major); and the journalism school into downtown Phoenix.

In fact, the partnerships and other creative financing helped ASU add about $3 billion in new space with only about 10 percent of it paid for by the state. Adding the space was necessary: Dr. Crow estimates that from the beginning of the recession to 2013, student enrollment grew by 20 percent.

The move also helped the city of Phoenix dust off its downtown. Near the new campus, two major hotels have opened up as well as a complex of stores and restaurants. With more young people in downtown Phoenix, the city developed a night life, which is often considered a plus in helping to attract new businesses.

At about the same time, ASU went about trying to internally create new revenue streams. In 2010, for example, the university had practically no revenue from online classes. Three years later, the university was bringing in $100 million. The number of students getting online degrees went from zero to 6,000 in three years.[11] The addition of online classes fits in with Dr. Crow's belief that technology can work in traditional face-to-face enterprises such as universities and health care.

The imperative of adapting to the economic situation has been good for the university, says Dr. Crow, who now calls ASU "more adaptive" and capable of making faster adjustments to economic shifts. "We already had some experience in making the university more flexible, but we didn't anticipate we would encounter anything like a $200 million reduction in that scheme," he says.

Dr. Crow has tried to use economics to convince lawmakers that there is an economic value in supporting higher education. "That has better prepared us to be of greater value as a force for economic competitiveness in Arizona," he says.

One way Dr. Crow has tried to illustrate the economic value of the university is through an office he created in 2005, called the Office of the University Economist, which, among other roles, measures the value of knowledge and skill in the workforce. For example, he asked the office, which is headed up by Dr. Hoffman, to write a white paper on the return on investment for tuition-paying students. His questions include:

- When we drive our tuition up as the state investment goes down, what are the economics of that?
- What is the return to the state for each graduate that we produce?
- What would be the projected performance of the state with a higher level of college degrees?

Dr. Crow hopes that mixing economics and education will turn on a light bulb in the legislature. "What we've done is move away from the simple model that has evolved in other states and really doesn't work in Arizona, which is that you should invest in this public university just because you should," he says. "I'm like, I don't think so. We've actually taken the legislature and tried to look at them as an investment community and to have them evaluate the case for investment in us."

In other words, an educator has become an economist.

The Business Owner as Economist

For most businesspeople, understanding their product and their market is what it is all about. Then they can decide on their marketing, hiring, production, and budgeting issues. But what most businesspeople don't directly recognize is that it is really all about the economy. Indeed, the business motto of Naroff Economic Advisors is "Linking the economic environment to your business strategy." If you don't know the economy, you are operating in a vacuum.

In the past, it seemed that the average businessperson suffered from tunnel vision. Their world consisted strictly of their industry. They knew all about production methods, new products, and emerging markets, but they had almost no idea whether their plans to grow and invest made any sense in the context of the current or projected economy and economic trends.

That is changing, and changing rapidly. We live in an integrated world where our competitors can and do exist anywhere and everywhere. The average businessperson, no matter what size business they operate, now recognizes that to succeed the economy and the trends implied by them matter.

For a business to prosper, managers need to know not only how to produce but also where to sell and the location and size of their market or markets. Demand is critical, and that comes from determining market size. That may sound simple, but even for a small retailer, sales can appear almost magically from anywhere. A mobile society means the customers you can attract are not limited to any single location. Add to that the Internet, where information about a business can be spread across the world, and it becomes clear that to succeed, a business needs to know what is happening close by and far away.

Understanding the market, then, means recognizing the condition of the economy in any location where sales could potentially take place. Businesspeople need to understand the local, regional, national, and even international economies not simply because customers come from anywhere and everywhere. The direction of a local economy is first and foremost determined by the direction of the national economy. It is hard for a small area to grow quickly if the nation is in recession since that probably means local companies are suffering as well.

But knowing the shape of the national or international economies is not enough. Regional economies can and do grow at different rates due to special factors. In the 1970s, the surge in oil prices caused large parts of the country to go into recession. But in the oil patch regions, it was "happy days are here again" as the higher prices led to a huge inflow of earnings. Rural parts of Pennsylvania or North Dakota that had stagnated for decades are booming as a result of the oil shale revolution. If you don't recognize what is special about your community, you don't know much.

Businesspeople have to understand markets as well as economic conditions. Commodity-market trends help determine the cost of their inputs and thus their expenses. If you are losing money on each sale, it is hard to make it up in volume. Things such as droughts, which affect agricultural costs, or wars, which affect energy prices, matter and have to be understood if a business is to successfully decide on what and how much to produce.

And then there is the little matter of financing the company. Where interest rates are going and what is the best time or rate to borrow can often be a make-or-break issue for the average business. That means a business owner must also watch the financial markets and have a basic idea of what the Federal Reserve, which helps set rates, is going to do.

Finally, there is the issue of evolving trends. The information revolution has and will continue to change the way businesses interact with customers. You can go online and market your product or buy inputs from around the world. That means that traditional concepts about the way to do business can change almost overnight. For example, who would have thought that Microsoft would ever lose its monopoly over the computer world? But Apple, Google, and the cloud are changing the way we use information technology. Does anyone really know what the computer industry will look like in five years?

Failure to grasp the emerging trends in industries that may not even be directly related to the one you are in can lead to planning decisions that are disastrous. For example, should vehicle makers invest in plants that make gasoline-powered engines, or should they move toward natural gas–powered engines? The surge in natural gas and the drop in price means that changes will come. How the companies grasp those changes will determine their success or failure.

To succeed, the businessperson has to be a good economist or, of course, hire a good one. There is no escaping the fact that it is not enough to know your industry. The good ones succeed, which we can see by the decisions made by Greg Parker, the head of a chain of convenience stores.

Greg Parker: From Fast Food to Economics

When Greg Parker graduated from the University of Georgia in 1976, he intended to go to law school. But his father had been planning to construct a convenience store. He just had not gotten around to it. Parker decided to temporarily forgo law school to get the store up and running. He never did go back for the law degree.

Instead, he built the Parker Companies into a 30-store chain of convenience stores, plus a gourmet market open 24 hours a day, two self-service laundries, and a real estate development arm. Becoming a businessman instead of a lawyer means that he spends a lot more of his time thinking about the direction of the economy, not torts.

Three times a year, Parker organizes a meeting with other CEOs from a wide variety of industries to discuss the economy and figure out ways to become more competitive. He says the high-powered group might discuss what is going to happen to the price of gold or what are the safest banks in the world. One of the highlights of the meetings is a presentation by Walter Zimmermann, an analyst with United-ICAP, an advisory service.

"He's a contrarian; some call him a pessimist," says Parker. "I call him the smartest man in the world." Parker says Zimmermann predicted the financial collapse of 2007 and the subsequent stock market debacle. But he also predicted that the market would implode in 2012. Instead, the stock market rose.

Parker says Zimmermann has him thinking about the opportunities that might take place if the economy collapses again. "Maybe I want to be more liquid and have cash for the opportunities that will present themselves."

Convenience stores seem like an unlikely place to make money, given the daunting economics of the business.

Convenience Store Economics

The average convenience store derives about 70 percent of its $4.6 million in annual revenue from gasoline sales. (About 80 percent of the gasoline purchased in the United States is from a convenience store).[12] However, gasoline consumption has been falling. In 2007, the United States consumed 9.3 million barrels of gasoline per day. By April 2013 consumption had fallen to 8.5 million barrels of gasoline per day.[13]

A typical convenience store gets 30 percent of its $12,600 per day in revenues from the products it sells inside its doors. Of that 30 percent, tobacco products, including cigarettes or smokeless tobacco, represent up to 40 percent of the store's sales, says Jeff Lenard, a spokesman for the National Association of Convenience Stores (NACS).

"While cigarettes still are the top revenue generator inside stores, they are still not considered to be a growth category like foodservice, in particular," says Lenard. "Dollar sales for cigarettes the past few years have held up because of escalating state and federal taxes as well as man-ufacturer-driven price increases." With that kind of economics, Parker thinks the industry should be contracting.

But, that's not the case. At the end of 2012, there were 149,220 convenience stores, up 14.2 percent from 10 years earlier. In 2009 and 2010—economically difficult years—the number of stores dropped by 1.19 percent compared to 2008 but bounced back some in 2010 and 2011.[14]

"Stores in our industry don't go away," says Parker. "Say I divest a store and someone buys it; they don't seem to go away. You say, 'How are they making it on those little sales?' But they do."

At the same time, an increasing number of companies, from drug stores to dollar stores to fast food restaurants, are trying to capture some of the consumers' dollars spent at the stores. For example, Lenard says stores such as Old Navy and Staples sell candy and soft drinks at their checkout counters.

Finally, the industry finds an increasing amount of regulation is headed its way. For health reasons, some local municipalities are try-ing to limit the size of sugary drinks that can be sold. Energy drinks, another big seller at convenience stores, are under attack for the amount of caffeine they contain. And, the way Parker describes it, federal inspectors are constantly buzzing around his offices looking at everything from retirement accounts to the height of cup and straw dispensers to make sure they comply with disability regulations.

Things Are Bad, So Expand

Despite all the problems, at the beginning of 2013, Parker Companies was starting an expansion push. This may sound counterintuitive but he is trying to grow because he is concerned that bad economic times are ahead for the nation.

He recounts how one of the CEOs who participated in his three-times-a-year Econ Group meetings has taken the approach of circling the wagons by divesting assets and paying off debt so he has a good credit rating for future borrowing. "I have taken a completely different approach," he explains.

One reason is that he believes even with contracting demand for gasoline and cigarettes, consumers will still be going to convenience stores for immediate consumables such as milk and bread. Even in a diminishing marketplace, the retailer who uses the best technology and listens to the consumer will win, he says.

But, he also thinks there could be significant opportunities for entrepreneurs like himself in the years ahead. "My position is, if you look from an economic standpoint, huge wealth was accrued at the end of the last Depression. And I am of the belief that huge wealth is going to be made in these times of hardship, and I think people who are well positioned that are smart and understand risk and are well collateralized have a huge opportunity."

To capitalize on this gloom-and-doom scenario, Parker took down a $10 million 15-year fixed-rate loan with a 3.03 percent interest rate. He views it as practically free money. "If you can't make 3 percent on your money, shame on you," he says.

With the money, he bought land that the owners had told him they would never sell. He "negotiated the hell" out of his construction costs and started buying larger quantities of materials to get more savings. Contractors who used to be difficult to deal with are now scrambling for work, he says. "This is an opportunity to grow because the economy is eventually going to turn," he says. "And we will have paid for this with very cheap dollars."

Kampp, Buckhorn, Dr. Crow, and Parker have all had to become economists in a way. They have had to adapt to what was happening around them, to make tough choices—some professionally, some personally. But what is the foundation for those decisions? In the next chapter, we look at the types of forces that make us economists.

Notes

1. www.nytimes.com/1992/10/31/us/1992-campaign-democrats-clinton-bush-compete-be-champion-change-democrat-fights.html.
2. www.tampagov.net/dept_Budget/files/recommended_operating_and_capital_budget_FY14.pdf.
3. Interview with Bob Buckhorn.
4. www.tampagov.net/dept_Mayor/Presentations/files/budget_mayors_presen tation_2014.pdf.
5. Ibid.
6. Among the faculty Crow has hired are two Nobel laureates, plus winners of many other awards. www.asu.edu/excellence/faculty/.
7. Dr. Dennis Hoffman of Arizona State University, using Bureau of Economic Analysis data.
8. Ibid.
9. Bureau of Labor Statistics, http://data.bls.gov/timeseries/LASST04000003.
10. Current Results. www.currentresults.com/Weather/Arizona/annual-days-of-sunshine.php.
11. Virgil Renzulli, vice president for Public Affairs in an e-mail on October 12, 2013. ASU Public Affairs Department.
12. Jeff Lenard, vice president National Association of Convenience Stores in an e-mail on January 28, 2013. NACS.
13. Energy Information Administration. www.eia.gov/todayinenergy/detail.cfm?id= 7510; www.eia.gov/dnav/pet/pet_cons_psup_a_EPM0F_VPP_mbblpd_m.htm.
14. Jeff Lenard, vice president of NACS in an e-mail on January 29, 2013. NACS.

Chapter 4

How a Perfect World Would Work

T his is no longer your parents or grandparents economy. As we saw, knowing that "it's the economy, stupid" and understanding how the economy actually operates, are two different things. Worse, the economy is a living, and therefore, changing thing.

Our standard of living, the types of jobs we have, our employment opportunities, what we can afford to buy with the money we make and even the full range of goods that we can purchase are all wrapped up in the way we organize and operate our economic activity not just now but also in the future. So, yes, it is the economy! But the key is not to be stupid about it and the way you do that is by understanding how all the players in the economy operate.

How We Got Here

The economic structure we currently operate in the United States is the result of centuries of trial and error. It is not something that came from the Founding Fathers, though there are many who think that is the case. Yes, the Constitution set out the basic principles for the nation, but it did not tell us how to run the economy. Indeed, there are economic positions in it that have been abandoned. So we cannot look to the eighteenth century for what we have today or what will emerge as we go through the twenty-first century.

The economy also didn't come from following the directions in an economic textbook or a self-help manual entitled "How to Form an Economy." Yes, economists like to take credit for just about anything good that has happened in or to the economy and disavow anything bad, but economic theory has evolved to account for the many changes in businesses and household activities that are the result of progress. And, of course, economists rarely agree on just about anything. There is an old saying that if you laid every economist end to end, you still wouldn't reach a conclusion.

What we are saying is that there is no one single economic concept that has or will drive the economy. Instead, it is a collection of ideas that have been fitted together in a patchwork of ways to create our current system. We have part free-market economics, part government controlled. And some markets have government run elements existing side-by-side with private-sector companies. Simply put, you cannot describe the form of this economy in simplistic terms. It is much more complicated.

As for Wall Street, it is doubtful that anyone there would or could claim credit for the structure. They would argue that Wall Street principles are critical to the success of the economy and maybe they should be used more generally throughout business, but the markets constitute only one element of this complex system.

While many current and past politicians, political analysts, and pundits like to say they helped create the intellectual foundations of the current system, few have actually had any real impact on the current structure of the system. Undoubtedly, politicians have helped push the economy in different directions, created short-term changes in the structure of business relationships and even affected the way we look at the economy. But politics played only one role in the evolution.

A lot of different forces, individuals, circumstances, and actions have come together to create the economic system we now live under. Thus, understanding how it evolved from a simple structure to the current complex world economy we now have is critical in comprehending how it actually works. And as conditions change, the perception of what is right or wrong may change, but the ability to evaluate the new ideas will still be founded in the understanding of where we came from and where we are going.

If you know why something came about, you have a basis for suggesting ways to change it to make it better. When politicians tell you their program is best for the economy while their opponent's will hurt it, you can make your own judgment. Knowing how the economy works will allow you to better critique those who claim they have the answers to all of our economic ills. Economics touches every aspect of our lives, and we shouldn't leave it up to others to tell us what to think.

Building the U.S. Economy: A Journey through Time

The transition from the early days of the country, when both the population and the number of businesses were fairly modest to the mind-boggling international colossus we currently have was quite slow. But is it necessary to describe that process in detail? Yes, at times this discussion about the historical evolution of our economy might seem tedious, proceed slowly, and often explain obvious facts and relationships. But when we get to the destination, it should be clear that the time was well spent.

The goal of this one geeky chapter is to give you the foundations to understand not only why we currently have the economic conditions we are dealing with, but also the means to evaluate where we might be going. And maybe most important, you will be able to participate in the discussion of the solutions.

The Very Beginning: Hunting, Fishing, and Doing Your Own Thing

Once upon a time, in a land of small populations but great abundance of natural resources, there lived a people. Actually, this is not a fairy tale. These were the original inhabitants of the country, and geography determined where they lived and how they survived. We are not talking about one group in one place, as this is a vast nation. Instead, even 400 years ago, there were a variety of economies that existed. Those primitive but successful organizations laid the foundation for the future, and how they evolved is the story of this section.

Since water was the most critical aspect of life, close proximity to oceans, lakes, and streams were where you had to be if you were going to survive and prosper. The people back then probably weren't told by their doctors that they should drink eight glasses of water a day, yet they still knew what they had to do. Clean, drinkable water was and still is the basic building block of any location.

That, of course, brings us to one of the foundations of economics: If there is a need for something, what economists call *demand*, it will be supplied in one form or another. The essential nature of water created the drive to find critical supplies of water, and that formed the basis for household locations. If the sources of water happened to change, people had to follow the water. That may have led to annual migrations or even periodic mass movements and complete changes in long-term living situations when water sources dried up.

Of course, what people did to survive, wherever their choice of location, was also determined by what Mother Nature managed to provide in addition to water. Since they lived close to the water, the inhabitants got a significant portion of their food from the seas or lakes or streams. The variety may not have been great, but as long as it was abundant, people could live and stay in one place.

At the same time, the food sources were not limited to what was swimming around. Water is needed for physical survival, but that didn't mean the source of food had to be from the bounty of the seas or streams. The land itself was fertile, and the growth of crops for food was extensive. Forests covered much of the land, and they were filled with a wide variety of food sources. Those were not limited to animals but plants as well. To secure the food supply, people became farmers, hunters, or gatherers, not just fishermen. These were means to an end that small families could pursue and survive at.

Wow. Think of it. All you need to survive is a place where there is water. You could hunt or fish or farm for part of the day and party the rest of the time. The streams overflowed with fish, the oceans were full of seafood, and the forests contained herds of animals and flocks of birds. You didn't have to worry about rent or mortgage payments, taxes, or even global warming. All you had to do was go out of your shelter, whatever that might look like, and find your living.

All that seems to be great, and for many it was. But it also had huge challenges. To survive, people were required to provide all their needs by themselves. There was only so much time to find the food, maintain the shelter, and enjoy life. Even then, context mattered. Food supplies were based on availability, which was frequently determined by seasons and weather. Shelter and clothing needs varied by climate and seasons, and so did production. But they did it all, and they prospered.

Evolution Phase 1: Specialization

The more things remained the same, the more they had to eventually change. The first critical part and maybe most meaningful development that moved the economy from the simple hunter/gatherer/fisherman system to what we have now was specialization.

Remember your first economics course? I know, most of us have done our best to forget that course as it was one of the dullest, most boring classes you ever had. But if you search your memory hard, you may remember you learned about specialization when the idea of the division of labor in producing goods in an industrial society was introduced in that freshman economics course.

The discussion of how labor can be best used to produce the most, or what economists call *productivity*, tended to be centered on the lessons of the industrial revolution. The factory collected people who had a variety of skills, threw them together, and gave them one specific job to do. Workers became adept at whatever it was, and the production-line method led to vast increases in output.

But what is missed in those discussions is the simple fact that the division of labor was introduced and in many ways perfected well before the sweatshops came into vogue. It actually started when a tribal leader said to one of the clan members, "Hey, dude, you are one a heck of a hunter. Why don't you go into the forest and get the family some deer for dinner."

The reality that chief recognized was that as extended families grew, the different skills needed to provide all that the group required were not evenly distributed. Not surprisingly, some people could hunt or fish better than others. The ability to build a shelter, no matter how rudimentary it may have been, was hardly universal, especially when there was only a small group to choose from. Making clothes, organizing activities, and creating safe keeping for extra goods were not capabilities that everyone possessed equally.

Thus, as time went on and the size of the society expanded and the needs increased even more, it became clear that it would be a lot more efficient (though I doubt that was the word used) if only a few of the most skilled secured the food, while those who knew what to do with the bounty prepared it, those that were good at construction created the shelter, and the rest did whatever it was that they were best at doing. That is, even in the small family setting of early America, some form of specialization made economic sense, as the standard of living, if not the simple survival, of everyone depended on all doing the best they could by producing as much as possible.

That restructuring from a strict self-sustaining activity to dependence on others for survival was the true beginning of the modern economy. The transition from individualistic economic activity to group production allowed for—indeed, even facilitated—the creation of the large tribes, clans, extended families, troops, religious orders, or whatever that came to populate the landscape. The advantage was that each person's skills would be used to support the general good. Interdependence, not independence, was what would guide all future forms of economic activity.

The evolution of the economy from one that produces all to all who produced for all was inevitable because it just made economic sense. With more skilled people producing the different types of goods and services, the quantity of goods produced expanded, the availability of food became greater or more varied, and the quality of everything tended to improve. As a consequence, everyone's standard of living increased. Not surprisingly, the radical change where individual efforts were now turned into coordinated economic activities didn't come easily. Some of the most basic issues of any society had to be resolved. The biggest and most important one was, "Who gets to do what?"

While it might sound nice that those that could did, while those that couldn't did something else, it was a lot tougher in the real world to make those decisions. Not everyone was going to agree with the determination of expertise.

Once the distribution of jobs was determined and the many varied responsibilities were divvied up, the next major concern had to be addressed: "How were the goods going to be distributed?" More may be the result of specialization but who gets the more was always going to be an issue of discontent. The distribution of income was a problem then as it is now.

Government: Benevolent Dictators and Other Fun Ways to Distribute Goods

In this early economy, you had people producing goods and people consuming goods, just like we do today, but not everyone made everything they needed. Critically, the means to transact the business relationship didn't exist. That is, it took something or someone to decide who did what and who got what.

Conflicts were naturally arising as to the fairness of any distribution. To resolve those disagreements, a "governing entity" of some form or manner had to be created. That could be an individual or a group, but it was entrusted with the process of structuring behavior to conform to the general good.

Someone had to do that, and the simplest way was to have a benevolent dictator make those choices. That is, the head honcho had to decide. Subsequently, a council may have been added to express their views and spread the blame. These were the people who told others what to do and what they were getting or at least oversaw the process so it didn't get out of hand and evolve into conflict, destroying the tribe.

Not everyone could be made happy. And you didn't have a choice once the decisions were made. There were no labor markets or alternative job opportunities. That is important to remember when issues of income distribution are considered.

Since authority was required in this new economy, the idea of "government" became a necessity. In essence, the "polity" was the inevitable consequence of going from an individualistic to group economy.

As such, it meant that government was supposed to do the bidding of all the people to create the most good and, in doing so, unify the group. Good luck with that. But it did work for those societies that accepted the leadership in a fairly unquestioned manner. When authority was questioned, battles broke out and the nations broke apart.

For a very long time in this country, tribes of different economic orders ruled the land, and those economies provided all the essentials: food, clothing, shelter, and defense. But the greatest challenge and change came when the types of goods and services that could be created began to take on even more specialized qualities as the nations came in contact with each other. That is where the next stage of development comes into play: trade.

We Are Not Alone!

While tribes may be able to create a number of different goods and services that people want, there are limitations to what can be produced. Variety is indeed the spice of life, especially when it comes to possessions. We have always been awed and desirous of things new and different.

Ultimately, the somewhat isolated tribes had to start intermingling with each other. Many of those meetings were not particularly peaceful. Just as we like new things, we also distrust others we don't know. But there were also opportunities to meet and greet different groups under controlled circumstances. Those connections formed the basis for the next great change in societies and economies: people saw that there were things in life other than what they were capable of creating.

Without any alternatives, groups had to be satisfied with what they made themselves. The options were limited to the way those particular clans did things. Variety may or may not have been highly valued. But once there was contact, people saw there were options that frequently they never had seen before. The reality of what they were missing became a factor in their lives.

The interaction of different nations producing different types of goods led to the first complex aspect of economies: trade. Seeing that others had products that appeared to be great ideas, or at least something worth having, fostered needs that ultimately had to be satisfied.

People wanted those products, and if they couldn't make them themselves, then they had to find means to secure them. Again, where there is demand, there is likely to be a way to create a supply.

Barter Can Only Get You So Far

In the beginning, trade occurred through the simple concept of barter. I have something you want and you have something I want, and we arrange to swap goods or services. Bartering was relatively easy because that is what had already been happening within the tribes. Those who provided the food swapped with those who provided the clothing, who swapped with those who provided the shelter, and so on. That is the case even if all the goods were put in one big pile and everyone chose.

However, when the swap meets were between nations rather than within tribes, there was a fundamental issue that created conflict: You had to agree on what constitutes a fair trade. Haggling and the ability to make the best deal became an essential skill. But it was also true that not all deals could be consummated.

Making a deal can become difficult since not all products have the same value to each person. You may like something but do you really need it? If you don't, that makes you less willing to part with the product that you have so painstakingly crafted. The differences in how a good is valued can be extreme, and it depends on the perceptions of the individuals doing the trading.

Indeed, when you start talking about individual desires, you finally get to the fact that we are simply a bunch of consumers. We want lots of things, and we want even more of the things we don't have. Trade accentuates that state of mind. It creates demand for goods and services that people might never have even thought about (which is also the foundation of advertising, but that is a different story).

But what is desirable and can be traded is a personal thing that is very dependent on where you live and what time of year it may be. That is, context matters. It is easy to sell wool blankets to people who live in the Snow Belt but not to those who live in the desert. If your air conditioner is working fine, you really don't have any need to trade for one, especially if it is winter—which reminds us of that old saying that you can sell ice in the summer but it's an awful lot tougher to do so in the winter.

Bartering thus has its limitations and frequently can fail to create an agreement between two willing bargainers. Even if there is a large number of certain goods, that doesn't mean the goods wind up being exchanged for something else.

The inability to complete the trade may have little to do with the desire to have the deal succeed. The issue that causes the deal to collapse usually comes down to price. The price of a good is simply the value that someone else places on it, not just the value the seller places on it. Essentially, it is how much you are willing to exchange one good for another, and each seller has his or her own opinion of value.

While a barter system can work under certain sets of circumstances, as it still does in many ways, no barter system could handle the growing number of specialized products that were being offered once populations expanded and came into contact with each other. It can be very hard to exchange a skateboard for an oil change. Worse, the way a price was determined often depended on goodwill and trust. When you didn't know someone well, you were usually quite leery of any exchange.

To have a successful barter trade, you had to have a good that someone wanted, and the other trader had to have a product you needed. But that was only the first step in the process. Each side had to be able to determine how much their good was worth in terms of the amount of the other good they were trading for. That becomes quite difficult when the goods are not divisible. It is unclear if someone would trade half an arrow for a smaller-than-needed length of rope. And nothing happened unless there was a need for the items being offered. If you weren't in the market for an axe, so be it.

Something had to be done about the problems inherent in a barter economy. The ever-expanding sizes of tribes made it possible to create a whole variety of products, but getting something in return for those goods was becoming more difficult. Out of that necessity developed the concept of money. Instead of trading goods, a generally accepted alternative item was used, and that is what opened up the world to full-scale economic development.

Money Makes the World Go 'Round

The conflicts created by the barter system were holding back economic activity. If only something could be found that would be accepted and used to make a deal, then people would not have to simply trade one product or service for another. That alternative had to be created and since need is the mother of invention, ultimately it was. Money, whatever it was called, looked like, or was made of, was the critical breakthrough that made it possible to move beyond the limitations imposed by the barter trade system.

What is money? No, it's not something we can never have enough of. Okay, we can never have enough of it, but that is not the point. Money, as any good first-year economics student will tell you, is a medium of exchange. It is something that can be used to secure a good. But the rub in all this is one simple problem: money has to be generally accepted. That is, people and businesses have to believe that if they hold the money, they can get something for it.

There is a great burden placed on money by the need that it be generally accepted: it must hold its value. If you are to hold money, you have to believe that it can be used not just immediately but, much more importantly, in the future. If it can't, then there is no reason to keep it in your wallet, put it in the bank, or stash it under your mattress, and you are back to a barter system. Therefore, anything that harms the value of money will limit its usage. And the last thing an economic system can afford is the loss of the usage of its money.

The concept that money is in effect a storehouse of value has clear implications for the economy of today. It means government must back it unconditionally. Public policy has to be managed in a way to lessen any potentially negative impacts on the currency.

One of the worst things that can happen to money is that it loses its purchasing power. Why hold something that gets you less in the future, especially if it has no intrinsic value? Ugly green pieces of paper that are full of germs are hardly something that you want any part of unless there is a really worthwhile reason to hold it.

Rising prices, which we call *inflation*, is unquestionably the worst thing for money. It means that the longer I keep some cash in my pocket, the less I can buy. The higher inflation, the more our savings are destroyed. As a result, I do whatever is possible to rid myself of this evil thing, and that means I buy everything as soon as possible.

No economy can persist if we don't look to the future but simply live in the present. If no one wants to hold money because of the fear that it will lose value, then we wind up with the equivalent of a barter economy. Money that has stopped being held and used as a vehicle to exchange for other goods is no longer money. It is just another filthy piece of ugly paper.

Thus, we fight inflation, which reduces purchasing power. That is the economic foundation for the Federal Reserve System. Someone or some group or government entity must be out there to provide some confidence that our money has value. The Fed was created largely to make sure that everyone is willing to hold money by insuring that it's not just in God that we trust but also the government itself.

Money Is Not Enough (Don't We Know That!)

Once we have money, the possibilities of the economy become unlimited. Thus, the creation of a monetary system is just the beginning of the modern economic story. We know the actors; they are businesses, households, and the government. We just don't know how they work together. We don't know what they do or why they do it, and that has to be explained.

Consider the most basic of economies where we have only those who make the goods and those who buy their products. That is, we have an economy that has only businesses and consumers. Let's focus on the corporate world for a while. In our simple world, one person made the goods. But it's time to get real, and since we have moved way past that point, we have to consider the workings of companies that make complex products.

In order to produce in today's world, a boatload of workers need to be hired. So the ad goes on the web site and the resumes are e-mailed, and the human resources group sorts through it all. Candidates are chosen, interviewed, offered a salary, and the person goes to work. Sounds great and it is. But there are still some issues to be resolved.

First and foremost, how does a company make money after all those workers show up? That may sound like a crazy question to ask since all you have to do is sell a product at a profit and, bingo, you're on easy street. But in our complex economy, not everything works in a simple manner.

First, after you have hired your employees, you have a small thing called payroll. If a firm is to pay its workers, it has to have the funds to do it. The only way it can get money is by selling its products. Who can the firm sell its products to? Either its workers or someone else's employees. So if a firm pays people wages to work for them, it is hoped and expected that they will buy lots of goods in return. That works out fine as long as everyone, no matter where they work, spends all their income.

So, if we all take our fantastic salaries that have made us all so fabulously wealthy (just kidding) and go out and spend them, then all the money given to workers winds up back in the hands of firms in the form of purchases of goods. That way, a company can get back what it gives up in payments for workers and for the other inputs to production.

But I smell a rat here. First of all, where are the profits? Well, they come from paying the business owner, and that is all. There's nothing left over. Okay, I can live with that for now. But I am still worried about the idea that to make that minimum profit everybody has to spend all their money. Okay, maybe that is not totally dumb as lots of people live from paycheck to paycheck and we do like to hit the malls really hard. But not everyone shops till they drop.

While lots of us do manage to spend everything we earn, some of us are a little more cautious. We manage to take a little off the top of our paychecks and hide it away for a rainy day. That's a strange thing called *savings*. When that happens, not all the payments to workers wind up being spent on goods. Some firms find they paid more to produce the goods than they earned. That's called *losses*, and it's hard to make up losses through volume.

If households need to spend all they earn but don't, Houston, we have a problem. How can firms survive if people decide to stop spending a little? Not easily. Could it be that this wonderful economy that has evolved over the decades has to collapse? Well, not really.

We have to find a way to get the money not spent back into the economy. How that happens is simple: get someone to collect all those savings and have them find a way to convince others to spend it. When there is a challenge, there always seems to be a solution that will ultimately be found, and this one is no different.

The way we get the money back into the economy is to create a company that buys and sells savings. What is that business called? Well, how about a bank! We need banks, or more generally, the financial system, to make sure what is taken out of the economy in the form of savings is put back into the economy. Essentially, a bank is nothing more than a way to collect and distribute all the funds that businesses and individuals don't want to spend right away.

The Banking System Made Simple

The economy we are following has really started to evolve. It began with self-sufficiency, moved to interdependence of production, then the need for money, and now we have the complexity of putting the money to work.

One of Ben Franklin's famous sayings is "a penny saved is a penny earned." Indeed, for a long time, saving money was considered a key to the economy's success. But there are two sides to every coin, and that is true when people don't spend all they earn.

As we have shown, if you set aside some of your hard-earned income, that is potential demand for goods that doesn't go to businesses who are trying desperately to sell their wares. You can buy things or save, but you cannot do both with the same money. So you have to look at savings as a loss of spending.

If savings means businesses get less money, is that bad? The answer is absolutely not! But it is a problem. Money coming out of the economy in the form of savings—with businesses, it is retained earnings—and not going into demand for all those wonderful things that businesses want to sell you has to find its way back into the economy. Maybe you don't really need all that stuff, but that is not the point. If you don't buy it, it cannot be made.

The savior of the economy put at risk by all those selfish savers is the financial system. It is the mechanism by which savings are recycled so what leaves the economy gets put back into the system. It is the original "green" industry. Okay, bad pun.

The recycling responsibility of the financial system is simple. Think of a bank as a very large piggy bank. Instead of people stashing their cash in their mattresses, strongboxes, or their backyards, they give it to a business to hold on to. That company has to convince everyone that it is safer to leave their money with them than if they kept it at home. They have nice big safes with huge steel doors that not even Jessie James can break into. Okay, that may not be totally true, but you get the picture.

So all those people who have been hoarding their money at home take it to the local building and loan association, thinking it's now a wonderful life. They have savings, it is in a safe place, and they are even getting a little payment for keeping their money with those nice people. Maybe the return savers get, which is called *interest*, is not a whole lot, but it is more than if they kept it in cash. And you don't need a security firm to protect it either!

Of course, that is only the first step in the process. The financial institution has lots of money that they have collected, but they are also paying interest on that cash. There is also the cost of the safe, the branch employees, loan officers, accountants, and, of course, lots of money for the bank executives. So something has to be done with the savings. That is where lending comes in.

In the real world, while some people don't spend all they earn, others need extra money to buy things they cannot pay for out of savings or income. Some of us do both. We save but want to buy a new SUV that costs a lot more than we have in the bank. Companies need cash to buy new machinery, equipment, and software or to build new plants. And, of course, governments tend to need money from time to time, and they go looking for someone to fill their coffers.

Into that gap between those who have money and those who need cash rides the banks. They make their money by making loans. The borrowers then run out to the dealer to buy the shiny new vehicle and businesses invest, and it is indeed a wonderful world. In essence, banks are simply redistributors of savings. They take money from households, businesses, and even governments and give it back to households, businesses, and governments.

The implication of this recycling responsibility is that the financial sector is the linchpin of the economy. For the business world to operate smoothly, the funds that come out in the form of savings, which are leakages from the system, have to be returned in the form of loans, which are injections back into the economy. If the financial system stops working, households don't get the loans they need to buy vehicles, houses, or appliances, and businesses cannot invest in new machinery or build new plants. Everyone is left holding their savings or retained earnings, and that would mean the economy would grow an awful lot slower, if at all.

But while banks are the linchpin of the modern economy, that doesn't mean they always know what they are doing. Indeed, most of the recessions in the nineteenth century had their roots in bank runs and failures. When banks made mistakes, they were usually doozies. But people needed to trust that their money was safe from the Jessie Jameses who rode in on horses or who inhabited the back offices. Once they lost that trust and panicked, they pulled their money out, and guess what—there was no money to grease the wheels of economic activity!

Eventually, it dawned on those who ran the financial system and the government that maybe there should be some overseer of banking activity. In 1913, the Federal Reserve was created, largely to ride herd on the banking sector so that credit would flow and bank failures would be kept at a minimum. And it did that, until the Great Depression, though you can hardly blame the Fed for that.

The Fed has evolved greatly over the past century. It is the sheriff of bankland as the system's key regulator. It now plays the critical role of making sure that the currency doesn't lose value; that is, it is the major inflation fighter. Did you really think Congress was capable of doing that? You cannot have a complex economy if the currency is under attack and not accepted by households and the business community, so someone who was not running for office had to keep control of things, and it is the Fed.

The Federal Reserve has also been burdened with other responsibilities, in particular, helping to ensure full employment. After World

War II, the Full Employment Act made full employment (what a surprise) one of the two mandates of the Fed. Now, the dual responsibility—full employment at low inflation—is what the Fed tries to balance.

That means the Fed has to lean against the wind. Its policy is wholly dependent on context. When things get going too boisterously, the Fed has to take the punch bowl away. You don't want things getting too out of hand and inflation rearing its ugly head. If the economy is weak or in recession, the Fed's job is not to worry about inflation but to put the pedal to the metal and get things going again. They might be concerned that inflation would come back eventually, but they will worry about that after the recession or Great Depression is gone.

Big Brother Is Watching Over Us

Okay, businesses are humming along, consumers are spending like crazy, and the financial system is greasing the wheels of industry with the guidance of the maestros at the Federal Reserve. Sounds great, right? Yes, but there is a missing link here. In the primitive world, a benevolent dictator or counsels made the decisions that ensured everyone followed the rules. In the modern world, that role is played by our favorite whipping boy, the government.

The role of government in society is wide ranging and depends on the wishes of the voters—or at least that is the theory. But there are a number of overarching aspects of government that directly impinge on the economy. Our fearless leaders like to spend money, and to pay for their insatiable appetite to give us all we want, they either tax us or borrow money.

As to how the economy is affected by government actions, let's limit the discussion right now to the concepts of spending, taxes, and borrowing. In a later chapter, the horrors and wonders of the spending and taxing decisions will be discussed, but right now it's all about the way the economy works in general.

So you run for office, get elected, and tell everyone that you will make the roads smooth, the schools great, and provide police and fire protection. At the national level, you are strong on defense and like to help those who are in need. There is something in those public services that just about everyone wants, and so we get them. That means the government is out there spending lots of money on things everyone or anyone wants.

How do our politicians pay for that largesse? They have really only two options: they can tax you or borrow money. What is a tax? As far as economists are concerned, it's just a transfer of income from the private sector, either households or businesses, to the public sector. Instead of you or me or the local business down the street having money to spend, our friends in Washington or state capitals or town halls have the money. That is a leakage out of private spending. We no longer have as much money to do with what we want, and the deeper government dips into our pockets, the less we have.

Thankfully, at least for economic activity, the tax money burns a hole in the pockets of the politicians even faster than it burns a hole in ours, and our friendly elected officials spend it on all those things that they think we want. What has happened is that private demand has been transferred into public demand.

The only thing missing in this discussion is a small thing called the *budget*. On one side of the ledger you have spending. It is a lot, and it is probably rising. On the other side are revenues. The basic source of that money is taxes. But sometimes—well, if you are the federal government, most of the time—the tax receipts fall short of the spending and you wind up with a budget deficit. To make that up, the government goes to the public and borrows money. That takes money that might have been lent to businesses or households and sends it to the public sector.

Basically, the government is also just a redistributor of income. It takes money out of the wallets of businesses and households, reducing their spending power, and spends it on things our elected officials think are needed. Taxes are leakages from private demand, while spending is an injection of money back into the economy. The larger the budget deficit, the more the government puts back into the system than it takes out.

Context should matter to politicians, even if their actions imply that they don't think it does. When the economy is booming, it would be really irresponsible to pour more fuel on the fire and possibly increase inflation by spending like crazy. It's tough enough for the Federal Reserve to deal with businesses and households without having to worry about what the big spenders in Washington are doing.

Alternatively, though, it was done as recently as December 2012, it really makes no sense to raise taxes when the economy is weak. Is it logical to take more money out of people's pockets or business coffers when there isn't enough demand to begin with? There is a time for every purpose, though we can never be sure who in Washington knows that. So the government must consider more than the next election when it makes policy. Did we really write that?

The World Is Our Oyster

The economy is almost complete. To this point, all we have done is look at the United States as if it exists by itself. To paraphrase John Donne, no country is an island, entire of itself; every country is a piece of the world. And that is just as true of the United States as it is of any other nation. Indeed, the remaining missing link in this narrative is the introduction of world trade.

We have seen how the interchange of goods between tribes changed the primitive economy. Trade among nations has done the same. It allows for the introduction of goods and services that might not be available without those relationships. It creates competition for products we produce and for our dollars.

While economists agree that trade can be good, there are some upsides and downsides that should be kept in mind. In a future chapter, a full discussion of the good, the bad, and the ugly aspects of trade will occur. Here, we are interested only in how trade affects the level of economic activity in the United States.

There are two parts of trade: we can sell goods to foreigners, or they can sell stuff to us. In the first case, when we ship products overseas, we are exporting the things we make. So ships leave our ports and wind up in Europe, Asia, South America, or wherever. What do we get in return? *Money!* We get cash that people in other countries could have used to buy their goods but instead they buy our products. That is great because we now have another source of demand. Instead of depending just on U.S. consumers, businesses can get sales and income from foreigners. The more the merrier, and the better off we are.

But the downside is that we love to buy everything foreign. When China ships products to the United States, those goods are called imports. They are frequently cheap, and we can buy lots of them. That's great because it always helps to have a supply of low-cost products available.

Unfortunately, there is no such thing as a free import. We have to pay for the products we lust after. We do that with our earnings. So we ship dollars out of the country to pay for the vehicles, clothes, appliances, and everything else that we purchase. However, that is the exact reverse of imports. We spend our hard-earned income that could have been used to buy goods made in America on goods made somewhere else. That means there is less demand for American companies.

Basically, an export of a good is actually an import of income or demand while an import of a good is actually a shipping out of our income or spending power. What that tells me is that you want to have as many exports as possible, for that increases sales for U.S. companies. However, you might want to limit imports since they reduce demand for American-produced goods.

The difference between exports and imports is the trade balance. When exports are greater than imports, it means more money is coming into the country, and that helps generate more demand. So a *trade surplus*, which is what this is called, is good for the economy.

When imports exceed exports, the economy suffers. More money is going out than coming in. This is called a *trade deficit*, and the larger it gets, the more money that leaks out of the U.S. economy and into the economies of our trading partners.

Keep in mind that imports by themselves are not bad. As I said, they allow for a wider selection of products, usually at lower prices. But there is a cost of trade, and that occurs when we run trade deficits, which reduce economic growth.

Now we have the basics of our economy. From a simple family that managed to survive on its own, a complex economic system has been created, with a variety of actors. We have people who produce things, and they are called businesses—at least the Supreme Court thinks they are people. We have individuals who purchase goods, and they are our consumers. We even have concept of world trade. Instead of neighboring tribes that are trading with each other, we have different countries. The government oversees all this securing the common good.

All that is great but what is left out is the concept of business cycles. People may want to buy, businesses may want to sell, and governments may want to do whatever governments want to do at any given time. But the willingness and ability to do that is greatly affected by where you are or frequently where you think you are in a business cycle.

What are business cycles? Basically, the economy doesn't go straight ahead. You have to think of it as being a roller coaster, with long stretches of growth. Indeed, since World War II, the growth periods have averaged five years, though the expansions have varied greatly in length. The shortest period was just one year, from July 1980 to July 1981. We barely were aware the recession had actually ended before a new one had started. In contrast, there was the 1990s, where we had growth during almost the entire period. The expansion started in March 1991 and ended in March 2001, a full 10 years of exuberance, which was sometimes irrational.

While there is no one single reason an expansion comes to an end and a recession starts, what we do know is that businesses, households, and our elected officials view the world differently, depending on where the economy is going. Thus, while we may know how the different actors in our economic passion play interact, understanding their behavior requires a lot more than simply saying that people like to consume, businesses want to produce and sell their products, and politicians want to provide public services. It is the context of those decisions that we look at in understanding what should or should not be done.

Having developed a general understanding of all the major actors in this economic play and the importance of business cycles, the next step is to see how consumers, businesses and the government really work and how context affects their decisions, for better or worse. In Chapter 5, we start off by taking a look at households and their spending decisions.

Chapter 5

Shopper Nation: Why We Buy or Don't Buy

We are a nation that likes to shop. Consumer spending represents about 70 percent of the annual U.S. gross domestic product, over $17 trillion at the end of 2013, the largest in the world.

Americans purchase all sorts of goods, such as vehicles, computers, houses, and clothing. But we also buy services such as health care, hotel rooms, and restaurant meals. In fact, two-thirds of all spending and over 45 percent of the economy consists of purchases of services.[1]

But the decision whether to buy something is complex. Anyone making a purchase has to decide if they can afford it. When was the last time the boss promised a raise? If there isn't enough money in the wallet or checking account, is it worth pulling out the credit card?

The decision to use the credit card or take out a loan to buy a car may entail how confident the consumer is in having a job in the future. Or maybe the purchaser has assets that are rising in value—a stock market portfolio or a house—so the job may not be as important. And if the consumer is approaching the so-called golden years, perhaps more of the spending will go toward health care or cruises and less on new sports cars or the latest smartphone.

In this chapter, we look at how the economic environment inter-acts with this critical part of the economy.

What Causes the Itch to Spend?

At 10:30 A.M. on a steamy mid-July day, consumers are start-ing to stream into Macy's Herald Square flagship store in midtown Manhattan. Some head for the men's floors, where Polo shirts, Calvin Klein shorts, and Alfani T-shirts are reduced by 25 to 40 percent. Others head for the women's floors, where the savings on such brands as DKNY, Ralph Lauren, and Style & Co. are equally as tempting.

Are the buyers in the store because the major retailer is holding a big well-advertised annual summer sale to make room for fall sweaters and jackets? Or are consumers shopping because they feel better about their own personal economic prospects?

Economic theory tells us for most consumers, what matters the most when considering purchases is wage and salary gains. The faster worker compensation rises, the better off households will be and the more they can spend. That would trigger more demand and more hiring, and you would think the economy would be off to the races. However, that's not what's been happening in the United States since the economic downturn.

One organization that has been chronicling eroding wages is the National Employment Law Project (NELP), which has a relatively long history of involvement in labor issues. NELP was founded in 1969 to provide legal assistance on employment issues as social changes began to convulse the nation. The organization then evolved into a legal ser-vices backup center that provided legal expertise on specific issues such as jobs for health care workers. But President Reagan went after such legal groups who received taxpayer funding. And after Congress took an axe to paying for the law groups, NELP evolved even more into a center that received a lot of its funding from foundations and did labor research and assisted grassroots groups involved in labor issues such as helping vulnerable immigrant day workers.

For the period 2009 to 2012, NELP found that real median hourly wages declined by 2.8 percent across 785 occupations. Even the workers in the highest-paying occupations, where median hourly wages ranged from $30.47 for the lowest-paying job category to $83.33 for the job that paid the most, saw their wages drop by 1.8 percent over the time period.

However, it was far worse for lower and mid-range occupations such as hairdressers, butchers, and school crossing guards. In the quintile of occupations where median wages ranged from $10.61 per hour for the lowest-paid position to $14.21 per hour in the highest-paid occupation, real wages fell by 4.1 percent between 2009 and 2012.[2]

Ironically, while wages were falling the most for lower- and mid-range workers, another NELP analysis looked at where the new jobs were being created. In the first two years of the economic recovery, low-wage occupations accounted for 21 percent of job losses but 58 percent of the jobs added. By way of contrast, mid-wage occupations such as municipal employees had 60 percent of the recession losses but only 22 percent of the jobs created in the recovery.[3]

"So what our studies show is that at the same time that we have disproportionate job creation in low-wage jobs, we've also seen the wages decline in these low-wage jobs," says Christine Owens, executive director of NELP.

Owens's pathway to NELP has taken her from the University of Virginia Law School to civil rights battles and women's issues. She eventually ended up at the AFL-CIO, where she became director of public policy. But she says her special concern has been low-wage and unemployed workers, which led her to NELP in 2007, when they were looking for a new executive director.

From her perspective, one of the major reasons why there has been a significant increase in people working in low-wage jobs is the oversupply of people desperate for income and willing to do any work. "It is just a matter of economics; the large number of people looking for work will drive down wages," she says. And when they do find work, many are starting at either the minimum wage or a wage that uses the minimum wage as a base.

Table 5.1   Older Workers Get the Jobs

Age Group	Recession (Dec 2007–Feb 2010)	Recovery (Feb 2010–Jun 2013)	Net
16 to 19	−1,366	−18	−1,384
20 to 24	−1,201	1,059	−142
25 to 34	−1,493	1,094	−399
35 to 44	−3,512	−3	−3,515
45 to 54	−1,434	−651	−2,085
55 and over	1,225	4,049	5,274
Total all ages	**−7,781**	**5,530**	**−2,251**

SOURCE: NELP, based on U.S. Census Bureau data.

Owens, who has been arguing for an increase in the minimum wage for years, notes the lowest of wages—$7.25 per hour as of mid-2013—has not kept up with inflation or productivity. "So that basic wage floor has eroded," she says. "It does not create that kind of upward lift that is needed to keep wages at the bottom of the labor market up."

Who is taking many of those low wage jobs? Most of the job gains since the recession have gone to people aged 55 and older who have seen a 20 percent net increase in jobs between December 2007 and June 2013—a period that includes the recession and recovery—according to a NELP analysis of U.S. Census Bureau data (see Table 5.1). The older workers are the only age group that has gained ground since 2007. They are showing up in grocery stores, retail chains, and fast food establishments.

Seniors Get the Jobs but the Pay Leaves Many Cold

Griffin Coxey is a 57-year-old who drives a forklift, and his situation is an example of what has happened to many people 55 or older who have lost their jobs.

Coxey has worn a white collar for most of his work life as an accountant and company controller (basically, the chief accounting officer) in the Sheboygan County, Wisconsin, area. He has both a bachelor's degree and a master's in business administration. But despite his long experience and education, after he got laid off from his last full-time controller's job in October 2010, he says he could not find anything until he landed a $9.25 an hour job at Home Depot. "Eventually you just get tired of sitting around," he says.

But there is a cost to taking a relatively low-paying part-time job. He estimates his family income—his wife works, too—has dwindled from $60,000 to $35,000 to $40,000. The shrinking of their income means they have to be very careful how they spend their money. "It is almost like going on retirement, living on a fixed income is what it is," he says. "You know we never did live extravagantly anyway, so we can keep our house, but the vacation that we wanted to take—we can't take the vacation."

But it goes beyond vacations. His son is getting married in 2014, and he won't be able to help out financially as much as he would like. His 2005 Hyundai has 110,000 miles on it, and he's not sure how he will pay for a car to replace it. Eating out a restaurant and going to movies are rare occurrences. "We make just enough to get by, but there's no extras," he says.

And Coxey is far from alone—especially where he works. He says his Home Depot is stocked with lots of people who are starting to get silver hair. "You would not believe how many people are like me—and I'm not criticizing Home Depot because they gave me a job when no one else would," he says. "I actually really love the work. I learned to drive a forklift, and I never thought I would be driving a forklift. The store treats you really good, but the only thing I don't like is the money."

All that we need for a great economy is for businesses to pay their workers more and more, right? Not so fast. There is a natural tension between corporate earnings and wages. The more workers are paid, the less that is left over for profits, everything else held constant.

That is where the business cycle comes in. When growth is strong and unemployment rates are low, there are not a lot of people out there looking for work who have the skills a company wants. Expanding the workforce becomes difficult. Consequently, firms have to bid up wages to get the employees they want and need. They often have to pay up for workers employed in other companies in order to get them to switch positions. That is when workers do really well. Labor has the upper hand, and workers shop their skills around, getting the best deal they can.

But the pendulum swings, and when the economy is expanding modestly and unemployment rates are fairly high, there is little reason for businesses to pay their workers a top salary. There are also a lot of skilled, experienced people beating the bushes for jobs. Businesses have the upper hand when there are many applicants for any position. Firms make use of that power position to limit labor income growth.

The importance of where you are in the business cycle, or context of economic activity, was no clearer than in the recovery from the Great Recession. Unemployment rates hit double digits, and the slow recovery kept rates high for an extended period. There were so many people looking for work that firms could essentially pick and choose as they pleased. Essentially, a job candidate had to have the right skills and enough experience to warrant an interview, let alone get an offer. There was minimal pressure on businesses to raise wages, and they didn't.

If businesses don't give their workers salary increases, there are real costs to the economy. Even with the prices of things people buy rising very slowly (i.e., inflation), people could not afford a lot of additional goods because of the stagnant income growth. Household buying power, which is compensation after price increases are taken into consideration, grew at an extremely sluggish pace.

Indeed, after declining in 2009, real or inflation-adjusted compensation per hour was essentially flat for four years. It is hard to generate strong growth, which would be above 3 percent, if incomes and purchasing power are going nowhere.[4]

So why don't firms simply raise wages, since it will cause the economy to grow faster and ultimately help the company? There is a little issue that we can ascribe to what economists call "The Free Rider Problem": that is, if everyone else does something and I don't, I will benefit the most without paying the cost.

Basically, it could be really great for the economy if all firms gave bigger pay increases. As wages rise, so would consumer demand, output, and ultimately employment. But if I were a business owner or executive, it would be very beneficial if I held my costs down and did not pay higher wages. That would give me a competitive advantage. So my best move would be not to raise wages. Essentially, I get for free what every other firm gets by paying higher wages.

Clearly, that is not sustainable. Each firm acting individually would make that same calculation. Indeed, if just one company raises wages and no one else follows, that company will lose. It will be paying higher wages, but it will have no impact on national income. Meanwhile, competitive companies will have lower costs, giving them a cost advantage. Since it makes no sense for any one firm to start raising wages faster unless circumstances require them to, wages will not rise faster. That creates a Fallacy of Composition: what is good for one firm (not raising wages) is not good for the economy as a whole.

Sluggish economic growth leads to limited job gains, which causes the unemployment rate to decline minimally which keeps wages down. Limited wage increases produce lackluster consumer spending, which gets us back to the beginning—sluggish economic growth. The only way out of this "growth trap" is for the unemployment rate to fall over time to a level where labor becomes scarce and firms must bid up wages. As we saw in the first half of the 2010s, that could take a long time.

If anyone is wondering why the recovery from the Great Recession was so tepid, one place to look is at the growth trap. Yet the economy continued to expand despite the issues with limited income growth. Consequently, there must be other factors involved with household decisions about how much to spend.

The reality is that two households, even if they have the same income, may buy different things and spend different amounts. Income just provides a baseline for spending. It is those variations between individuals and income groups that drive the economy. This is where factors such as confidence, wealth, and debt come into play.

That it is not just the money you make that determines what you spend is a reminder that context is the most important factor in economic activity. Thus, in order to understand if people want to shop till they drop or drop shopping, we need to look at things such as consumer attitudes, what is happening to the value of their investments, including the prices of their homes and where people may be in their lives. All these come together to determine consumer spending and ultimately, for a consumer-based economy, economic growth.

"Charg-It"

Income is only one aspect of the ability to purchase things. Despite worker income's falling during the recovery from the recession, the economy continued to grow. Consequently, there must be other factors involved with household decisions about how much to spend.

One of those factors is debt.

The bank-issued credit card has changed the way many of us live. But, who created it and where did they do it?

Try a young banker from Brooklyn.

Anyone who wants to find the birthplace of the first bank credit card type of system has to go to Flatbush Avenue, deep in a neighborhood full of Caribbean accents.

Looking for a bank? Long gone. Instead, search for a store that sells furniture and appliances.

Inside the Fulton Stores on Flatbush Avenue is an artifact that gives a clue as to what used to be in the building: a large, round, steel bank vault—the type featured in bank robbery movies and still used by fiduciary organizations to illustrate the safety of their deposits. Instead of money and valuables, the vault holds a queen-sized bed with tan-and-red-striped reading pillows and assorted vanities and dressers—all for sale, of course.

The vault once belonged to Flatbush National Bank, which proudly ran ads in the spring of 1945, calling itself "the only independent commercial bank in Flatbush."[5] The Flatbush bank was run by John Biggins, a manufacturer who went into banking in 1927, only two years before the great stock market crash and the Great Depression.[6]

Around 1946, Biggins's son, John C., came up with the idea that changed personal finance: merchants and customers could sign up for something called "Charg-It." He had observed that local merchants were losing business to the downtown department stores, which offered credit. So why not offer a system that the smaller local merchants could use to entice consumers to shop local and the bank could supply the credit instead of the shop?

If bank retail customers passed a credit bureau check, they would receive a "Charga-Plate," writes Louis Hyman, the author of the book

Debtor Nation: The History of America in Red Ink. They could use the Charga-Plate at any store that took it. The merchant sent the receipts to the bank and received their money the same day. If consumers did not pay their total bill, they were charged an annual rate of 6 percent, Hyman writes. Merchants gave up 8 percent of each purchase to the bank.[7]

Yes, a credit card system that worked at more than one establishment had been born. Fast-forward from Charg-It to 2013. About 75 percent of Americans have a credit card. Consumer revolving debt—in large part, credit card debt—was over $850 billion in 2013, according to the Federal Reserve Board.[8] Divided by the population of 315 million, this comes to almost $2,700 dollars for woman, man, and child in America.

When we look at just households, the numbers are even more amazing. The average American credit card–holding household has credit card debt of about $10,550. Finally, if you really dig deeply into the number, as some analysts have done, and look only at households that carry balances, he average outstanding balance could be over $15,000.[9]

For those who do have a credit card, there are myriad options. There are standard credit cards available from most banks. There are credit cards with rewards programs such as cash back or cards that allow a user to earn points for an airline or hotel. Places such as Disney have cards that require points to be redeemed at specific retailers. There are even cards for people with bad credit or for students who have a short credit history.

By 2000 there were so many different variations on cards that John Oldshue, a meteorologist for an Alabama television station, decided to try to make it easier for consumers to compare interest rates and card terms by developing a web site called LowCards.com. While it may seem like a strange business for a weatherman, Oldshue had done the same thing in 1999 for long distance telephone plans.

Oldshue and his wife needed a long-distance calling plan and found there were 200 options out there.

Bill Hardekopf, a partner at LowCards, which is based in Birmingham, Alabama, says, "He researched what the best plan was and put that up on a web site so he could share it with his friends. That developed into a business that was called SaveOnPhone.com."

Within a year, Oldshue and Hardekopf were analyzing the growing credit card business, looking at about 1,000 credit cards to see what
was new and what trends might be developing. From some 14 years of
studying the industry, Hardekopf thinks the main reasons why people
carry credit cards is to avoid the need to carry lots of cash and to buy
things that they may not have the money for at that moment.

But he thinks there are yet other reasons people are pulling out the
plastic: some like the rewards, such as cash back or the possibility of air
travel; others like the protections that come with using a credit card.
And at the end of the year, he says, "It's a great accounting system, since
at the end of each month you get an accounting of all the purchases
you have made on your credit card, so it makes it easier to do your
taxes or keep a budget."

But does their credit card usage vary depending on the state of the
economy? In other words, do people look around themselves and ask,
"Is this a good time to charge something?" Probably not directly, says
Hardekopf. Instead, he thinks credit card usage relates more to how
people view their own personal finances.

"I think people make decisions based on their own personal financial scenarios," he says, but adds, "the overall economy can affect their
personal finances." For example, if a worker has had his or her hours
cut back or been laid off, the odds are good they will cut back on their
credit card use.

And, indeed, that is what has happened since the economic
downturn. Between 2008 (the peak in credit card usage) and 2011
(the bottom), the total amount of revolving debt (mostly charges on
credit cards) had dropped 17.5 percent, according to Federal Reserve
statistics.[10]

"I think people have tightened their belts," says Hardekopf, "And
I think people got used to not putting a lot of transactions on their
credit card or running up a lot of credit card debt."

Back in Brooklyn, Biggins's effort to market Charg-It was short-
lived. In 1946, his father sold Flatbush National to Manufacturers Trust,
which promptly shut down the card system, according to Hyman's
book. The son moved to New Jersey and restarted the credit card
scheme at Paterson Savings and Trust Company, where Biggins became
head of the personal loan department.[11]

Manufacturers Trust later became Manufacturers Hanover Corporation, which was then purchased by Chemical Banking Corporation. Chemical in turn was bought by Chase Manhattan Bank. Chase later purchased J. P. Morgan & Company to become JPMorgan Chase, which is one of the largest credit card issuers in the nation.

Why Debt Is Good—or Bad

We know that people love to use their credit cards and borrow money for not just small purchases but big ones as well. But is that a good thing? The typical answer is yes, but in reality, the answer is that it depends on how much is borrowed and where the economy is going. In other words, it is all about context.

Economic theory tells us debt is a boon to commercial activity. Early in an economic slowdown, people look to their savings for support, but when that runs out, they turn to debt. When people are stretched, they borrow in order to maintain their standard of living.

Typically, people start out optimistic about the future, no matter what the circumstance. The philosophy is that a financial setback is only temporary, so if I borrow a little now, I will be able to keep going. When I get my job back, I will pay off the debt. Sounds great, right? Maybe. Whom you borrow from matters, and for many people, the choice is limited: It's the credit card or nothing. It's hard to get a loan from a bank if you don't have a job.

As long as the financial problems that households face are relatively short term, going into debt makes sense. While that is good, as it limits the extent of the downturn, it sets the stage for problems later on, especially since credit card debt is expensive.

The longer the slowdown, the weaker the recovery, the greater the future problems. After a while, households become maxed out. Ultimately, they use up all their savings and cannot repay their loans. That leads to a collapse in spending. If that occurs after the recovery begins, the expansion is weakened.

But it doesn't stop there. Eventually, people start reducing their borrowing in order to lower their debt loads and improve their personal balance sheets. Even when they are working again, they need to pay down the debt they accumulated. That stretches out the recovery as households, even if their wages are rising again, use some of those gains to get their financial houses in order.

Reducing debt burdens may be good for the individual, but if lots of households do it, it is not good for the economy. That is another example of the Fallacy of Composition.

Debt is not just a concern when economic conditions falter. Some of the biggest problems are created when the economy is booming. People feel that the good times will never end and they borrow like crazy. The ratio of debt to income rises during good times, indicating that people are piling on the borrowing.

But the good times don't last forever, and when households get overextended, an economic slowdown leads to an inability to pay back the debt and ultimately a drop in spending, which raises the question: is frugality better than debt?

Without borrowing, economic growth is limited to income growth. Too much borrowing, though, leads to huge upswings in demand, which is usually followed by a large cratering in spending when the pendulum swings back as people stop borrowing and start rebuilding their balance sheets. Like everything, debt is good as long as it is done in moderation.

If too much of a good thing is not good, what factors drive all that borrowing? One thing that leads the debt boom is wealth. When your stock market account is surging, you might feel comfortable about putting more charges on your credit card. So you have to take into account the stock market and home values when it comes to consumption.

The Rich Worry, Too

How many people do you know who are worth $10 million or more? Unless you work on Wall Street or hang around the right country clubs, the answer is probably not very many. But as Parker, a wealth management adviser, sits in a "client room" on Fifth Avenue, he reels off story after story about people who are worth millions and millions of dollars.[12] Their view of the economy is different than most middle-class Americans, whose main dream of getting rich involves picking the winning lottery ticket.

To illustrate a point that wealth is relative—that you can have a lot of money but not feel rich—he recounts how he was driving with a friend who had just received a check for just under $1 million for a partnership he's involved with.

"I say to him that you must feel really great about that—and he's sitting there holding the check," says Parker. "And a plane takes off from Westchester County Airport right where we are driving, and it's a private jet, and he goes, 'You know, the guy who handed me this check got $4 million.'"

Despite getting the big check, Parker says his buddy still mows his own lawn—of course, it is 10 acres in a very upscale suburb and he rides a big tractor. But why not hire someone else to do it? Because, Parker says, his friend does not feel wealthy.

"As I think about the folks I work with, I have plenty of clients who have $10 million, $20 million, $30 million," says Parker. "They certainly have a lot of money, but they don't have what I would view as a wealthy lifestyle. Oh, they have a bunch of homes, but they don't have time to live in them. And, they are always sort of paranoid about running out of money and all that stuff."

Rich people paranoid?

Yes, indeed, says Parker, recounting how he has a client who used to have in excess of $100 million. Parker managed only a piece of it—maybe a little over $10 million. The rest was run by Bernard Madoff, who was running a Ponzi scheme with the money and will spend the rest of his life in jail for the swindle, which took in billions.

"And I am sitting there post-Madoff, and the family still has $10 million or $11 million, which by most definitions means you are well off, and the patriarch of the family is telling me, 'This is worse than death.'"

Beg your pardon?

"Well, I was having a hard time understanding it, too," confesses Parker. "But it just meant that on $100 million, you could generate $4 million to $5 million a year in income to maintain your lifestyle—the plane, the houses, all that. But, on $10 million, you can't do that anymore, so they had to get rid of the plane, some of the houses, and cut the living expenses, so everything they had become accustomed to no longer works."

From his experience with the wealthy, Parker has had a number of clients who never quite got into acting like the Great Gatsby even if they were wealthy. He recounts how he has a client whose worth is in the $20 million range. "He hates spending money," says Parker. "He has a boat on the Jersey shore, which keeps breaking down. He could probably afford a $150,000 boat but he just keeps fixing the old one."

That particular client earned most of his money through his acumen. But Parker says the clients who have the most difficulty with wealth are those who have inherited large sums "because they don't have the experience, they don't understand the grind to save and build," he explains. "They have the money, and they are incredibly insecure about it."

On second thought, maybe the insecurity is somewhat understandable given Parker's experience with some old New England families that had large holdings of inherited IBM shares. Back in the 1980s, IBM was the darling of Wall Street. The stock sold for as much as $160 a share, and the company would declare an annual dividend of 5 percent to 6 percent—enough to afford the winter vacation in Gstaad or spend a few weeks at St. Bart's—and still put the children through private school. Oh, and not have to hold a nine-to-five job. Parker would argue in vain for them to diversify, sell some of the stock.

"It represented a disproportionate amount of people's wealth, and there was this notion that we would never invade the principal, we'll just live off the dividend," says Parker. "And, then IBM went from $160 to $40 a share and they cut the dividend, and these people's lives were devastated."

In his experience, what happened to the IBM families is not unique.

Parker knows financial executives—in theory, sophisticated investors—who rode their Bear Stearns stock or Lehman Brothers stock all the way to zero. "Now, you have a bunch of these guys walking around with worthless Lehman stock. I would suggest they have the company that issues the physical stock certificates send them some so they can hang them on the wall as a reminder."

And he wonders if Apple, Inc. is the next IBM in regard to the wealthy. "At the end of 2012, it was selling at $700 a share, and the next year it traded below $400 a share," he says. "So, look, there are a lot of people who owned it on the way up, would not part with it, and in the summer of 2013 it's at $450 a share, a 40 percent drop, and it's represented a third to a half of some people's liquid net worth."

What is that these wealthy people want to use their money for?

Parker says from his experience the rich have four things that really concern them. The first is making sure they take care of themselves for the foreseeable future. Second is to take care of their family, their children, and grandchildren. Third is having enough money for their charitable interests. And fourth is having enough money to pay their taxes.

However, people's priorities may not always fit neatly into this order. For example, Parker has a client—a former executive—who gives away a couple of million dollars per year to his philanthropic interests. "We got together and he drew this hill, which represented his wealth," says Parker. "And he said his goal was to give away everything he has. He has four or five kids, all well educated, but he said, 'They have to do it on their own.'"

Although some metrics seem to indicate the rich are just getting richer, Parker thinks being wealthy has now become more stressful. Many of the rich saw their net worth sag sharply in the Great Recession—as both their home prices and stock portfolios fell. "So 2008 was a panic of mass proportions," he says. "Affluent people felt incredibly vulnerable, and on top of that, the institutions they trusted and relied upon got themselves in trouble and sold them a bunch of stuff that Warren Buffett has described as "weapons of mass destruction."

Add the possibility of losing money to yet another Madoff, says Parker, and life is just more stressful. "You think if I had $10 million, all my problems would be solved," he concludes. "My experience has been, yeah, not the case. Everything is context."

Economic Theory of Wealth

Economic theory views wealth differently. When your 401(k) is growing like crazy, you feel comfortable about your retirement. The future is supposedly secure, and as a result, people start to spend, spend, spend, and then borrow so they can spend more. You have to take into account the stock market when it comes to consumption.

Equity markets, and to the extent they raise or lower wealth, affect household spending regardless of the changes they may be seeing in their incomes. When people feel that their futures are set and they don't have to worry about it, they spend more.

The best example of the impact of the equity market on consumer spending occurred during the dot-com bubble in the 1990s and the rebound in stocks in the middle of the 2000s. With all the equity markets hitting record highs, people saw their retirement plan values soar. They felt they could spend all they wanted, and this even spilled into borrowing. With the wealth being built up in their stock holdings, they could take it to the bank and get loans. And they did that.

Of course, when the stock bubbles burst, so did wealth and spending. The result was a recession that began within a year of the peaking of the stock markets in both 2001 and 2007.

If you think stocks matter when it comes to debt and spending, consider the impact of housing. Home equity comprises about one-quarter of household wealth, and many have considered the value of the house a "savings account." When prices rose, people felt good about their financial situation. This wealth effect, especially during the period from 2004 to 2007, when prices rose sharply in many metropolitan areas, contributed to the boom in the economy.

Housing, though, had an added impact on consumer spending. The advent of readily available home equity loans and lines of credit allowed people to use their houses essentially as piggy banks that they could break into anytime they wanted to, and which they did. So households not only felt good about the future but also were able to readily translate those euphoric feelings into spending in the here and now. This led to a surge in consumption and powered the strong growth in the middle part of the decade.

The economy went into recession when the housing bubble burst, just like with the tech bubble. Wealth collapsed, and so did the feeling of comfort. But things got even worse as the ability to borrow from the house disappeared. That exacerbated the slowdown.

When you add the decline in wealth due to the collapse of the stock markets and the housing markets to the inability to borrow from credit cards, from banks, or from home equity, is it any surprise that the economy went into such a deep decline that the downturn has been nicknamed the "Great Recession"? And given that it takes a long time to rebuild that wealth, is it any surprise that the recovery was so slow? And is it any surprise that when stocks and housing prices recovered, so did growth?

We know that you cannot just look at income; you have to look at wealth and a household's balance sheet. Indeed, the changes in wealth and income have impacts separate from the levels of income and wealth, as that is what affects perception of their well-being. People worry about whether the future looks brighter or darker. And that is where consumer confidence comes in.

Feeling Good? Buy a Car

Anyone who has sat through a basic macroeconomic course will know that you cannot just look at income, debt, and wealth to understand the consumer. You have to know what people think and feel, not just what they have, when it comes to household spending. That is where consumer confidence comes in.

What are the key factors that drive consumer confidence? Maybe most important is the perception of job security. If you think you will be losing your job, it is not likely you will be going out and spending lots of time at the mall. Alternatively, when your company is expanding and hiring lots of people and you think that the good times are here to stay, it is easy to open the wallet really wide.

How do people come to the conclusion that they have, or don't have, job security? They look at the economy. Are jobs being created or destroyed, and what is happening to the unemployment rate? The labor market is clearly key.

Was it a surprise to anyone that consumer confidence collapsed in late 2008 and early 2009? The economy was losing hundreds of thousands of jobs each month and the unemployment rate rose to double digits, so it only made sense that people assumed the turtle position and stopped buying. Fear, which is another way of saying "I have no confidence," drove household buying decisions regardless of household incomes. Basically, if you think you are going to lose your job, nothing else matters.

In December 2008, during the dregs of the recession, the Gallup Economic Confidence Index, which polls 1,700 adults on a daily basis, found that over 60 percent had a net negative view of the U.S. economy's current state and future direction.[13] (By way of contrast, by mid-year 2013, there was a considerable improvement, with a net negative view of the economy by 7 percent of those polled, though it has continued to bounce up and down.)

The auto industry is a good example of what happens when confidence tumbles. During the worst months of the Great Recession, the nation's automobile showrooms were quiet places. Many consumers had trouble getting loans, and yet others were not sure if they would still have a job to pay off a loan. Gasoline prices were rising even though people were driving less.

As a result, many people put off buying new cars. One of those procrastinators was Kathy Simmons of New York City. In 2012, Simmons owned a 1995 Honda Accord station wagon, a dependable car, but as it aged, mechanical issues started to crop up. A simple oil change was costing over $1,000 as the Honda specialists kept finding issues such as important bolts or bushings that needed to be replaced. Spending the money was a necessity since the Honda service representative insisted whatever needed to be done was a safety issue. On top of that, like many people, her stock portfolio had gotten "dinged up," as her investment manager termed it. So why spend $30,000 on a new car when it would only cost a few thousand dollars per year to keep it running?

It was a situation lots of other people were facing as they tried to tease more mileage out of their clunkers or they decided they couldn't afford a new car. The procrastination or hesitation at buying a new car showed up in the numbers. In 2005, the automobile industry sold 17 million cars and light trucks, according to the U.S Bureau of Economic Analysis. But in 2009, that was down to 10.4 million. Even in 2013, well after the end of the Great Recession, the industry was still not fully recovered, with sales of about 15.5 million units.

In yet another way to look at the auto slowdown, the number of total registered vehicles declined between 2008 and 2011, says Dan Meckstroth, an industrial economist at Manufacturers Alliance for Productivity and Innovation (MAPI), an education, research, and professional organization. Citing private databases, he notes that car registrations continued to decline into 2013 even though the auto companies were selling more light-, medium-, and heavy-duty trucks.

"The drop in car registrations really reflects the poor financial condition of consumers and the fact they have postponed spending as well as a preference for utility vehicles," he says.

Although the auto industry is cyclical, in the past it had one metric going for it: the natural increase in the population, which results in more teenagers' getting their driver's licenses. In theory, the new drivers should become car buyers. Historically, points out Meckstroth, the driving-age population increases by about 0.9 percent per year. However, even that's changing, moderating in recent years to 0.6 percent. "It is decelerating but it's still growing," says Meckstroth.

Some of the decrease in car buying may be associated with the difficulty young people were having getting jobs. Even by the end of 2013 the unemployment rate for ages 16 to 19 was still over 20 percent on a seasonally adjusted basis. Young adults could not afford the payments on a car or just did not have the credit rating for a loan.

At some point, consumers will begin to feel better about their economic situation, which should help car sales, says Meckstroth. "There is plenty of pent-up demand," he said in mid-2013. "People who kept their cars and did not replace them will be replacing them more," he says.

That turned out to be the case for Simmons. By the end of 2012, her stock portfolio had recovered significantly. Consumer confidence by then had improved considerably, with the Gallup poll showing a net negative of 13 percent. That's when Simmons purchased a new station wagon. "It gets to the point where the cost of repair is more than the market value of the car," says Meckstroth.

The impact of wealth on confidence is important, but not the end of the story about how the consumer spends. There are other factors that can affect confidence, and most of them have to do with income. For example, if inflation surges, that is not good news for spending. Why? People are worried that their costs are rising faster than their income and they will not be able to sustain their standard of living.

In contrast, other, non–income-related issues don't have a major effect on spending decisions. Political uncertainty caused by crazy doings in Washington, D.C., may drive people bananas and cause confidence to decline. But being disturbed that Congress has gone over the edge and sharp changes in the willingness to spend just don't necessarily go together.

Over time, people worry more about their incomes than anything else. Factors that threaten their jobs or their wealth are translated into lower spending. Positive events that cause people to believe their salaries will rise will loosen the purse string. Those positive and negative factors are the ones that we need to look at if we are to understand the direction of consumer purchases, and as we have shown, that means understanding the context in which those decisions are being made.

Thus, we have seen that income, wealth, and debt play a huge role in consumer spending. Changes in those components do affect confidence, a wild card in any discussion about where retail and vehicle sales or even the housing market will go. But those factors still don't tell us the whole story. One other issue must be considered: changes in the patterns of spending as people age.

Where a person is in his or her life cycle not only cannot be dismissed, but with the aging of the Baby Boomers, it might have to be considered almost critical. A person's propensity or willingness to spend changes with age.

When you are young and carefree, you make money and you spend it. As you age and start a family, you begin to concentrate on the future. Instead of spending, you start saving and investing. After you've reached your peak earning years and put away all the money you need, you think about retiring, during which time you start drawing down on your wealth.

Why does that matter? Because of demographics. The U.S. economy has been a captive of the Baby Boomers, those born between 1946 and 1964, for the past 60 years. They have been the largest age group their whole lives and have been catered to because if you can get Boomers to buy something, you have a great market for your product no matter what other age groups want or need.

That has had enormous implications. As Boomers' preferences have changed, so has production, be it for clothing, homes, or vehicles. Fast food became popular for lots of reasons, one of which was the Boomer generation hitting their teens and young adult status.

As Boomers have aged, their tastes and income levels have changed as well. Small cars became luxury vehicles. Apartments in the city became McMansions in the far-out suburbs. And now that they are beginning to retire, the next change is occurring. They are looking for high-density, amenity-rich locations in which to retire and are therefore changing their location patterns. As any Boomer will tell you, their aging is creating rapidly increasing demand for health services.

Similarly, as Generation X hits middle age and the Millennials take their role in the economy, patterns of spending and production will continue to be altered in order to account for these groups. And as Boomers pass on, their importance in the economy will wane, and spending patterns will change once again.

Will consumers shop till they drop or drop spending? It depends. It depends on their incomes and wealth, their debt levels and their willingness to take on debt, confidence, and where they are in their lives. And that means that context is critical in any discussion about consumption. All of these are factors that businesses have to watch closely when they determine their business plans and that corporate sector is what we will look at in the next chapter.

Notes

1. U.S. Bureau of Economic Analysis, GDP report. www.bea.gov/newsreleases /national/gdp/gdpnewsrelease.htm and Naroff Economic Advisors, Inc. December 20, 2013.

2. National Employment Law Project, "The Inequality of Declining Wages during the Recovery," July 2013. www.nelp.org/page/-/Job_Creation/ NELP-Fact-Sheet-Inequality-Declining-Wages.pdf.

3. National Employment Law Project, "The Low-Wage Recovery and Growing Inequality," August 2012. www.nelp.org/page/-/Job_Creation/ LowWageRecovery2012.pdf.

4. U.S. Bureau of Labor Statistics, Productivity and Costs release, and Naroff Economic Advisors, Inc. December 6, 2013. www.bls.gov/news.release/ prod2.nr0.htm.

5. *Flatbush Magazine*, published by the Flatbush Chamber of Commerce, March 1945.

6. Clipping from the *Brooklyn Daily Eagle*, 1927, exact date indecipherable.

7. Louis Hyman, *Debtor Nation: The History of America in Red Ink* (Princeton, NJ: Princeton University Press, 2011), 146–148.

8. Federal Reserve Board. January, 2014. www.federalreserve.gov/releases/g19/Current/.

9. Nerdwallet, a commercial web site. January, 2014. www.nerdwallet.com/blog/credit-card-data/average-credit-card-debt-household/.

10. Federal Reserve Board. January, 2014. www.federalreserve.gov/releases/g19/Current/.

11. Hyman, *Debtor Nation; Flatbush Magazine* reports sale of the bank in its June 1946 issue.

12. Parker is a real person, but his name and some other personal details have been changed.

13. www.gallup.com/poll/122840/gallup-daily-economic-indexes.aspx, January 9, 2014.

Chapter 6

How Is a Can of Tuna Like a Smartphone? Yes, Context!

The corporate world can be like a pressure cooker. Shareholders want higher returns. The workers grumble about their pay increases. CEOs have to make critical decisions on where or whether to build a new factory. To understand new regulations a company may need legions of lawyers.

How does the company get all this done? Part of the answer is through assessing the context around decisions it has to make.

In this chapter, we look at factors such as corporate taxation and regulation. How much do they influence CEOs when it comes to important decisions? We examine the rationale for taxes on small business.

We also take a closer look at how a company, in the middle of the recession, made a decision to build a major new factory that will be producing the computer chips that power our tablets and smartphones and whatever else Silicon Valley types can invent in the future.

Another important fact of life for a company is that corporate life can be Darwinian. In others words, acquire a competitor or be swallowed up yourself. To better understand the context around the decision to buy and sell companies we talk to a deal maker who tries to find creative ways to merge companies.

A Company Decides to Build Chips

A recession can scare a company away from making big investments. Lenders may turn down loans to anyone but the most creditworthy. Stock market analysts may clamor for cuts, not investments. And boards of directors may simply decide to wait for the storm to blow over.

But sometimes a business sees the economy and the context surrounding its decisions in a different light and decides to plow ahead. Let us introduce you to one of those fearless firms: GLOBALFOUNDRIES, a company that wasn't in existence until March 2009, the worst period during the Great Recession.

Today, GLOBALFOUNDRIES (GF) owns a state-of-the-art semi-conductor factory—in Saratoga County, New York, about 20 minutes north of Albany. The building with a white and gray metal shell covers an area roughly the size of six football fields. Inside are miles of pipe and wire and hundreds of very sophisticated machines designed to produce tiny transistors used in electronics such as games and smartphones.

The initial cost to build the enormous factory was about $4 billion, a very large investment in the middle of the recession. Since breaking ground on the project in 2009, the company has already expanded the campus with additional production capacity and a new research-and-development (R&D) facility, bringing the current project budget to $8 billion.[1]

Given the state of the economy in 2009, who would do this? And why?

Part of the answer revolves around the semiconductor industry itself, which has a history of making big investments almost every year. Historically, annual R&D investment by U.S.-headquartered semiconductor firms has averaged about 15 to 20 percent of sales per year, according to Falan Yinug, director of industry statistics and economic policy at the Semiconductor Industry Association in Washington, D.C.

"No matter whether it's a good year, economically speaking, or a down year, high levels of R&D investment is just the cost of participating in the industry," says Yinug.

At the same time, the industry has been on a powerful growth track. Yinug says that global semiconductor sales in 2012 were $292 billion, over double the sales of 10 years ago. Global sales a decade ago were over double the sales 10 years prior to that.

This strong growth leads to more spending just to keep up with the demand. "There comes a time when there is just not enough global semiconductor capacity to keep up with growing demand," he explains. "When this occurs, semiconductor firms start thinking about actually investing in new plant and equipment to meet the ever increasing needs."

And those investments can be huge. Yinug estimates the typical leading-edge semiconductor fabrication facility costs about $5 billion. "The only type of facility currently more expensive to construct is a nuclear power plant," he says.

The investor in GF is Advanced Technology Investment Company (ATIC), which is based in Abu Dhabi. On its web site, right under where the company tells visitors, "Real change takes time," ATIC enumerates why it could look at the world economy and shrug off the downturn: "We recognize that value creation is more about sustainable wealth generation than short-term profit."

ATIC can afford to be somewhat patient because it is investing some of the sovereign wealth of Abu Dhabi, which has about 4 billion barrels of oil reserves, according to the U.S. Energy Information Administration. However, Abu Dhabi has as one of its goals shifting from an oil and gas economic base to a knowledge-based economy by 2030.[2]

"So they are making strategic investments in certain key industries to make that switch happen," says Travis Bullard, a spokesman for GF.

Bullard has some unique perspective on the investment since he was involved with it from the start—in 2006, before any oil money became involved. That's when the company he worked for, Advanced Micro Devices (AMD) of Sunnyvale, California, said it would spend $3.2 billion to build the chip factory in Malta, New York. In 2006, AMD had ambitions to expand beyond the single chip factory it owned in Dresden, Germany.[3]

But building a semiconductor plant, referred to as a *Fab* by the industry, requires billions of dollars. Even with a big package of financial incentives from New York State, AMD needed more financial help. Two years later, it partnered with ATIC. By the fall of 2008, AMD decided to exit from the chip manufacturing business and sold the Dresden Fab to the Abu Dhabi investors.

"The original press release of October 7, 2008, essentially said, 'Watch this space, a new company will form in a few months,'" recalls Bullard. But that fall, the economic news deteriorated. Lehman Brothers was in bankruptcy. The U.S. Treasury had announced it would fund the Troubled Asset Relief Program (TARP) with $700 billion to bail out the banks. And Bullard recalls that as the headlines got worse, people kept asking, "Is this thing still going to happen?"

Looking back on it, he thinks the reason that AMD was able to complete the deal is that no one knew how bad things were. "Everyone knew it was a big deal, but I don't think anyone understood how big a deal it really was," he recalls. "If it wasn't for the cash that was available from Abu Dhabi, there was no way—in my humble opinion—that this was going to happen because all the investment dollars were drying up."

But the deal did not require financing: ATIC was paying cash. According to the press release, the Abu Dhabi fund paid AMD $700 million, assumed $1.2 billion in AMD debt, and added $1.4 billion in new capital.[4]

However, to be a player in the business, ATIC required more than just deep pockets because there were some serious competitors. In the United States, Intel had many Fabs producing chips for the computer industry. In Asia, the Taiwan Semiconductor Manufacturing Corporation had a long list of customers from its 27 years of making chips. And China was quickly getting into the business as well.

Owning one chip plant in Germany would not give ATIC the ability to be competitive. So in June of 2009, ATIC paid $3.9 billion for Singapore-based Chartered Semiconductor Manufacturing. Now, ATIC owned a company with six Fabs, all in Singapore. ATIC was suddenly sprouting corporate muscles to compete against some of the large players.[5]

However, most of Chartered's business was in what Bullard terms "mainstream" technology, in other words, older computer chips. ATIC had given GF the ability to compete with both the older technology and the newest "leading-edge" computer chips. Sitting at a conference table at the Fab campus, Bullard explains how part of the context of the business is the shrinking size of the chips themselves and the increasingly expensive machines to make them.

The industry measures the chips in terms of nanometers. A single nanometer is a billionth of a meter. A human hair is about 50,000 nanometers. Today, mainstream computer chips are manufactured using measurements of 65 to 90 nanometers. But a leading-edge chip includes components measured at just 20 nanometers or smaller. By way of comparison, Bullard says a single silicon atom is about 5 nanometers.

"So we are basically talking about lining up four to five atoms—that's how small we're talking about here," he says. "We are basically moving molecules around."

Moving molecules around to produce tiny transistors starts with a "clean room," where there are no particles in the air. The air is 10,000 times cleaner than an operating room and recirculated every three minutes. Technicians working in the clean room look like they are wearing moon suits so that no pieces of skin or hair contaminate the room. To prevent vibrations, which might jar the sensitive machines, some parts of the concrete foundation are 12 feet thick.

At the same time, the Fab requires copious amounts of ultra-pure water. In the case of GF, the factory uses about 3 million gallons of tap water per day. But the tap water is put through an intense purification process so there are no impurities in it. The water is necessary because lithography is the main way that chip manufacturers imprint silicon wafers. Lithography is basically a photographic process where an image of the electronic circuit is imprinted on the basic silicon wafer.

"You take a silicon wafer, you clean it, and then you pattern it and then you etch it and then you wash it off," explains Bullard. "There could be a thousand different processing steps, so those processes include the application of chemicals and you have to rinse away those chemicals . . . and so it's a constant rinsing," he says.

At the same time, the business is getting increasingly expensive because the imprints on the chips are getting tinier and tinier. "The reason it's getting so expensive is that the width of the lines (the circuits) are way smaller than the wavelength of light," says Bullard. "So we're using a bunch of tricks basically to be able to draw lines that small."

The tricks, however, are expensive. Many of the hundreds of machines in the clean room cost $35 million to $40 million each. But Bullard says the next generation of tools to make semiconductors is getting closer to $100 million.

"These tools are so big and so complicated it takes several 747s to deliver each machine," he says. They require a special attachment on a crane to minimize vibration. The attachments cost $1 million, says Bullard. "And it is designed only to move these machines," he says.

Why spend all this money?

In part it is because of context: the changing nature of electronics. There is a very large premium to be the first company to introduce a new technology. "The industry is very competitive, and our customers place a gigantic premium on being first, so it's a very time-sensitive industry," explains Bullard. A good example of this is that when Apple (which does not produce its own chips) introduces a new product, consumers line up outside the company's stores hours or even days in advance.

In addition, the demand for smaller and smaller chips can come from customers who barely existed only a few years earlier. Bullard pulls out a chart that shows who requires the newest technology. One new area: the huge server farms that are involved in cloud computing. "They don't just want performance, they want lower power usage because those server farms consume huge amounts of electricity," explains Bullard.

However, for a chip manufacturing company, there is a big risk that it will miss a burgeoning market because it takes so long to develop the technology to produce the chips. In press interviews, Intel's CEO has admitted that the giant company missed out on mobile devices. Intel now says it will be more responsive to smartphones and the next hot trend—intelligent glasses and watches.

Another contextual element in making the investment in the middle of the recession was financial aid. Because governments all around the world as well as state governments consider Fabs to be economic drivers, they are quite competitive in offering financial incentives in any number of combinations: grants, subsidies, tax relief, road construction.

"Texas gave Samsung over $1 billion, and Dresden gave AMD about the same amount," recalls Dennis Brobston, the president of the Saratoga Economic Development Corporation in Saratoga Springs, New York, which was competing to get the new investment.

"At the time, we were competing with Israel, China, Malaysia, Dresden, and in the U.S., Texas and Phoenix," recalls J. Shelby Schneider, who at the time worked for Brobston.

New York's package to woo GF included $500 million for construction, $150 million that had to be spent on R&D in the state, and tax incentives of about $650 million over 10 years, says Brobston.

Bullard says the package "helped to make New York a more competitive option versus other places around the world."

There were still other factors that also led GF to locate in upstate New York. About 15 years ago, an AMD executive had helped the University at Albany-SUNY develop a nanotechnology center. Today, GF recruits engineers and scientists there. At the same time, locating in Saratoga County puts GF close to IBM's research facility in East Fishkill, New York, where over 100 GF engineers are doing research.

In the fall of 2013, it was still too early to know if ATIC's investment would pay off. Bullard agrees that the start-up costs have been so high that the company was still in the red in the fall of 2013. However, the potential is quite large.

Brobston says GF has said it hopes to ship 60,000 silicon wafers a month to clients. The average wafer costs about $100,000. This comes to about $6 billion a month in revenue or $72 billion for the year.

"So you can see how your investment gets paid back rather quickly, which is why the ATIC folks got involved because it is a business that gives high returns," says Brobston.

Computer Chips: Five Factoids on Making Computer Chips at GLOBALFOUNDRIES

1. Working 24 hours a day, seven days a week, it can take GLOBALFOUNDRIES as long as 90 days to physically produce a single sophisticated computer chip used in a smartphone.
2. On its way to becoming a computer chip, a piece of silicon travels on an automated system around the inside of a fabrication plant that is six times the size of a football field. The total distance the silicon wafer travels on its way to becoming a working chip could be as much as 10 miles as it goes from machine to machine.
3. Making computer chips takes 3 million gallons per day of super-pure water. That's enough water to fill a pool that is almost three times as long as a football field, 150 feet wide, and 30 feet deep, using numbers by the U.S. Geologic Service (http://ga.water.usgs.gov/edu/mgd.html).
4. Producing computer chips is also very energy intensive. The GLOBALFOUNDRIES plant uses 75 megawatts of electricity or about the amount of electricity consumed by a town of about 75,000 to 100,000 depending on the season.[a]
5. The semiconductor industry measures sizes in nanometers, which is one billionth of a meter. A human hair is about 50,000 nanometers. GLOBALFOUNDRIES is producing chips that are 20 nanometers or 0.04 percent of the size of a human hair.

---

[a]The Edison Electric Institute estimates about 1 megawatt services 1,000 people, depending on where they live.

The Urge to Merge Depends on Context

While some companies grow by building new factories, others use context to decide when is the best time to expand by buying someone else. Indeed, American businesses love to merge, acquire, and fight over who gets to take control of someone else.

Hardly a day goes by when the business pages don't have some announcement of a takeover. In 2012, a record year for corporate weddings, there were 11,957 acquisitions. This worked out to almost 48 every workday. In 2013, M&A was even stronger in the United States, up 20 percent over the prior year, according to Dealogic.[6]

The announcements are full of phrases lauding the takeovers as a way to make a "strategic investments" or "expanded service" or lifting an acquired company "to the next level." All these phrases are quoted from takeover announcements by just one New York firm that buys and sells companies regularly.[7]

There is hardly a day when Wall Street is not buzzing about the prospect of a takeover probably put together by an M&A (mergers and acquisitions) shop.

Meet David Braun, one of the matchmakers, and the founder and CEO of Capstone Strategic, Inc., which advises companies on potential acquisitions. Braun is somewhat unusual in that his office is not on Wall Street or even in New York. His 25-person firm is based in McLean, Virginia, close enough for Braun to drive to the American Management Association (AMA) in Crystal City, Virginia, where he teaches a class on mergers and acquisitions.

He is an affable storyteller who can easily talk about vastly different client mergers such as a company that cans tuna and a firm that tries to save money for hospitals and health care systems.

Although it's natural for a CEO to get excited about an acquisition, Braun tries to keep his clients focused on the most important part of the merger—what happens after the acquisition. "I think that too often people think an acquisition in itself is the strategy; they get excited about the deal and forget that it has to make sense," he says in a meeting room at the no, the American Management Association (AMA) as mentioned earlier "The transaction part is not the hard part. We can get the lawyers and accountants together and make all that stuff work. The hard part is that you actually have to implement it."

Sounds logical, doesn't it?

But then the conversation turns to one of the largest mergers in U.S. history: the combination of AOL with Time Warner in 2000, which cost an estimated $160 billion to $182 billion.[8] Braun keeps a copy of the January 10 announcement of the merger in his office as a reminder of how not to write press releases about these types of combinations. An example of the corporate hype:

> The merger will combine Time Warner's vast array of world-class media, entertainment, and news brands and its technologically advanced broadband delivery systems with America Online's extensive internet franchises, technology and infrastructure, including the world's premier consumer online brands, the largest community in cyberspace and unmatched e-commerce capabilities.[9]

Braun figuratively scratches his head. "My question is, did the press release tell me at all why they did this? I've talked to the AOL executives and they say, 'One of the biggest things we struggled with is have we overcomplicated this?'"

By way of contrast, he says the announcements from legendary investor Warren Buffett are quite simple. "Most of them are one sentence explaining why they made the acquisition," he says. "They are extremely purposeful."

As it turns out, overcomplication of the press release was the least of their problems. The merger is now considered a huge failure. AOL, for example, had a market value of only $2.7 billion in mid-2013. "I think the vision of it is very inspiring," says Braun. "But the execution of it is the difficult part."

However, looking back at the context of the merger, it becomes a little more understandable why the executives would call the new company "uniquely positioned" in their press release.

When the AOL–Time Warner merger was announced, the dot-com era was still in full swing, recalls Braun. He compares it to a modern-day gold rush. "These dot-coms were gold," he says, "and no one knew where e-commerce was going." This led to one of those periodic Wall Street buying panics. Mutual funds, hedge funds, and investors from Peoria all wanted a piece of the action.

"Companies were being bought who not only did not have any profits, they did not have any revenues because it really was a feeding frenzy where people said, 'We don't know what's going on so consequently we better buy stuff or we are going to miss out.'"

To Braun, an element of negative context around the merger was the millennial shift. There were plenty of news reports questioning whether computers, phone systems, and other electronic devices would still work on January 1, 2000. He terms it an issue of bad timing—no pun intended—since it began to raise an element of doubt just when the mega-merger was in the works.

"Remember, people got up in the middle of the night to check to see if their phones worked, people took cash out of the bank in case there was chaos at the banks," he says. "So there was this background of fear."

Add in yet one other issue of context—there was also plenty of money around to invest in these types of deals. "As a result of that, it was a lot of the 'other people's money' phenomenon," he says, referring to how deal makers used investor funds to enrich themselves.

But that was then. Does context still matter in the world of mergers and acquisitions? Indeed, it does, says Braun, who observes that some of the contextual issues include whether a company is in a position to take advantage of changes in the economy, whether it is a good time to borrow to do a deal or use cash, and whether it is a good time to enact a merger from a tax standpoint.

One example of how taxes matter to corporate buying and selling happened at the end of 2012. Congress was wrestling with ways to resolve a budget impasse that had gone on for months. Unless some agreement could be reached, there was a real possibility that capital gains tax rates might rise. Wall Street advisers beat the drum: sell now to avoid paying more taxes in 2013.

The pitch worked: according to Dealogic, the volume of acquisitions was up 67 percent compared to the prior quarter. The rate of mergers slowed slightly in the first half of 2013 but then roared back later in the year.[10]

The slowdown did not worry Braun because of the pressure for CEOs to always "move the needle." What's the needle? The needle, says Braun, is the stock price, which is also another part of context.

But moving the needle is not that easy, he points out. For example, if a company with $90 billion in revenues buys a $100 million company, the needle doesn't move. The same with a $1 billion purchase.

"But if they make a $10 billion acquisition, what happens?" asks Braun. "It moves the needle."

However, most deals are smaller, says Braun, who estimates that 97 percent of acquisitions are under $500 million. "If I am a $200 million a year company and buy a $10 million a year company, you will never know about that," he remarks. "I don't have to report it; you can't track it and find out if it was a success or failure."

In fact, many of the most successful acquisitions don't necessarily make the headlines, but they can move a company into a dominant position in an important industry.

Look at GE, he says. While many people know that the giant company makes cooktops and dishwashers, Braun says the company has been steadily making acquisitions in the water business, which has been estimated to have about $2 billion to $2.5 billion in revenue by Wall Street sources. (GE does not break down its water revenues.)[11]

"Most people don't realize it but GE has a major position in water—municipal water, potable water, ultra-pure water used for chemicals," he says. "They did it by cobbling together very strategic assets and very patiently brought them together with one single purpose, which is to say, 'We're going to own the water business.'"

Braun thinks one of his own deals involving the seafood company Chicken of the Sea is more typical of the types of smaller deals that make sense. In 2003, the CEO of the San Diego–based company asked Braun for some ideas to grow. Buying another canned tuna company was unlikely since the industry had consolidated to three companies. All three competed so fiercely that margins were low and consumer demand was far from robust.

"So we said, 'Let's think about this: what do you really have to leverage?'" says Braun. "Number one is the name brand; everyone knows their brand name. Coca-Cola, Apple, Cadillac, they spend tons of money to get you to remember their brand name. But here's a company that doesn't spend any money and you remember it."

At the same time, Braun started to look more deeply into what Chicken of the Sea actually did. Yes, they catch or buy tuna around the world. Once the white albacore are caught, they have to be packed and shipped to a cannery.

"So you know what they are really good at?" asks Braun. "Logistics." So what do you buy that capitalizes on this? In Chicken of the Sea's case, it was Empress International, a Port Washington, New York, importer and distributor of frozen shrimp.[12]

"It created a whole new category for them to grow that business but at the same time leveraging what they were good at," says Braun. He adds that the acquisition added new products, new customers, and new sources of supply—all critical factors in the seafood business.

Will corporate America ever tire of the continuous dog-eat-dog world? Not likely because the tax code makes mergers compelling. How so?

Braun says a common scenario is for one company to buy another for its real estate that has already been depreciated. The acquirer gets to redepreciate those assets at current value, he says.

"We had one deal where part of what the acquirer bought was 11 or 12 facilities, mostly office buildings. But the seller did not realize the value of those assets. So our client buys them, ends up selling them and getting the tax benefit for it which basically paid for 50 percent of the cost of the deal."

For Braun, there is a bit of personal context in making deals. Two of his favorite board games are Risk and Monopoly. And, he confesses, he was always a fan of *Let's Make a Deal*.

The Corporate Tax Conundrum

It all sounds so simple. All you have to do is cut taxes and reduce regulations and the economy will boom and all will be right with the world. At least that is the approach to economic policy that many believe makes sense. But not all tax cuts have the same impact. Not all changes in regulations create additional economic activity or come without costs. It depends on the type of business tax cuts and regulatory changes and how far they go. That is what context is all about.

While the Supreme Court may have ruled that businesses are like people, the reality is that people run a business.[13] How the corporation operates; what it does with its funds; how it reacts to changes in taxes, regulations, or economic factors are all determined by who, at the time, happens to be running the company. It cannot be said that two different CEOs will always behave in the exact same manner even if the issues they face are precisely the same.

It is in that context that company actions and reactions must be evaluated. It is not enough to say that all you have to do to expand the economy or create new jobs is to reduce corporate taxes. Lowering business operating expenses is not even a necessary condition for companies to hire more workers. There are many circumstances where increased costs and a growing economy occur simultaneously. So let's look at a few so-called givens and determine if they really do what they are supposed to do.

Corporations Are People, Too, and They React Accordingly

We talked about how consumers' reaction to tax policy is dependent on their incomes, confidence, wealth, age, and the business cycle itself. Well, since people run businesses, it should not surprise anyone that the same can be said about corporate responses to changes in taxes.

It seems that whenever the economy is in trouble, the proposed solution, at least by some, is to cut corporate taxes. That seems to make total sense. If the business of business is business, lowering the cost of doing business should cause firms to expand, right? Not necessarily. Indeed, cutting taxes could be a waste of time and money under a variety of economic circumstances.

Let's go back in time to 2009. The housing sector had collapsed, banks and vehicle makers were failing and being bailed out by the government, and the world financial sector was teetering on the edge of collapse. And that is not an exaggeration. Essentially, the economy, which had actually entered the recession in December 2007, started going downward with a vengeance.[14]

With fears of a major recession, if not a depression, looming, consumers assumed the turtle position: they basically stopped shopping almost completely. So how did businesses react to demand falling apart? They did what we have said they did: they revised their business plans so that the goal was to be open on January 1, 2010. In order to do that, they cut expenses to the bone, and that meant laying off work-ers. In the first six months of 2009, nearly 4 million jobs were lost.[15]

Let's review things: The financial and housing sectors collapsed, households stopped buying, and the labor market was a blood bath. Into that breach, some people actually thought that it was a good idea to cut business taxes. Indeed, the stimulus bill passed in the spring of 2009 contained not only tax cuts for households but tax cuts for busi-nesses as well.

How much of those tax cuts do you think went to adding jobs? Think of it this way: If you are a CEO who is trying to survive and you are cutting jobs, cutting output, and planning for a depression, how much new capital are you buying? Do you really need to add a new machine or a new plant when your sales are crumbling and could fal-ter further? What is the potential return on that potential investment? It cannot be very high. Indeed, it is likely to be negative, especially if those fears of a depression turned out to be correct.

The lesson: When the economy is falling apart, businesses are not going to hire more people or invest, so giving firms new tax breaks is simply a transfer of income: It goes from taxpayers to owners and managers of the firms. It doesn't find its way back into the economy as more output or employment. In short, cutting taxes makes no eco-nomic sense when the economy is a mess. Some politicians thought that was the way to go during the recession and it remains the com-mon wisdom for many.

What about when the economy is booming? When we have hit the sweet spot in growth, and profits are high, wages are rising, and households are confident, shouldn't we cut taxes then? The better question would be: why would we even think of cutting taxes when happy days are here again?

What is the purpose of a corporate tax cut? It is to incent compa-nies to expand their hiring, production, and/or capital spending. That is usually done when companies need some help or a push. It is best done when, without that assistance, firms are likely to act cautiously. In other words, tax cuts should increase growth when it is lagging.

When profits are soaring and the economy is booming, firms already have the wherewithal to hire and expand. They don't need more money; they already have enough, or at least should have enough.

They should not want to be supported by government subsidies, though they will always take a handout when offered.

Indeed, during the good times, when chief financial officers do their calculations on the economics of growing the business, it is usually quite positive. Thus, adding to cash flow by lowering taxes doesn't do a whole lot to change the calculations. Again, it is more likely to be just a transfer of income from taxpayers to owners of capital as well as management. Conclusion: Tax policy needs to account for the thinking of business leaders, and they are worried about the same things that consumers worry about.

To Regulate or Not Regulate, That Is the Question!

If you ask any businessperson, they will tell you they can deal with tax increases as long as they know what those costs will be. What they hate the most, though, are regulations, or what most executives think is the tendency to overregulate the economy. Not only does it cost businesses money to comply with all the crazy quilt of requirements, but regulations keep firms from operating in ways they would like to or prevent them from getting into markets they consider good opportunities.

Why is government so obstinate, demanding that firms conform to so many rules and regulations? Well, it comes down to the basic calculation of the cost to society of underregulation versus the cost of overregulation. It can be hard to fully calculate the cost of regulations. You have to ask what firms would do if they could enter a market or could operate differently. Essentially, you don't know how successful the firm would be if the regulations didn't get in their way.

There are also the compliance costs, which have been estimated a number of times, though the range is extremely wide. For example, in 2011, the Office of Management and Budget's 2009 report to Congress estimated annual costs at around $50 billion to $60 billion. Meanwhile, a September 2010 report prepared by Nicole V. Crain and W. Mark Crain for the Office of Advocacy within the Small Business Administration (SBA) stated that the annual cost of federal regulations was about $1.75 trillion in 2008.[16]

The cost of regulation is either small or extremely large. Clearly, both approaches to the problem have been criticized vehemently, usually from groups who have one axe or another to grind. Those who worry about businesses running wild have sided with the Office of Management and Budget (OMB), while those who want businesses to be unleashed believe in the Crain and Crain report. Of course, we can talk about the cost of regulations all we want, but the discussion makes no sense without balancing it with the benefits. And the benefit analysis can be as touch-feely and questionable as the cost analysis. For example, an OMB report in 2013 put the benefits of the regulations in place over a 10-year period at "somewhere between $112 billion and $678 billion."[17] To say the least, that is a very wide range, and it makes it hard to have much confidence in any economic research on the subject.

Well, if the studies don't come to a conclusion, is there any way for us to judge what would happen if regulations were relaxed? Well, yes, we can try it in the real world. That is precisely what former Federal Reserve Chairman Alan Greenspan did during his term of office. He led the charge to eliminate the Glass-Steagall Act, which had put a wall between banks and investment companies. The Financial Services Modernization Act of 1999 officially allowed finance firms of all types to essentially become one.[18] Banks, investment companies, and insurance companies could now merge, and they did.

Mr. Greenspan also took a laissez-faire approach to regulating these companies. He strongly believed in the "self-regulatory approach" to central banking. He called it, in his testimony in front of Congress in October 2008, the *"self-interest of lending institutions to protect shareholders' equity."*[19] As a consequence, financial institutions were given leeway in operating in a wide variety of ways and were allowed to use just about any and all financial products they could create.

Well, we know the cost of deregulation and the laissez-faire approach to financial regulation: the Great Recession. What is not clear is what the cost would be from overregulation. Undoubtedly, it could stifle the truly aggressive competitive juices of those firms and individuals that operate at the outer edge of the regulatory envelope. They push it as far as they can, and if it breaks, so be it.

Much of business experimentation derives from doing things in ways that have not been thought of before. That is called *innovation*.

Stifling innovation is probably the worst thing that a regulator can do, as it slows not only current economic activity but future activity as well.

When you consider the long-run potential for an economy, additional output can come from two sources: employing more workers and employing workers more efficiently—that is increased productivity. One example of a way to expand productivity is better use of machines. In other words, a lot fewer auto workers can make a lot more vehicles with the help of robots.

If regulation slows the rate of growth of investment and innovation, it will reduce the potential growth rate of the economy. Regulators must therefore consider the cost of overregulation with the cost of underregulation. Like the rest of us, regulators cannot look into the future with any certainty. It is doubtful that Alan Greenspan would have looked the other way as financial institutions created all those innovative new products if he had known that those products would wind up collapsing the economy, which means the regulators have to assume they are going to make some type of error.

But which error should regulators make? Should they overregulate and slow current and future growth, or should they underregulate and risk another calamity. It depends on the potential cost of the mistake.

Take the example of the minimum wage. This is a regulatory action in that it forces a certain, specific pay scale on businesses. Should there even be a minimum wage, and if so, what should it be? The minimum wage has been studied many times by a large number of economists. Not surprisingly, the conclusions are hardly consistent. The logic is simple: If you put a floor under wages, then firms will limit or reduce hiring of workers who don't produce enough to make themselves profitable. In economic terms, a company hires someone only if the value of the output they create exceeds their costs. It's hard to make a profit if your workers don't earn their own way. Therefore, if you raise the minimum wage, employment will go down, right? That is not exactly what the literature shows.

In a comprehensive review of the literature, John Schmitt showed that while there are some indications that for low-wage workers raising the minimum wage could have a small negative impact, overall there is no definitive proof that the effects are significant.[20] Indeed, there are some studies that actually find a positive relationship between raising the minimum wage and employment, which seems to make no sense at all.

The point here is that something that appears obvious may not be true in the real world. How is it possible that raising the minimum wage doesn't cause firms who employ many low-wage workers to cut back? Like anything else, avoidance and adjustments are the operative factors. It's not the regulation itself as much as how the costs can be spread around that really matters.

And there are frequently many ways to do that. As Schmitt wrote:

> The most likely reason for this outcome is that the cost shock of the minimum wage is small relative to most firms' overall costs and only modest relative to the wages paid to low-wage workers. In the traditional discussion of the minimum wage, economists have focused on how these costs affect employment outcomes, but employers have many other channels of adjustment. Employers can reduce hours, non-wage benefits, or training. Employers can also shift the composition toward higher skilled workers, cut pay to more highly paid workers, take action to increase worker productivity (from reorganizing production to increasing training), increase prices to consumers, or simply accept a smaller profit margin. Workers may also respond to the higher wage by working harder on the job. But, probably the most important channel of adjustment is through reductions in labor turnover, which yield significant cost savings to employers.[21]

Regulations are rarely welcomed or appreciated by the firms being regulated, but they are not necessarily all bad. Some may restrain growth, while others may limit the ability of entrepreneurs to do what they believe is needed to get things done. Some executives believe that just about any regulation would reduce profits, not just immediately but for a long time.

But not all regulations turn out, over time, to be nearly as bad as they are initially perceived. Few vehicle makers welcomed the Corporate Average Fuel Economy (CAFE) standard. Car makers believed the new regulations would kill the vehicle sector when they were introduced in 1978. Fast-forward 35 years—and with fuel prices pinching consumers—companies are now battling it out to have the highest average for their fleets and their individual vehicles.

What the examples of the minimum wage and vehicle mileage requirements show is that regulators need to understand that their actions have impacts that may not be obvious. These two examples turned out well, or at least not badly, for the economy. Not every regulation is so lucky, and not every attempt at reducing regulations turn out well. There are costs and benefits from regulations, and they depend on the context of the economy.

Essentially, what we are saying is that regulators must directly recognize what every statistician knows: There are two types of errors. You can do something you shouldn't do, or you can fail to do something you should do. When it comes to regulation, the first error is that you put in too much regulatory oversight and too many requirements. That is doing something they really should not do. In the second case, you don't put in enough regulations when you should be regulating more aggressively. That allows businesses to do things they probably shouldn't be doing also a bad move.

The regulators must decide which error to make. If they make the wrong one, we all suffer. But keep in mind that they are going to make a mistake. The one they make will cause problems, whether it be slower growth or a massive recession. And businesses must adjust accordingly. As we saw with both of the examples in this chapter, firms do adapt to tax and regulatory constraints. It is the context in which those adaptions occur that determines the success or failure of a firm.

While companies are busy trying to make money, Washington is often busy debating how to spend it. In the next chapter, we look at some of the contextural issues in the $3.7 trillion the Obama administration estimated it would spend in FY2014 and a mystery surrounding an important part of it.

Notes

1. GLOBALFOUNDRIES, press release of January 8, 2013. www.globalfoundries .com/newsroom/2013/20130108.aspx.
2. ATIC. January 13, 2014. www.atic.ae/vision/abu-dhabi-2030/.

3. Luther Forest Technology Campus history. www.lutherforest.org/about_concept.php.

4. AMD press release, December 8. 2008. The Foundry Company was later named GLOBALFOUNDRIES. www.amd.com/us/press-releases/Pages/Press_Release_129458.aspx.

5. GLOBALFOUNDRIES press release, September 7, 2009. www.globalfoundries.com/newsroom/2009/20090906.aspx.

6. Data from Dealogic, a financial and technology company. Press release of January 2, 2014 titled Global M&A Review Full Year 2013.

7. Various press releases from KKR&Co, LP. One example: KKR's acquisition of ReSearch Pharmaceutical Services, Inc. on July 31, 2013. http://media.kkr.com/media/media_releasedetail.cfm?ReleaseID=781663.

8. Merger estimate from various news sources. For example, the *New York Times* said the merger was worth $160 billion (http://learning.blogs.nytimes.com/2012/01/10/jan-10-2000-aol-and-time-warner-announce-merger/?_r=0), while *CNN Money* said the value of the merger was $182 billion (http://money.cnn.com/2000/01/10/deals/aol_warner/).

9. Press release, January 10, 2000. www.timewarner.com/newsroom/press-releases/2000/01/America_Online_Time_Warner_Will_Merge_to_Create_Worlds_01-10-2000.

10. Dealogic data. January 2, 2013. www.dealogic.com/media/55516/dealogic_global_ma_review_-_1h_2013.pdf; http://www.dealogic.com/media/81237/dealogic_global_m_a_review_-_first_nine_months_2013.pdf.

11. One estimate came from Global Water Intelligence. October, 2009. www.globalwaterintel.com/archive/10/10/general/ge-stresses-its-commitment-water-market.html.

12. Chicken of the Sea press release, October 21, 2003. http://chickenofthesea.com/multimedia/?p=264.

13. *Citizens United v. Federal Election Commission*, No. 08–205. Argued March 24, 2009. Reargued September 9, 2009. Decided January 21, 2010.

14. National Bureau of Economic Research, "Business Cycle Expansions and Contractions." www.nber.org/cycles.html. January 13, 2014.

15. Bureau of Labor Statistics. Current Employment Statistics, Naroff Economic Advisors, Inc.

16. Nicole V. Crain and W. Mark Crain, "The Impact of Regulatory Costs on Small Firms." Lafayette College, Easton, Pennsylvania, contract number SBAHQ-08-M-0466. Release date: September 2010.

17. Office of Management and Budget, 2013 Draft Report to Congress, "On the Benefits and Costs of Federal Regulations and Agency Compliance with the Unfunded Mandates Reform Act." May 21, 2013.

18. The Financial Services Modernization Act of 1999, enacted November 12, 1999.

19. Testimony of Dr. Alan Greenspan, Committee of Government Oversight and Reform October 23, 2008, Federal Reserve Board of Governors.

20. John Schmitt, "Why Does the Minimum Wage Have No Discernible Effect on Employment?" Center for Economic Policy and Research, February 2013.

21. Ibid.

Chapter 7

When to Spend, When to Cut, and When to Scratch Your Head Over the Federal Budget

Putting together a budget may sound easy: you try to balance what you make with what you spend. Then, there is the U.S. budget.

The last time the fiscal affairs of the U.S. government were in the black was 2001. That makes some politicians see red, and they want to cut, cut, cut. Others see the budget as an opportunity to help provide jobs in their districts so the deficit isn't so bad.

In this chapter, we look at the importance of context in determining what to do about government spending. What is the state of the economy when the president sends his version of the budget to

Congress? What are the dynamics needed to keep investors interested in buying U.S. Treasury bonds? And how does a government make significant changes if it won't touch entitlement spending such as Medicare, Medicaid, and Social Security?

Every year, government accountants, legislators, and their staffs and analysts pick through the budget, examining its nooks and crannies. But sometimes even the experts don't understand what's going on. As we will see in this chapter, a fog hangs over one of the most critical segments of the U.S. budget—the spending for health care, which represents about 25 percent of federal spending.

Impact of Health Care on the Budget

In the summer of 2013, the government needed Sherlock Holmes to help solve a mystery about one of the largest U.S. government expenses: health care. Something unusual was going on in the doctors' offices, clinics, and hospital wards. The rate of growth of expenditures was starting to slow for Medicare, Medicaid, and even private health plans.

The slowdown was significant. Health care expenditures came down from an annual growth rate of about 7 percent between the years 2000 and 2005 to 3.8 percent between 2007 and 2010.[1] In 2012, the growth rate had declined to 3 percent, a rate that was last seen in the 1950s, when doctors made house calls and charged $4 for an office visit.[2]

Could the change be related to the economic downturn? Were people using less health care because they were out of work? Maybe seniors and others were taking fewer prescription drugs? Was there some obscure change in the federal repayment rates that was giving health care providers less money for their services? The people who study these things were perplexed.

The Congressional Budget Office (CBO), which produces independent analyses of budget and economic issues, put on its detective hat. Two CBO analysts looked at possible changes in Medicare's payment rates and the possibility that seniors were not going to the doctor as much.[3] Perhaps seniors felt they couldn't afford health care because their stock portfolios had shrunk or their homes had declined in value.

What they found was a big question mark. Yes, they found that the recession cut into health care use but not substantially. They used complex economic formulae that looked at the data over a long period of time. But even after the economy started to recover and the stock market rose, the lower rate of growth continued.

At the same time, the CBO analysts looked more closely at individual seniors. "They looked at microeconomic data, households who had suffered larger wealth losses or other bad effects of the economic conditions, and those households did not seem to have any different reaction in their Medicare spending," said Doug Elmendorf, the director of the CBO at a September 17, 2013, press briefing. "That leaves open the question: if it's not the financial crisis and recession, then what is it?" he asked.[4]

Table 7.1 shows the factors they looked at and the effect on the declining growth rate. At the end of the exercise, the CBO researchers could not account for 2.4 percentage points of the declining growth rate.

Other health care researchers tried to solve the mystery as well. On September 19, 2013, three health care experts, Amitabh Chandra of Harvard University and the National Bureau of Economic Research (NBER), Jonathan Holmes of Harvard University, and Jonathan Skinner of Dartmouth College and NBER, presented a paper at a Brookings Institution conference asking if the slowdown in health care spending was different from other periods when it slowed down only to soar again.

They agreed with the CBO that the recession itself was not the main reason. They wrote in the paper, "On theoretical grounds we question whether GDP growth itself should have a large impact on health care spending—short run income effects for health care spending are notoriously small (McClellan and Skinner, 2006), and it's not clear why Medicaid or retired Medicare enrollees should seek more (or less) health care when markets are in free-fall."[5] So they started with a hypothesis that only part of the reason for the slowdown was associated with the recession, and they turned to other possible reasons.

Some of the candidate factors included the possibility of patients faced with rising prices, a declining federal reimbursement rate to health care providers, cuts in Medicaid benefits, a reduction in technological advances, and a slowdown in the spread of older technologies.

Table 7.1   Contributions of Various Factors to Annual Growth in Per-Beneficiary Spending for the Elderly in Parts A and B of Medicare (percentage points)

	2000 to 2005	2007 to 2010	**Difference**
Overall Spending Growth	7.1	3.8	−3.2
Potential Contributors to the Slowdown			
Growth in average payment rate	2.7	2.5	−0.2
Growth in demand by beneficiaries			
Changes in the age and health status of beneficiaries[a]	0	−0.3	−0.3
Growth in the proportion of beneficiaries enrolled only in Part A[b]	−0.1	−0.3	−0.2
Growth in the use of prescription drugs	−0.5	−0.6	−0.1
The financial crisis and economic downturn	0	0	0
Change in supplemental coverage[c]	★	★	★
Unexplained Contribution to Growth			−2.4

SOURCE: Michael Levine, CBO, and Melinda Buntin, Vanderbilt University calculations in Working Paper Series, CBO, August 2013.

Note: The analysis covers spending under Parts A and B for beneficiaries age 65 or older in the fee-for-service portion of Medicare. It excludes spending on beneficiaries in private health plans as well as spending under Part D of Medicare.

[a]Changes in the health status of beneficiaries reflect changes in the age distribution, obesity status, and smoking history of the elderly population in the fee-for-service portion of Parts A and B.

[b]The estimates represent changes in the share of beneficiaries enrolled only in Part A after accounting for changes in the age distribution of beneficiaries.

[c]On the basis of a qualitative analysis of trends in supplemental coverage, we conclude that any contribution to the slowdown in spending growth would have been small.

They checked to see if stagnant wages for health care workers might be a factor or maybe people were holding off on going to the doctor in anticipation of Obamacare.

The Brookings analysis also put the drop in spending into the context of what was going on around the globe. Using an Organization for Economic Cooperation and Development (OECD) report, they found that aggregate health care spending fell even more around the world between 2008 and 2011.

They wrote, "We hypothesize that this more dramatic drop in health care expenditures than in the United States reflects both the larger share of publicly financed non-entitlement spending in other OECD countries, and a sharper drop in GDP for many countries such as Greece and Ireland. . . ."[6]

The paper's authors also looked at the effect of technology, such as the widespread growth of hip and knee replacements and pharmaceutical advances in treating cancer. In the past, the increased usage of new technologies added to the cost of treating patients.

The Brookings authors wondered if there could be a slowdown in the spread of these leading-edge and expensive technologies. For example, in the 1990s, there was a large increase in the use of stents (tiny devices inserted into a heart's arteries to ensure blood flow). However, as the researchers noted, later trials in the mid-2000s suggested only modest health benefits for the most common types of heart diseases in the use of these procedures.

One new technology that could drive up the cost of health care in the future, they noted, is proton beam therapy, which its maker claims is more accurate for treating early signs of prostate cancer as well as other tumors near important organs. Treatment with the machines can cost as much as $50,000, or double conventional radiation, said the paper. The total number of these expensive machines was expected to double between 2010 and 2014.

However, even this technology was bumping into resistance. In the summer of 2013, Blue Shield of California told doctors in the state that there was no scientific evidence to justify spending tens of thousands of dollars more on the technology than for conventional radiation, and the big insurer said it would limit its payments to certain tumors in children.[7]

The three Brookings experts also asked whether the slowdown in the rate of health care spending might be temporary. They noted that in the early 1990s health care costs as a percent of gross domestic product (GDP) declined but then resumed growing at a faster rate in the late 1990s.

The CBO's Elmendorf wondered if the slowing growth rate might not last as well. "Previous periods of slower spending growth have been followed by a pick-up in growth again. And in those previous periods, some of the stories one heard, anecdotes, sound like some of the stories heard today. So I think we can't rule out that possibility" said Elmendorf.[8]

In addition, Elmendorf noted that costs could again start rising just because of the nature of the system. Medicare remains a fee-for-service system in which the incentive to provide more care is built in.

Perhaps because of doubts that the declining growth rate will continue, Elmendorf says CBO remains cautious in quantifying the impact on future expenses. Basically, no one really knows what is happening with health care costs and what the future trends will look like.

Doubts from a Doctor

While medical policy experts try to figure out what's going on with health care spending, pediatrician Dr. David Waters is on the front lines of health care at the 16th Street Community Health Clinic in Milwaukee, Wisconsin. From his perspective of treating children every day, he wonders how anyone could expect the growth rate of medical expenditures to keep slowing.

"I can clearly speak from the 26 years I have been at the clinic that the patient population that we care for is less healthy progressively over the time I have been here," he says. And that decline in health in the young should be a red flag for the nation and its battle to control health care costs, he says.

In mid-September 2013 he had examined an 11-year-old girl who weighed 197 pounds, up from 169 pounds the year before. In 2012, he had referred the girl and her mother to a program at the clinic that promotes healthy choices for cooking and exercise. But the young girl still gained 28 pounds.

On another day in September, his first patient of the day was a girl who was almost 13 years old. She weighed 204 pounds. "A daily occurrence for me, I'm not even shocked by it anymore," he said.

Well, not quite. On another day, he had a 14-year-old Latino boy who had ballooned 54 pounds to 256 pounds in 15 months. "Yikes," he says.

These children are far from alone. He estimates that 40 percent of the pediatric patients at the clinic are overweight, and 25 to 30 percent are obese.

What's happening in that part of Milwaukee is true elsewhere but to a lesser extent. According to data compiled by the National Health and Nutrition Examination Survey in 2008, 16.9 percent of all children ages 2 to 19 were obese. Boys were worse, with 19.3 percent obese, compared to 16.8 percent for girls. About 2 percent of children were in the category of extreme obesity.[9]

Overweight children are especially common in Latino communities such as those served by the Milwaukee clinic. Nationally, 26.8 percent of Mexican-American boys and 17.4 percent of Mexican-American girls were obese between 2007 and 2008, according to the Centers for Disease Control and Prevention (CDC).[10]

"The obesity epidemic is disproportionately affecting minority communities," says Dr. Waters, who estimates about 70 percent of the patients at the clinic are Latino. He thinks there are a number of reasons for the larger number of unhealthy people. For example, some urban areas are so-called food deserts, areas where there is a paucity of healthy grocery stores. In addition, he notes the Mexican population has a food culture that cooks with oils and makes fried foods. "And there is just a higher incidence of diabetes among Mexican-Americans," he says.

Dr. Waters says people who use the clinic now expect their children to be fat. "One thing I have noticed just anecdotally is I get women who bring in their 15-year-old son to see me because they are being told by the family that he's too skinny. By comparison to everyone else in their community or school, they look too thin, so that's what people are sort of judging by," he observes.

The children are not only having weight problems, but a rising number are developing diseases related to the excess weight such as type 2 diabetes, which used to be mostly an adult disease. "The prevalence of diabetes is creeping down into the pediatric population because people are getting obese at such a young age," he says. "I think by early teenage years more and more people are going to end up with diabetes, insulin resistance. I know I see anecdotally more type 2 diabetes than I ever saw. The fact that it is in the pediatric population at all is a very scary thing."

Once the children become adults, they have an even higher chance of becoming too heavy. Waters estimates that 77 percent of the adults the clinic sees are overweight or obese. This is higher than the national average, which is closer to 69 percent, according to the CDC.[11]

There will be future cost implications for so many overweight or obese people. The overly fat are more likely to end up with blocked arteries, which could result in a heart attack or a stroke, he says. "And those with diabetes may end up with kidney disease, eye disease, and vascular disease, and caring for those people is going to be a big expenditure for our country," says Waters. "Obviously, the care that goes into that cardiac intervention with potential surgeries, coronary artery transplants, bypasses, and stuff like that is costly."

Waters's clinic has not been just a passive observer of the obesity epidemic among their patients. In 2012, the health care facility held a "South Side Bicycle Day" in a nearby park. One hundred people came, and the clinic gave away 50 bicycle helmets, made up T-shirts, had bicycle mechanics to repair bikes, and provided salads and other healthy food. In 2013, 400 people showed up. The police donated 45 bikes that were auctioned off, and the clinic gave away 150 helmets.

"We had Zumba classes and we just had a really fun day," recalls the doctor. "Next year (2014) we want to do it even bigger."

If Waters and the clinic can start to change the mind-set and waistline of his patients, he has plans. Waters, who rides his bicycle 7 miles to work every day, wants to give up his practice by 2017 and promote walking and bicycling in Latino communities across the nation.

Waters may have dreams, but he does not have illusions, which is one of the reasons he is skeptical about the slowing rate of growth on health care spending. To him, the key factor is the growing health problems of the country's population. "They seem to be considering people's health status as a static thing," he says. "But it's not."

What If Lower Health Care Spending Continues?

What does the falling spending growth rate mean? Despite lots of skepticism that the growth rate of health care expenditures will continue to shrink, there are huge implications if it does.

In 2013, the CBO decided to incorporate lower growth rates into its forecast for future health care spending.[12] The nonpartisan agency reduced the estimate of how much Medicare and Medicaid will cost between 2010 and 2020 by about 11 percent compared to an earlier estimate in August 2010. By 2020, Medicare will cost $137 billion less than previously expected and Medicaid will cost $85 billion less. The total savings over the decade could be as much as $785 billion.[13]

There are two dynamics taking place that have an effect on this estimate, according to Elmendorf. First, the overall level of health care spending is coming down. A lower historical level reduces estimates of future costs.

"In fact, over the past three years, we have reduced federal spending for Medicare and Medicaid in 2020 by about 15 percent," said Elmendorf. This downward revision matters even as much as 25 years down the road.[14]

"But in addition to the downward revision of the first 10 years, we have taken on more data in terms of the slowdown in health costs," he explained. "Our estimate of the underlying rate of growth of health spending, which comes from a historical average, is lower than it was, so we have a lower level of health care spending to jump off from and a lower rate of growth beyond that. A combination of those factors is to reduce the federal health care spending by 0.6 percent of gross domestic product in 2038, which is a significant difference."[15]

The slower rate of federal expenditures for senior health care, a program that affects 49.4 million Americans or about 15.1 percent of the population, could have significant ramifications if it were to continue for the next several years.[16] The U.S. budget deficit could be lower. If the deficit were to fall, this could take some pressure off Congress to cut programs.

In part because of health care spending growing at a slower pace combined with the congressional mandated cuts through the sequestration process, the CBO expects the budget deficit to decline to 4 percent of GDP in 2013, down from 10.1 percent in 2009. The agency estimates that by 2015 it could be as low as 2.1 percent of GDP and remain below 3 percent for the following four years. That's all good news for those worried over the amount of red ink in the budget.[17]

But, as Elmendorf was quick to point out, it does not mean that spending on health care will be lower—just the rate of growth. Spending on health care in pure dollar terms will continue to rise, he says, for at least three reasons.

First, there will be a large number of Baby Boomers retiring and enrolling in Medicare. As a share of GDP, health care spending for the aging population accounts for 35 percent of the growth. The CBO estimates by 2023, about 60 percent of all health care spending will go toward people 65 or older.[18]

Second, there is the specter of a rising rate of health care per person. This is related to the possibility of advanced technology, such as new ways of fighting cancer or improved heart-related devices. The CBO estimates the fast growth per person segment represents about 40 percent of the growth of health care spending.[19]

Third, under the Affordable Care Act (ACA), also known as Obamacare, there will be an expansion of federal support for health insurance for low-income people, especially in the form of expanded Medicaid coverage and the creation of subsidies for insurance exchanges. This will represent about 26 percent of the growth, the CBO estimates.[20]

All these increases will mean that health care as a percentage of GDP will continue to climb. Between 1973 and 2012, health care was 2.7 percent of GDP; by 2013 it had grown to 4.6 percent; and the CBO expects that by 2038 the ratio will rise to 8 percent.[21]

The declining growth rate, even if it's only for a number of years, has its own implications. In an analysis in July 2013, Moody's Investors Service cited it as one of the reasons the rating agency decided to upgrade U.S. Treasury securities from a "negative outlook" to a "stable outlook."[22]

But as of the fall of 2013, the mystery remained over the slower growth rate of health care.

How the Budget Interacts with the Economy

Any discussion about government spending needs to start with the basic idea that a budget is fundamentally a political document that has implications for both short-term and long-term economic growth.

As we pointed out in the business sector, companies need to invest in order to increase output. Well, the same can be said for governments. The more that is invested in building the future economy, what economists call infrastructure, the greater potential future growth will be.

But the government doesn't just spend money on things such as roadways, schools, water, sewer, or electrical capacity. It doesn't just invest in health care research or support technology incubators. All of these are critical to building a bigger and better economy. What it also does is provide a variety of social programs.

When government does things such as fund unemployment insurance, food stamps, and welfare payments—to both individuals and corporations—pensions and other transfer payments from one group to another, it is spending money on concerns that are not necessarily considered to be investing in the future, as it is sustaining present economic activity.

The first question is: how should we, or even should we, balance the budget? It may surprise many, but the answer could just be: don't bother.

How you resolve the problem of revenues and expenditures being out of whack is not as simple as it may appear to the casual or even professional observer. The standard but way too simplistic view is that all you have to do is cut spending or raise taxes. While that may be the case initially, there are real economic impacts from any of those decisions that complicate the ultimate effectiveness of the actions. No matter what you do, some people gain while others lose.

Let's face it—the Congress and the president have not done a very good job in balancing the national budget. Indeed, the U.S. federal government has run budget deficits every year except for four during the past 40 years. The only time there were budget surpluses was during the fiscal years 1998 through 2001. (The U.S. fiscal year runs from October 1 through September 30.) For the rest of the time, revenues didn't come close to matching expenditures.

Looking at the size of the deficits, you see that they differ over time dramatically. It is hard to simply compare dollar values, as things such as the size of the economy, the size of the budget itself, and inflation all factor in. For example, in 1983, the government ran a $208 billion deficit. That was about 6 percent of the GDP at that time.

In contrast, the $203 billion deficit in 1994 was only 2.9 percent of the entire economy, while the $248 billion deficit posted in 2006 was a mere 1.9 percent of all the goods and services produced.[23] Clearly, it is not enough to simply say that the federal government is running a deficit. You have to put it into perspective.

And that raises the first issue that must be considered: should we ever run budget deficits, or should we always balance the budget or maybe even run surpluses? This is really the heart of the matter because there may be reasons to run deficits, or even more critically, deficits may be inevitable. Let's explain.

A budget is essentially a political document that has economic implications. The president presents a budget, and then the 535 members of Congress get together and in ways that are largely mysterious to even those in the know, pass a series of bills that ultimately create the means to spend a huge amount of our money and collect usually less than that total.

Of course, the passage of all the budget bills is just the beginning of the spending process. Emergencies occur during the year, so there are special spending bills. And the economy matters as well. If there is a recession, a lot of workers wind up on the unemployment and welfare rolls, so spending can surge. In good times, people find jobs and stop receiving government payments, so spending might even be less than expected. Sometimes war breaks out, and that raises spending. So the budget is just the first attempt at describing what the government will spend. What it actually does is determined by the course of events during the year.

And then there are taxes. In times of economic troubles, taxes may be cut after the budget is passed so that people can keep more of their hard-earned income and hopefully spend it. But that reduces government revenues, at least in the first few years after a tax cut occurs. However, if the deficit is getting out of hand or the politicians want more spending, they sometimes raise taxes to increase revenues.

That the budget passed is just a guide to spending and taxation may be troubling, but it also points out that coming up with a balanced budget is no easy task. Indeed, it is likely to be impossible since there are so many moving parts during the year. The reality is that only by accident will spending and revenues wind up at the end of the fiscal year to be in balance.

Let's skip the idea that we should have a balanced budget and instead ask: why should we ever run a deficit? The answer is actually straightforward: you want to run a deficit when the economy needs to be kick-started.

A classic example of when lots of additional government spending made sense occurred in the spring of 2009. The financial markets had crashed in the fall of 2008, and the economy was rapidly following suit. With consumers fearing a depression and spending disappearing, corporations were facing an economic meltdown. Instead of looking to grow, firms assumed the turtle position and hunkered down. They adopted a simply strategy: survive until the end of the year. Hiring turned into firing, and payrolls were being reduced by 700,000 a month.[24] Near panic was taking hold.

Under those circumstances, the major worry was how to stop the free-fall before it snowballed into another Great Depression. Obviously, with the economy spiraling downward, neither businesses nor households were going to go out and spend money. Thus, the burden fell entirely on the government.

If the economy was going to break its fall, either it had to hit rock bottom or the government had to become the spender of last resort. Would tax cuts help? Not really. Since people and businesses were looking to hoard money, most tax cuts went into savings. Though about 30 percent of the stimulus bill that was passed was for tax cuts, at least during the first half of 2009, little was turned into spending on the part of households or companies. Therefore, the government had to spend money.

The federal government was the only economic actor who had the ability to spend more money even if they didn't have the revenue coming in. All it had to do was borrow it from people either in the United States or around the world. And that is precisely what happened.

Did the stimulus, as it was called, make a difference? That will be debated for years to come, but the massive collapse in the economy came to a halt in June 1999.[25] Did that happen by magic? Did Harry Potter wave his wand and the recession ended? Does anyone seriously think that was the case? The huge inflow of government funds into the economy had to play a role in turning things around.

When it comes to the budget, whether the government spends more money itself or reduces taxes and lets businesses and consumers shop till they drop, the deficit is going to rise. Tax cuts reduce revenues in the short term since it takes time for the funds to be spent and growth to accelerate that ultimately causes some of those tax losses to disappear.

However, government expenditures directly add to the deficit. That is true whether new projects are being funded or there are greater demands for safety-net programs. When the Great Recession hit, all those people who were out of work, as well as all the members of their families, were in need of support, and that meant even more spending on social programs and unemployment compensation. In times of major trouble, the only course of action, if action is to be taken, is for the government to run a deficit.

If deficits are run during bad times, when should the government actually start paying down the debt by accumulating surpluses? That, too, is fairly straightforward: when the economy is running full out. During boom times, revenues are rising sharply, and as long as spending is kept under control, government revenues might actually exceed outlays. That happened at the end of the 1990s when strong growth and a surging stock market created rivers of revenues for the government. Huge surpluses followed that actually could have continued if events and politics had not intervened.

Alas, anyone who understood Washington, D.C., knew that budget surpluses would never last, and they didn't. But at least for a few years, the nation's debt load was being paid down a little. The point is that it is good to run surpluses when the economy is strong, and if some money is taken out of spending and put into debt reduction, the economy can handle it.

The lesson is that there is nothing special about a budget deficit or surplus. Whether a deficit or a surplus is run depends on where we are in the business cycle and how the government reacts. It is all about context and the condition of the economy, income growth, and gains in equity. All those combine to create a revenue flow that may or may not balance out with the wants and needs specified in the spending portion of the budget.

It is economic reality that causes the government to run deficits or surpluses, and no policy can possibly stop that. Indeed, a balanced budget requirement would exacerbate problems. We have seen that a spiral into recession, which causes income and tax revenues to fall quickly, will create a deficit. If there were a balanced budget requirement, either taxes would have to be raised and/or spending cut. That would result in the economy's faltering even more, further depressing revenues. A never-ending negative cycle of higher taxes, lower spending, and slower growth would be initiated.

The only way out of the crises that would be caused by a balance budget amendment would be for the requirement to be flexible. When the economy was faltering, a deficit would be allowed. But by how much? If it is not enough, and few would have expected the huge decline that occurred after the financial sector's near collapse, then the negative cycle would be set off.

Even if politicians wanted to, spending could not be cut quickly and the social safety net would ensure that spending would jump. If you are unemployed, you get unemployment insurance. It is not easy or frequently not possible to control costs when the economy cycles downward. You can try, but it is doubtful you will succeed.

Similarly, long periods of strong growth generate rising household spending and income, which leads to improving corporate profits and stock values. Ultimately, that creates much stronger flows of revenues into government coffers, and surpluses become possible.

In good times, it might make sense to either spend more or tax less. But we already know how that ends. In the spring of 2001, when we had already benefitted from a string of surpluses, Congress decided to cut taxes. At the time, the forecasts were for budget surpluses in the $650 billion range for years to come. Within a few years, we were running $650 billion deficits. So much for managing the budget when the coffers are flush.

When asked the question, "Are deficits or surpluses good or bad," the answer will be: it depends on the condition of the economy."

It's Not the Deficit but the Interest That Matters

When you run a surplus only four times in 40 years, you can basically conclude that Congress and the president are not too worried about deficits. It is a lot easier to simply spend more than you take in and borrow to make up the shortfall.

Should we be worried about deficits? The answer is, of course, it depends. First, understand the difference between a deficit and the national debt. The deficit is the annual shortfall between revenue and expenditures. For example, in the fiscal year that ended September 2013, the government ran a deficit of about $680 billion.[26]

Now $600 billion is a lot of money, to say the least. But that was the shortfall that was run in just one 12-month period. To get the national debt, you have to add that to the deficits that have been run since we became a nation. At the end of 2013, that had reached $16.5 trillion. And that is an extraordinarily large number.

Indeed, if you think that we can pay off that debt, forget about it. The debt is about the same size as the GDP and about four times the entire budget. Even with revenues running about $3 trillion a year, if we saved 5 percent of the revenues, that would not be much more than $150 billion a year. It would take us 110 years to pay off the debt—and that assumes we don't run anymore deficits! Gulp!

So if national debt is a perpetual burden, is it really possible to afford to run additional deficits? Yes! You do that by paying only the interest on the debt and then borrowing more money for the next year's deficit. It is the interest on the debt that is the true burden of the debt since those payments must be made every year, by all of us, forever! In other words, when we don't balance the budget this year, every generation that comes after us has to pay something for that inability to keep our fiscal house in order.

The concern about the interest payment burden of the debt is something that cannot be dismissed or even taken lightly. Low interest rates make it relatively easy to fund the debt. When you can borrow money at close to zero percent for short-term funds, that is a great way to fly. The interest payments are really low. But the real issue for the U.S. economy is what will happen as the debt rises and so do interest rates?

Consider the projections made by the nonpartisan Congressional Budget Office. Interest payments could double over the next five years, from about $225 billion to about $460 billion.[27] That is based on the fairly realistic assumption that the deficit will be cut in half over the next five years. Indeed, the deficit has been basically cut in half since its peak.

Nevertheless, even as the deficit shrinks, debt payments are likely to become a major problem because we have to make those payments before we spend money on anything else. We have to maintain our credit rating to keep those rates low, so we cannot miss a payment. Default is not an option.

But if the required interest payment doubles, it ultimately means there is less money for other purposes. In essence, the interest payments crowd out funds that could be used for other programs. The fear that the debt will become the beast that devoured the budget means that you cannot run large deficits for extended periods of time.

If the deficits must be reduced, how should that be done? That is, of course, a political decision since Congress and the president must come up with a budget that has smaller shortfalls.

To reduce the amount flowing into the debt load every year, either taxes will have to increase and/or spending will have to be reduced. Both of those actions, however, have significant implications since there is no such thing as a free tax increase or budget cut.

Consider spending cuts. First, you have to realize that even with a budget that is closing in on $4 trillion, there is not a lot of flexibility. Mandatory spending accounts for about 60 percent of the entire spending. This includes programs that we know as entitlements such as Social Security, Medicare, and Medicaid. When you add in interest payments, the total approaches two-thirds of the entire budget, and when the Defense allocation and Homeland Security are included, you are looking at about 90 percent of the budget. In other words, if you don't cut entitlements or security spending, you cannot make any major dent in the deficit.

If you have decided that budget cuts are the way to go to reduce the deficit, what do you do, and what of the implications of those actions? Here you have to always keep in mind that when you cut the budget, you are making winner versus loser decisions. That is, someone will no longer receive the spending, while others continue to drink at the government's trough.

For example, let's say it makes sense to reduce spending on education but not on defense. Who are the winners? Clearly, if you do manage to buy more security with the higher defense outlays, then all of us win. But as we all know, not all the money that goes to the Pentagon buys us more security. It is not as if there isn't any waste in the defense budget. Actually, there is a lot of unnecessary defense spending, especially when it comes to creating real security.

And that gets us to the issue of pork. One of the biggest reasons it is so hard to cut the defense budget is that over the years, the Defense Department has managed to embed itself into large numbers of House districts. Cutting spending, then, might require a congressperson to vote for a cut in spending in his or her district. That is rarely good politics and tends to lead to a member of Congress becoming a former member of Congress.

Basically, everyone in Washington would like to tighten the government's belt, but only if someone else's belt is tightened. That is because pork is in the eye of the beholder. Rebuilding the Jersey shore after Hurricane Sandy devastated it seemed like a no-brainer, at least for those in the region. But for those in the heartland, it was nothing but wasteful spending. Meanwhile, northeastern politicians view farm subsidies as nothing but a waste of money, while farm-belt Congressmen think it is the linchpin upon which the nation's economy runs. It only matters if it matters to you.

Regardless, the winners of keeping defense spending up and reducing other outlays are all those firms that supply goods and services to the military.

Who loses when you cut education spending? Just as it is not clear that you buy more security with more defense spending, it is not clear that you have lower-quality education with less spending. It depends on where the cuts are made. If the government funds student loans at a lower level, the educational system is not affected, but some students simply will not be able to afford higher education and they may have to drop out of school.

If funds for school districts are cut, then it is likely that teachers or programs will have to be reduced. Those students who no longer have music, art, or advanced placement courses will be paying the price of reduced funding. Those students who are in larger classes but have trouble learning in those settings also are affected. However, those students who don't take art, music, or advanced placement courses or who can learn just as well in the larger classes suffer no loss. Even the losses are not evenly distributed.

Clearly, the trade-offs that must be made when cutting the budget are not simple or even obvious. In this example, if defense expenditures that don't add to security are continued but activities are cut that reduces educational attainment, there is a clear loss to the nation. However, it is also very possible that there is little change in educational attainment. It might even be possible to cut defense spending and not change our level of security.

The uncertainty about outcomes of budget cuts doesn't mean they cannot be made. They can and have to be. But there should be a clear-cut principle that determines what spending is reduced and what is sustained. Essentially, cut those programs or spending activities that create the least loss to society. Of course, since so much of that is judgment, and that determination is made in a political arena, it is likely that favored programs are saved, even if they add little to the economy, while those that have political enemies or little political backing will be reduced.

Keep in mind one last thing: The spending cuts do affect economic activity. If you cut the budget, you reduce government spending, and the demand for goods and services has to decline. That is simple math. That slows the economy, and an economy growing at a slower pace than expected will produce lower tax revenues than projected. That is also simple math. In the year that spending is cut, there is less demand. Period. That winds up offsetting, at least to some extent, the deficit reduction effects of spending reductions.

If you think that spending cuts are difficult, consider the alternative: tax increases. What taxes should be increased? Should we raise corporate taxes or income taxes? What about fees, which are really just taxes in disguise? The first question that has to be answered is who should be taxed.

Let's assume that you want to raise business taxes. There are dozens of ways of doing that. How it is done determines who is affected the most. Some taxes fall largely on large corporations, some on smaller ones.

How the tax is raised then will affect different types of companies in different industries. It is important to understand the negative impacts on businesses of any tax change. For example, if you implement a tax that falls heavily on small rather than large companies, will that accelerate the demise of the small business sector, which creates so many jobs?

According to the Small Business Administration, one-quarter of all small businesses fail in their first year, and that is a low estimate.[28] Other studies have shown that rate rising to as much as 50 percent. Regardless, less than half the businesses make it to the five-year mark, showing how fragile that segment is. While larger businesses will also be hurt by tax increases, they might have greater capacity to withstand an increased burden. Who gets taxed matters, and thus the negative impacts depend on the type and the level of tax.

But most of all, the tax has to be able to raise the revenue that is needed to cut the budget deficit. That means it cannot be avoided. There are many ways to avoid a tax, but one way you don't want firms to react is by deciding to take their activities to another country. If a tax leads to a reduction in production in the United States, you wind up slowing economic growth, and that ultimately cuts the revenues from the higher tax.

Similar issues arise if you want to raise taxes on individuals. Should the tax change fall on all levels of income or just the wealthy or the middle class or even lower-income families? What you don't want to happen is for the tax increase to reduce demand. Why? Because if households cut back their purchases, the economy slows, and just like the problem with higher business taxes, the amount of taxes raised is not likely to be anything close to what is projected.

What is a good deficit-cutting person to do? Does all this mean taxes should not be increased? Hardly. Indeed, there are plenty of business and personal tax breaks that don't create any additional economic activity at all. What that means is that the tax break can be modified or even eliminated without reducing either business activity or household spending very much. That is where tax changes must be directed.

In other words, if the budget deficit is to be narrowed, you can cut spending, but only in certain ways, or you can raise taxes, but only in certain ways. There are no easy or simple answers to the question: "How do you reduce the deficit?" It depends on the context of the tax changes: who, what, when, and how.

Deficits continue to be run and the debt continues to grow. And that brings us to the little issue called the *debt ceiling*. The debt ceiling is the maximum amount of debt the U.S. Treasury may issue.

Interestingly, until 1917, the United States had no debt ceiling. Congress made its spending and tax decisions, and what could not be covered by revenues was simply borrowed. But the Second Liberty Bond Act of 1917 subjected the Treasury borrowing to a limit that could be changed only by an act of Congress. While the Treasury has basically free rein to decide how to manage the debt, it cannot just issue as much as it wants to.

While the Second Liberty Bond Act seemed to be a logical way for Congress to oversee domestic borrowing, chaos, not oversight, was introduced into the basic act of paying U.S. debts. Remember, the borrowing is being used to pay for spending that Congress already authorized. This is not new expenditures or outlays the president decided to make unilaterally. The new debt is used to pay for IOUs, including interest on the debt, which the government has already run up.

As benign as that act might have appeared when first passed, in Washington, no good deed goes unpunished. Instead of simply saying, "We bought it, we should pay for it," some in Congress like to threaten not to raise the debt ceiling.

If Congress ever decided not to raise the debt ceiling, chaos would reign. While some bills could be paid as there was money coming in, there is no authority for the president to pick and choose what to spend those funds on. Indeed, it is not even clear the president could spend any money.

Though it is generally accepted that certain things such as defense and health care are essential functions that would be funded, what other bills would be paid are unclear. Either Congress would have to pass a bill stipulating the spending priorities in detail, or it would have to give the president carte blanche to determine how to spend the money. Could you imagine any Congress giving any president that kind of control?

But the real risk is that interest on the national debt might not be paid in a timely manner. That could be catastrophic to the economy. The United States is considered to be the safe haven for world investors (see Table 7.2), and Treasury rates are viewed as riskless. Thus, there is tremendous demand for our securities, and that raises prices and lowers the interest rates we pay. Being a riskless security means investors

Table 7.2   Major Foreign Holders of Treasury Securities (in billions of dollars)

	October 2013	% Grand Total
China	1,304.5	23%
Japan	1,174.4	21%
Caribbean banking centers	290.7	5%
Brazil	246.7	4%
Oil Exporters	236.6	4%
Taiwan	184.5	3%
Belgium	180.3	3%
Switzerland	174.3	3%
United Kingdom	158.4	3%
Russia	149.9	3%
Top 10	4,100.3	73%
Grand Total	5,653.5	

DATA SOURCE: U.S. Treasury.

don't need a little extra money to hedge against a potential default, and that also means our interest rates are lower.

Defaulting on an interest payment would change all that. Investors would pull money out of the United States and start demanding a higher rate to accept what is now a risky asset. Those factors would lead to a surge in interest rates and a major slowdown in the economy.

In addition, the dollar is considered to be the reserve currency of the world economy. Individuals, companies, and governments around the world hold dollars for transaction purposes. That is based in part on the safety of U.S. assets. A default would also end that status. The dollar would become a risky asset, it would be held less, and that would lead to a fall in its value.

What happens if the dollar falls sharply? The cost of imported products would rise rapidly. They would trigger rising inflation, further increasing interest rates. Rising prices would reduce consumer spending, and in conjunction with the higher interest rates, it would be very likely the economy would wind up in a recession.

If you doubt that a default would be a disaster, just ask the Greeks. When that country found it could no longer pay its debts, it had to be bailed out. Government spending was slashed; the economy crashed and unemployment rates soared, rising by 10 percentage points in a little over one year. Need we say more?

Ultimately, if Congress failed to raise the debt ceiling, the president might have to break the law by spending money as he pleased or act unconstitutionally by issuing bonds that Congress did not authorize. In other words, the president, the nation, and the economy would be in a pickle—or a constitutional crisis at the least.

Why would anyone think it is a good idea not to raise the debt ceiling and risk a default? A good question that seems to have no rational answer.

It is nice to think that fiscal responsibility means only balancing the budget and controlling taxes and spending. And even if you could pick and choose how to spend and tax, you have to recognize that you are also determining winners and losers. Deciding who are worthy to be the beneficiaries and who should be gored is something that only Solomon could determine.

Even if your wisdom were unlimited, you would still be at risk as projected levels of government expenditures and tax revenues ebb and flow with the business cycle. In other words, failing to recognize the context in which a budget decision is made is to make a failing budget decision. Context matters and, unfortunately, our politicians don't recognize that. We must.

Integral to budget decisions is the issue of taxes. In the next chapter, we look at how context does—or more often does not—affect how government decides to tax.

Notes

1. Michael Levine, Congressional Budget Office and Melinda Buntin, "Why Has Growth in Spending for Fee-for-Service Medicare Slowed?" CBO Working Paper Series, Vanderbilt University. August, 2013. www.cbo .gov/sites/default/files/cbofiles/attachments/44513_MedicareSpending Growth-8-22.pdf.

2. Amitabh Chandra, Jonathan Holmes, and Jonathan Skinner, "Is This Time Different? The Slowdown in Healthcare Spending," Presented at the fall 2013 Brookings Panel on Economic Activity, p. 6. www.brookings.edu/~/media /Projects/BPEA/Fall%202013/2013b%20chandra%20healthcare%20spending .pdf.

3. Levine et al.

4. Doug Elmendorf, director of the Congressional Budget Office, press briefing, September 17, 2013.

5. Chandra et al., p. 2.

6. Chandra et al., p. 5

7. California Healthline daily digest, August 29, 2013. www.californiahealthline .org/articles/2013/8/29/blue-shield-reduces-coverage-for-proton-beam -cancer-treatment.

8. Elmendorf press conference.

9. Cynthia Ogden, PhD, and Margaret Carroll, MSPH, Centers for Disease Control and Prevention, study of the prevalence of obesity among children and adolescents by Division of Health and Nutrition Examination Surveys, June 2010. www.cdc.gov/nchs/data/hestat/obesity_child_07_08/obesity_ child_07_08.htm#table1.

10. Ogden et al.

11. CDC Faststats. www.cdc.gov/nchs/fastats/overwt.htm.

12. CBO, 2013 Long-Term Budget Outlook, p. 27.

13. Elmendorf presentation at Brookings. Table: "Changes in Projected Medicare and Medicaid Spending between 2010 and 2020," citing technical revisions that add up to $785 billion. September 19, 2013. www.brookings.edu/~/ media/Projects/BPEA/Fall%202013/Fall%202013%20BPEA%20elemendorf %20presentation.pdf.

14. Elmendorf press conference.

15. Ibid.

16. Medicare estimate from the Henry J. Kaiser Foundation. Population from U.S. Bureau of the Census. http://kff.org/medicare/state-indicator/total -medicare-beneficiaries/; www.census.gov/popclock/.

17. Elmendorf press conference.

18. Ibid.

19. Ibid.

20. Ibid.

21. Elmendorf, Brookings presentation, chart. www.brookings.edu/~/media /Projects/BPEA/Fall%202013/Fall%202013%20BPEA%20elemendorf% 20presentation.pdf.

22. Moody's Investors Service, Analysis, United States of America, July 18, 2013.

23. U.S. Department of Treasury, Financial Management Service, Bureau of Economic Analysis data, Naroff Economic Advisors, Inc. analysis.

24. Bureau of Labor Statistics, Current Employment Statistics data, Naroff Economic Advisors, Inc. analysis.
25. National Bureau of Economic Research, "Business Cycle Expansions and Contractions."
26. U.S. Department of Treasury. Joint Statement of Secretary Lew and OMB Director Burwell on Budget Results for Fiscal Year 2013, October 30, 2013.
27. CBO, Updated Budget Projections: Fiscal Years 2013 to 2023. July 2013 update.
28. Small Business Administration, Office of Advocacy, "Frequently Asked Questions." September 2012 from Bureau of Labor Statistics, Business Employment Dynamics table on Entrepreneurship and the U.S. Economy."

Chapter 8

Tax Policy: Does Cutting Taxes Cure All Ills?

When it comes to government policy, nothing causes more arguments than taxes. Everyone knows that to provide services you have to pay for them. But what are "good" taxes, if there actually are such things, and which ones should be cut is a totally different story. Basically, everyone wants their taxes cut while keeping taxes on everyone else.

But even if you cut taxes, you can do it the right way or the wrong way. Some tax breaks can create significantly more economic activity but many others do almost nothing to improve the economy.

We need also recognize that cutting taxes is expensive, as every person or company is eligible for the tax if they meet certain conditions, regardless of whether they make use of that extra money. Some firms get a tax break even if they continue operating exactly the same as they did before the tax break happened. And since households of varying income levels spend the extra income from reduced taxes at a different pace, who gets the tax break makes a significant difference. Therefore, the distribution of income is a major player in the effectiveness of tax policy. In other words, if the tax cut doesn't make economic sense, it simply becomes a way to redistribute income, not a way to expand growth.

But politicians still love to say that all you have to do is cut taxes and everything will be right with the world, which is why one of our favorite sayings is: if you get your tax policy from a politician, you get the tax code you deserve.

There Is No Such Thing as a Free Tax Cut

Benjamin Franklin is credited with saying that "in this world nothing can be said to be certain except death and taxes." That may be true, but few people like to pay taxes so we do everything possible to escape them.

Tax reform, or how we should cut taxes and who should get those tax cuts, will forever be a hot-button issue. This anger about taxes is not something the modern Tea Party, invented as it came from the original Tea Tax protesters. But the fact that a tax is cut doesn't mean the tax cut makes any economic sense. Indeed, there are many examples of abusive tax subsidies hidden in the tax code that did little other than benefit a specific firm, industry, or group.

Since most of us cannot afford the best tax lawyers to scour every nook and cranny of the tax code to ensure that we pay the least amount possible, we demand tax breaks through the ballot box. That raises the question, "What taxes should be cut?" The usual response is "mine!" Unfortunately, that is not the best answer for the economy.

How, then, do you determine when a tax break makes economic sense? Use the *Acid Test* for tax changes: That is, *Only cut a tax if it adds significantly to economic activity and if a current tax break doesn't, it should be repealed.* A tax break that does not pass the Acid Test is a social welfare program that transfers money from the Treasury to those who get the break.

This is a simple concept that hinges on the basic fact that there is no such thing as a free tax cut. When you reduce a tax, to start with, the government loses revenue, and either households or corporations have more money in their pockets or banks. It is what is done with those additional funds and the cost to the government of providing those breaks, in other words, the benefits versus the costs of the tax cuts, that determine if the action on the part of our elected officials to provide tax relief actually accomplishes anything.

The purpose of the tax cut is to generate more spending on the part of either households or businesses. If personal income taxes are reduced, people find their paychecks are fatter. Individuals have the capacity to buy more goods or services, and that would, at least in theory, grow the economy. Businesses that benefit from the greater consumer demand can hire more people, adding to personal income and ultimately creating additional consumption.

When corporate taxes are cut, the company has more cash. A business tax reduction could, in theory, allow firms to expand production, hire more people, or invest in machinery, software, or even a new plant. That, too, should lead to greater economic growth.

All that makes total sense, as long as the tax cut actually achieves those goals. But not all tax cuts actually generate very much additional economic activity. If they don't, there are still some people or businesses that have more money, but the economy doesn't grow very much as a result, and tax revenues fall, expanding the budget deficit.

There are many examples of tax reductions that on the surface seem to make a lot of sense but in reality don't do a lot. Here are three:

Example 1: The inheritance/estate/death tax. A reduction or ending of this tax completely would add absolutely nothing to economic growth. Nothing. Nada. And there is no way around that. This is purely a social welfare program for the heirs of those who have created lots of wealth. That may not be bad, but that is all it is.

Why doesn't cutting the inheritance tax make any economic sense? Simple. The key is that the tax falls on the heirs, not on those who actually create the wealth. They are dead, thus the moniker *death tax*.

Since the wealth creators don't pay taxes as long as they are alive, it does not affect their economic or business decisions. Successful businesspeople don't sit around saying they will not create more wealth because after they die their heirs might have to pay more taxes.

They may hire tax specialists to protect their wealth, but they will not stop creating it.

The reality is that lowering the inheritance tax will not encourage any additional wealth-creating economic activity. Consequently, an inheritance tax cut simply amounts to a transfer of income to the heirs. Worse, if the tax is repealed, it could lower activity by ending the need for the tax-planning industry. Now we are not arguing that there is any economic value derived from having all those tax accountants and lawyers running around devising ways of preventing the government from getting its hands on their clients money, but to the extent that they are no longer needed and their businesses fail, the economy is negatively affected.

Regardless, the Acid Test argues that this tax should not be lowered.

Example 2: Carried interest. Carried interest is, in simple terms, a reduced tax rate available to those who manage alternative investments, usually private equity and hedge fund managers. Part of their income is taxed at the lower capital gains rate rather than the higher wage rate.

Should this tax break exist? It is hard to see why. Does anyone really believe hedge fund or private equity managers would get out of the business if they had to pay regular income taxes rather than the reduced rate? Really, come on now.

But let's say some managers do quit—would that even matter? Since they are investing other people's money, their investors would simply have to find new managers who have remained in the business. And there will be many other very successful investment advisers and managers who would be glad to take the money from their former competitors and employ those funds.

There could be some short-term dislocations as investors transition from one hedge fund to another, but ending the carried interest deduction would not reduce the availability of capital or economic activity significantly.

The Acid Test argues that the carried interest break should be terminated, as all it does is transfer money to a special class of money managers by lowering their tax rate.

Example 3: Mortgage interest deduction. The mortgage interest deduction is supposed to lower homeowner payments, thus increasing housing demand. Wrong. Interest payments are only one part of the "price" of a home: Homebuyers look at total monthly payments, which include principal and taxes as well as interest. Critically, mortgage companies don't qualify people on the basis of after-tax payments.

But, more importantly, when making their monthly mortgage payments, do homeowners really perceive they are paying less? Doubtful. Instead, when they file their taxes, they see it as lower tax payments or higher refunds, not a reduction in housing costs. That is, homeowners don't look at their tax returns and say that the tax refund that could be ascribed to the mortgage deduction all goes to the house. They allocate it across their entire living expenses, of which housing is just a part.

Ending the mortgage interest deduction would not significantly affect housing sales so the Acid Test would say end it.

There are many other examples of major tax breaks, including the investment tax credit, reduced dividends tax rates, zero taxes on municipal bonds, and lowered rates for interest and capital gains, all of which fail the Acid Test. These sound good on the surface, but when you look at their economic effects, their value disappears.

But it is not just a specific type of tax that could fail the Acid Test. How the tax is implemented, that is, who gets the tax break and how much, is always critical.

How Much Do Americans Make and What Are They Taxed?

Here are some things that are not very common: blue moons; no-hitters in baseball, and income tax increases.

Yes, read my lips, Congress does occasionally raise taxes on Americans' paychecks. It's painful for many legislators to raise taxes, but sometimes they are left with few places to get some revenue.

A recent case in point: a piece of legislation called the American Taxpayer Relief Act (ATRA), passed by Congress on New Year's Day 2013. That's also the bill that temporarily prevented the United States from going over the so-called fiscal cliff, a series of across-the-board tax increases and spending cuts that would have been implemented if Congress did not act.

As it turned out, two months later, the automatic cuts went into effect but the ATRA maintained what is referred to as the Bush-era cuts *and* increased taxes on high-income wage earners, specifically for couples earning more than $450,000 a year or single filers earning more than $400,000 a year. Their top tax rate went from 35 percent to 39.6 percent. They also got hit with a higher capital gains rate that went from 15 percent to 20 percent. And they ended up paying a surcharge on income of over $250,000 for a couple ($200,000 for singles) related to President Obama's health care bill.

But, most taxpayers avoided higher income taxes though they did once again pay their full share of Social Security taxes, which had been reduced. How much more will higher income wage earners have to pay in taxes?

In July 2013, the Tax Policy Center (TPC), a joint venture of the Urban Institute and the Brookings Institution, published a model estimating Americans' incomes and tax burdens for tax year 2014. For its computer projection, the TPC incorporated a variety of factors such as historical tax records, government revenue estimates, and the economic projections of the nonpartisan Congressional Budget Office, which projected the gross domestic product would grow by a moderate 3.4 percent in 2014. In estimating income, the TPC used a broad measure that included the value of employer-provided benefits, interest from tax-exempt bonds, and money saved for retirement that is not subject to taxation. In estimating taxes, the TPC included four federal taxes: income taxes, payroll taxes (Social Security and Medicare), the individual share of corporate taxes, and the estate tax.

The TPC's estimates of Americans' incomes and taxes are shown in Table 8.1. All the tax rates are permanent unless Congress decides to change them again.

While the Distribution of Income Is Good or Inevitable, It Still Matters When It Comes to Tax Policy

Consider the issue of income distribution and how it could affect the way we tax income. This is not a class warfare issue; it is an economic

Table 8.1 Estimated Income and Taxes for 2014[a]

| Expanded Cash Income Level (thousands of 2013 dollars)[b] | Tax Units[c] | | Average Income (Dollars) | Average Federal Tax Burden (Dollars) | Average After-Tax Income[d] (Dollars) | Average Federal Tax Rate[e] |
	Number (thousands)	Percent of Total				
Less than 10	11,769	7.2	5,807	249	5,558	4.3
10 to 20	23,032	14.2	15,378	374	15,004	2.4
20 to 30	19,434	11.9	25,214	1,227	23,988	4.9
30 to 40	15,837	9.7	35,514	2,696	32,818	7.6
40 to 50	13,117	8.1	45,663	4,694	40,970	10.3
50 to 75	25,154	15.5	62,882	8,614	54,268	13.7
75 to 100	15,494	9.5	87,922	13,764	74,158	15.7
100 to 200	28,016	17.2	140,177	25,510	114,667	18.2
200 to 500	7,709	4.7	293,075	65,867	227,208	22.5
500 to 1,000	958	0.6	694,817	195,152	499,665	28.1
More than 1,000	567	0.4	3,327,569	1,150,364	2,177,205	34.6
All	162,816	100.0	84,346	16,203	68,142	19.2

SOURCE: Urban–Brookings Tax Policy Center Microsimulation Model (v. 0613-1).

Number of AMT Taxpayers (millions): 4.2

[a]Calendar year. Baseline is current law.

[b]Tax units with negative adjusted gross income are excluded from their respective income class but are included in the totals. For a description of expanded cash income, see www.taxpolicycenter.org/TaxModel/income.cfm.

[c]Includes both filing and nonfiling units but excludes those that are dependents of other tax units.

[d]After-tax income is expanded cash income less: individual income tax net of refundable credits; corporate income tax; payroll taxes (Social Security and Medicare); and estate tax.

[e]Average federal tax (includes individual and corporate income tax, payroll taxes for Social Security and Medicare, and the estate tax) as a percentage of average expanded cash income.

activity issue. If you start with an economy that is largely dependent on consumer spending, you want an economy where as much of the income earned will be spent. That is where income distribution becomes a real factor in the level and make up of consumer spending.

Economists have a term called *marginal propensity to consume*, which comes into play when you deal with the issue of consumption and income distribution. This is really a very simple concept wrapped around a complex term. Essentially, it comes down to this: how much does an individual spend when he or she gets another dollar of income? Okay, it's not just another dollar; it could be a hundred or a thousand or a million dollars, but you get the point.

The theory argues that low-income households tend to spend just about all the income they earn because they have to. Most of the money is used for essentials such as food, shelter, heating, transportation, and clothes. The poorest frequently don't even have enough money to cover their basic needs. Therefore, any additional funds that these households receive generally get spent. Their propensity is to spend everything.

As incomes rise and people can meet their basic needs, they start buying discretionary goods. They don't need them, or at least all of them, but they like to have them. Whether it's a shoe fetish or the desire to have different shirts for every day of the year, once incomes reach a significantly high enough level, people purchase products they want rather than need.

Once a household's funds reach what we will call "middle-income" levels, families have the choice to save some of their earnings or spend it all—or more, which is the issue of debt that we have discussed. Generally, some of the income is saved, even if it is a small amount. That is, as middle-income households get more money, their propensity is to spend most but not all of their income. It is lower than the poor but often not that much lower.

Finally there are "upper-income" households. They can buy all they need, all they want, and still have some left over. They save a lot, generally by investing their extra funds. That is good because these are resources that the capital markets can make available to households and businesses to borrow. However, it also means that propensity to consume by the household that earns tons of money is a lot lower than those who are either middle income or lower income. Very simply, the higher the income, the more that is saved, and therefore the less that is spent.

The Occupy Movement made Wall Street a symbolic target in its effort to highlight income disparity. But lower Manhattan is not the only place where households have large incomes.

In September 2013, the Brookings Institution Metropolitan Policy Program, using IRS data from taxes filed for 2011, looked to see where those with the highest incomes lived.

Although the Occupy protestors focused on the top 1 percent, the IRS does not break down income on the basis of zip code until $100,000 because of privacy concerns. What that reveals is where the top 12 percent live, calculates the TPC.

The Metropolitan Policy Program found that 75 percent live in the 100 largest metropolitan areas as opposed to rural areas. In some of the metro areas, wealthy suburbs help to boost incomes such as the suburbs around Washington, D.C., or the Cambridge area of Boston.

Four out of the top 10 metro areas in terms of percentage of filers with returns of over $100,000 are on the West Coast. Think of the entertainment industry in Los Angeles, Silicon Valley in northern California, the financial and creative hub of San Francisco, and Seattle, home of Microsoft.

Elizabeth Kneebone, a fellow at Brookings who put together the analysis, observes that the metro areas with the highest incomes have certain characteristics: a high level of education, an entrepreneurial bent, the proximity to a major financial or creative center, and an industry or corporate entity that pays its employees relatively high wages.

"Many of the areas have a highly skilled and highly educated concentration of workers," says Kneebone, who is the co-author of *Confronting Suburban Poverty in America* (Brookings Institution Press, May 2013).

The New York metro area is not in the top 10 on the basis of share of filers earning over $100,000. It ranks fourteenth. However, many people who work on Wall Street actually live in coastal Connecticut, which ranked third. In addition, as Kneebone notes, New York has over 1.4 million people making over $100,000, the most numerically of any metro area.

Using the $100,000 or higher criteria, Table 8.2 shows the Brookings Metropolitan Policy's top 10 most wealthy areas.

Table 8.2 Shares of Tax Filers with Adjusted Gross Incomes of $100,000 or Higher in Tax Year 2011

Metro Area	Total Returns	Returns in Top AGI Category (greater than or equal to $100,000)	Percentage $100,000 and Above	Rank
San Jose-Sunnyvale-Santa Clara, CA	782,089	204,474	26.1%	1
Washington-Arlington-Alexandria, DC/VA/MD/WV	2,532,099	606,486	24.0%	2
Bridgeport-Stamford-Norwalk, CT	388,994	92,936	23.9%	3
San Francisco-Oakland-Fremont, CA	1,893,015	420,954	22.2%	4
Boston-Cambridge-Quincy, MA/NH	2,100,534	415,357	19.8%	5
Poughkeepsie-Newburgh-Middletown, NY	288,818	54,723	18.9%	6
Hartford-West Hartford-East Hartford, CT	556,938	104,963	18.8%	7
Seattle-Tacoma-Bellevue, WA	1,538,502	285,408	18.6%	8
Baltimore-Towson, MD	1,189,866	220,183	18.5%	9
Minneapolis-St. Paul-Bloomington, MN/WI	1,517,084	268,963	17.7%	10

SOURCE: Brookings Institution, analysis of IRS data.

Why should income distribution matter? An example is the best way to show how income distribution and spending matters. Let's assume that a household gets an additional $10,000. Someone living in poverty is likely to spend just about all of it. It is enough to allow them to buy what they need but not enough to make them rich, however that is defined.

Meanwhile, if it's the middle-income household who gets the extra money, they are likely to save some of it but still spend a significant portion of it. They have lots of discretionary items they would like to purchase. They can afford to put some away for a rainy day, which they are likely to do. Thus, they spend less of the extra money than a poor family would.

What about upper-income households? The extra money is nice but does not change the standard of living a whole lot. They are already buying all the necessities and discretionary items they want and they are still saving and investing extensively. Not much of the extra funds, if any at all, get spent.

Given this example, what happens to spending if incomes go up by $10,000? It depends on who gets the money. If it goes to the poor, probably all of it gets spent, so demand rises robustly. If it goes to middle-income households, most of it is spent, and demand goes up strongly. If it goes to upper-income households, little is spent, so demand barely rises.

Now consider the distribution of income. This is something that has been worrying economists, politicians, and average households for years. Basically, it should seem clear now that how the income that is earned in the economy gets distributed between income groups can have a major impact on economic growth.

That raises the basic question of whether there is a good distribution of income. While there may be implications for growth of different types of income distributions, it is difficult to say that over time one type of distribution is best. However, when it comes to economic growth, some are better than others.

For example, if 1 percent of the population gets 99 percent of the income and those "1-percenters" don't spend a lot of the money, economic growth is likely to be quite sluggish. However, if everyone has the same income, there may be limited savings, and that could reduce capital availability and investment, reducing future growth. Clearly, somewhere between equal distribution and total concentration of income is a "good" one, but it is hardly clear what that is.

In addition, there may be nothing that can be done about it even if we wanted to. Technological change, which puts a premium on high-skilled workers, is a major factor. Technology also reduces the demand for lower-skilled employees, keeping their wages in check.

Similarly, the globalization of economies is creating tremendous restraining pressures on wages as labor supply is now international in scope, not just domestic. If you can produce anywhere, workers all across the globe become potential employees. That allows owners of capital to keep wages down and reap a larger share of the returns. Since there is no turning back on globalization or technical change, the changing patterns in income distribution may be inevitable.

That doesn't mean there is no reason to consider the changes in income distribution: it creates political issues and problems even outside the economic concerns. The Occupy Wall Street movement, which came and went quickly, should not be dismissed. It represented a group of disenfranchised individuals that may not have moved a lot of people to action but whose ideas may be present in a lot of workers.

Disenfranchised employees are not nearly as productive as those who feel they can make their way up the corporate and income ladders. They do their jobs, but a firm doesn't make a lot of profits because a worker gives them a dollar's day of work for a dollar's pay. It is the worker that goes the extra mile that creates the added product and ultimately the most earnings. Profits come from firms paying for a day's work but getting more than a day's output.

While there are reasons to consider the impacts of the income distribution, the attempts to politicize the issue, especially the incessant use of the phrase *class warfare*, hides the economic discussions. It is not whether the distribution of income is good, but what are the implications for economic growth, consumer and government spending, the budget deficit, and the availability of capital of the changing income distribution.

With that in mind, in the short term, the shifting distribution is already having real economic implications. In the United States, the income distribution has been moving more toward upper-income households. This has been nicknamed the "bar-belling" of income as more gets concentrated in upper- and lower-income groups.

A report by Linda Levine for the Congressional Research Service concluded that "inequality has increased in the United States as a result of high-income households pulling further away from those lower in the distribution."[1] It is in that context that the economic implications need to be discussed.

The winnowing out of the middle class is restraining consumer spending and therefore economic growth. The middle class has been the driving force for the economy since the 1950s. They are the key to the consumer-based spending. But as income flows upward and more people move down the income ladder, consumption growth potential declines.

The more income that moves to households with lower propensities to consume, the lower the growth of the economy since the share of income going to spending would decline. That is particularly worrisome for an economy that depends heavily on household spending.

In addition, there is a potential change in the types of goods demanded both in terms of categories and where they are produced. Upper-income households buy more discretionary products and fewer necessities. Are more of those goods imported, or are they produced domestically? Since most food and housing are domestically sourced, changing income patterns might lead to rising imports. That is not clear, but it is a potential outcome.

While income distribution per se is not the most important factor in the economy, how incomes change matters. Thus, understanding how the economy is growing requires not just income growth but also income distributional issues. The context of income change—when and how quickly that is occurring—makes context once again a key factor in evaluating the economy.

Indeed, was it any surprise that the economic recovery was so slow given that workers' incomes hardly kept up with inflation but management and business owners' profits soared? If it was, it was because observers didn't account for who was getting the earnings from the growing economy, only that those earnings were expanding. They missed the whole idea of income growth in the context of who gets the growing income.

Is the Answer to Every Economy Ill to Cut Corporate Taxes?

We talked about the reality that businesspeople respond in ways that are similar to households in that their reactions to tax policy is greatly affected by the context in which those policies were implemented and their corporate financial outlook. If the Acid Test is to be used, those factors need to be considered when corporate tax changes are considered.

Since companies create jobs, helping firms along is always a popular approach to economic policy. The problem is that tax cuts are very expensive because of the way they are structured: everyone who is qualified gets the tax break even if the tax break doesn't induce them to do anything differently from what they would normally do.

Consider the investment tax credit. The logic of this break is to increase the level of investment in the economy. That makes total sense, as improving technology and production expands the economy's capacity and therefore its growth potential. There is nothing better for long-term growth than robust business investment.

How could implementing something like an investment tax credit be anything but good? While the purpose of a tax cut is to induce additional spending, it is not limited to those firms who are incented to invest. Anyone who actually invests gets to take advantage of the reduced costs.

A simple mathematical example can best illustrate the issue. Let's say that business investment is running at $1 trillion a year and the economy needs a boost. Let's also assume that without an investment tax break, we would still have only $1 trillion in investment. That is, the level of business investment would be flat without some government incentives.

It would seem that the prospect of no growth in capital spending would be a really good time to cut business taxes, and it would be. And let's say it works extremely well so that instead of zero additional investment, capital spending grows by a whopping 15 percent. The tax break creates $150 billion more spending. Wow, what a great move, right? Maybe. Maybe not.

Before you take out the axes and start cutting investment taxes like crazy, you also have to consider the costs to the Treasury of reducing the tax. Here is where the difference between economics and politics can be seen the clearest. An economist would say that you only give the tax break to those firms who would not have invested in the new machinery but because of the reduced costs, they decide to make the investment. The politician says you cannot do that (and in reality it would be impossible to make that determination), you have to give everyone who invests the deal.

It's the universality of the tax break that creates the real problems with tax policy. The government has not only reduced taxes on the firms that decided to purchase the additional $150 billion of new capital, but it has also given a tax break to all those companies that were going to invest anyway. Remember, without the cut, there still would have been $1 trillion in capital spending.

Without the tax break, the firms that spent the first $1 trillion on capital would pay the government the old, higher tax rates. Instead, the Treasury collects reduced taxes from those companies, again, not because they were induced to invest but because they did what they were going to anyway. That is, the government's tax take from all those companies is reduced.

Let's say that the tax credit reduces corporate taxes by 10 percent of the cost of capital. That would mean the government loses roughly $100 billion—10 percent of $1 trillion. But only an additional $150 billion is spent by firms. That implies the government pays for about two-thirds of the cost of the new capital. What a deal!

The dirty little secret of corporate tax cuts is that firms benefit simply because they exist. Believe it or not, lots of politicians actually think it is a perfectly acceptable thing for the government to pay firms for doing nothing, but that is precisely what happens with tax breaks.

Clearly, this is just an example, and there are a lot of other factors that go into determining the benefits and costs of a tax cut. For example, the additional spending would multiply though the economy and could generate more than $150 billion in growth. The taxes on that would offset some of the lost revenue. But the point still holds: When government reduces taxes, everyone benefits even if they do not change their behavior one bit. And that costs the Treasury real money. The economic research on tax cuts is clear: they do not pay for themselves, at least in the first few years after they are implemented.

Should we ever cut taxes on businesses? The answer is yes, but you need to get a really big bang for the bucks that the Treasury loses. The best time is early in a recovery, as the impact will be multiplied. The impression that the economy will strengthen because of the increased investment activity caused by the tax breaks would lead to rising corporate confidence. That could generate significant additional growth even in unrelated industries, as most business leaders build a better economy into their business plans. But once there is a solid, broad-based expansion and most sectors are standing on their own, those added impacts are limited and business tax cuts only transfer income from the Treasury to businesses. It is a form of income redistribution.

That said, there are some taxes on businesses that really do need to be reexamined extremely closely. One is the so-called double taxation of small-business owner income. Basically, most small-business people pay personal, not corporate, income taxes. As such, all revenues their businesses earn are essentially personal income.

Unfortunately for the average small-business owner, when they take home a paycheck, they pay taxes for Social Security (FICA) and Medicare twice. First, they pay it out of their own paycheck. But that is not enough for the government. Since small-business owners are also employers, they have to pay the business share of FICA and Medicare taxes, which as it turns out is exactly the same as the employee pays.

What does that mean? The Social Security tax rate is 6.2 percent of income up to a cutoff point. The Medicare portion is 1.45 percent on all income. Thus, the small-business owner pays 12.4 percent for Social Security (6.2 percent for being an employee and 6.2 percent as the employer) and 2.9 percent for Medicare (1.45 percent for being an employee and 1.45 percent as an employer). The result is that before paying anything else, including income taxes, small-business owners pay the federal government 15.3 percent of their income up to the Social Security maximum.

Since most small-business owners earn less than the Social Security maximum, the starting tax rate is a real business killer. What that tells us is that one of the best ways to generate more hiring is to allow small-business owners to be responsible for only the employee portion of the payroll taxes. That would generate significant savings. Since most small-business owners plow much of their earnings back into the business, they will likely be able to afford more inventories and/or part-time workers.

The lack of rational approaches to small-business taxes makes no sense at all. These firms create most of the jobs. At times during the first few years of the recovery from the Great Recession, ADP, a payroll services company, indicated from their surveys that almost all the private-sector payroll increases came from firms that employed less than 500 workers.[2] Similar results can be seen in the U.S. Bureau of Labor Statistics (BLS) Business Employment Dynamics reports for the past few years. Indeed, the importance of small businesses in job creation has not just been during the latest recovery but BLS's data show that between 1993 and 2013, nearly 64 percent of the net new jobs came from businesses employing fewer than 500 workers.[3] If you don't pay more than lip service to small businesses, you don't get much growth.

These issues of income distribution and the costs of tax breaks matter because of their impacts on the deficit. Basically, if you lose tax revenues through a tax change, the deficit widens. That growing debt can be paid in just three ways: by reducing spending, raising other taxes, or borrowing. Each has redistributional impacts.

Let's assume that the rising budget deficit that results from an inefficient tax cut is dealt with through cutting spending. We cannot afford to pay for everything, so let's eliminate some programs. While that sounds good, government spending cuts don't come without a price. Some person, group, or company loses.

If the government reduces its purchases of goods and services, businesses that had contracts to supply those products now are looking at reduced order books. Their incomes fall and they cut back on employees and buy fewer inputs. That reduces economic activity further. We have a redistribution of income from those firms that lose business and their employees and suppliers to those who pay lower taxes.

If the tax cut is paid for by borrowing, a similar redistribution takes place. Future generations pay for the spending of the current generation. Of course, if those tax breaks do create a lot of new investment that increases society's long-term productive capacity, we could have a trade-off. But, in general, as we saw in the example about all those firms that get the tax break for simply breathing, that is usually a stretch of the imagination.

Finally, we can raise other taxes. That redistribution is very obvious. Those who pay the higher taxes give money to those who pay lower taxes. Is that fair? Only if you are comfortable saying that one group of people should have more money while others have less. And that gets us back to the entire distribution-of-income discussion.

But the discussion of tax changes and their impacts on the economy doesn't stop with the high cost of businesses taxes or the problems of how the distribution of income affects tax policy; there is the key concern about messages that it sends: if tax breaks are given to those activities that are deemed to have special value, what does it say about those activities that are taxed at higher rates? Policymakers are indicating they consider the competing activities to be of lower value.

Think about it. The tax code seems to be saying that people should earn their income from almost any means other than labor. Why? Wages and salaries are taxed at just about the highest rate of any income source. There are special lowered rates for dividends, capital gains, and interest income—especially from state and local debt—but if all you do is make your money from wages and salaries, you pay a higher tax rate.

Consider the tax-free treatment of interest on state and local government securities. Most state and local governments issue bonds for schools, roads, and other infrastructure projects, and no federal income tax means that interest on the securities can be reduced. That increases construction by making the projects more affordable.

Interestingly, the federal government taxes interest paid on its own debt. That creates a strange commentary about federal activities: If you lower the tax to encourage one type of activity but don't lower it on similar types of activity, you are basically saying the higher-taxed activity is less worthy. Do members of Congress really believe that their spending has less value than what municipal governments do? And do we really want to encourage more local construction or borrowing?

It is possible, if all your income is municipal bond interest, that you could pay no taxes at all. At the least, those who earn interest from munis will pay much lower taxes than those who earn the same amount of wages or salaries. What is the government saying? Investing in municipal debt is an awful lot more desirable than working for a living. Quite an interesting message, isn't it?

Similarly, there is the issue of the so-called double taxation of dividends, which are currently taxed at a 15 percent rate rather than the more typical 25 percent to 35 percent rate on income. The argument is that corporations already pay taxes on that income. If the owners of the corporations, the stockholders, have to pay taxes on that income as well, the company income is actually taxed twice.

While the double-taxation argument may have merit, the reduced tax rate affects only those stockholders of companies that pay dividends. Stockholders in so-called "growth" companies, which tend not to pay dividends, don't get that benefit. Is the government really trying to encourage dividend payouts rather than faster business growth? Once again, those who receive income from dividends rather than wages will pay lower taxes.

Finally, there are capital gains, where the reduced tax rate of 15 percent for most filers was supposed to foster saving and investment. However, over the long run, neither households nor businesses invest based on tax rates. Also, capital is raised internationally, so why a lower or higher tax rate would affect a foreign investor is anyone's guess. The result, though, is those who earn income from capital gains pay lower taxes.

By imposing higher tax rates on wages and salaries compared to interest, dividends, or capital gains, the tax code clearly values investment income more than labor income. If Congress really wants to encourage work effort, it should show it by lowering the tax on wages and salaries compared to other income sources. If it doesn't want to show a preference, then it should consider all income as being equal and tax all sources similarly.

When it comes to taxes, it is not clear that cutting taxes is the answer. It could be, but you have to cut those taxes that create the most additional economic value and don't send negative messages to certain groups or businesses. It is not very often that we see our friendly politicians talk about how much more economic activity is generated by their tax proposals or compare the positive impacts on the economy with the costs. Normally, the tax cuts occur in the dead of night when no one is looking so the hard questions don't have to be answered.

Unfortunately for all of us, there are few politicians that haven't seen a tax cut that they couldn't support and explain why it is so great, even if it isn't. Which gets us back to another favorite saying: If you get your tax policy from a politician, you get the tax code you deserve.

While politicians wrestle with taxes, the Federal Reserve often has to adjust its monetary to policy to what it sees happening in the halls of Congress. In the next chapter, we look at how the Federal Reserve tries to adapt and keep the banking system on track.

Notes

1. "The Distribution of Household Income and the Middle Class," Congressional Research Service, November 13, 2012.
2. ADP National Employment Report, various reports.
3. NFIB Research Foundation. U.S. Bureau of Labor Statistics, Business Employment Dynamics, various releases and Supplemental Firm Class Size Tables.

Chapter 9

Monetary Policy: Money, or Maybe the Federal Reserve, Makes the World Go 'Round

T he Fed is assumed to be all-knowing and all-powerful: wrong and wrong. How monetary policy works is discussed in this chapter, but much more important, how the same policy can be successful or a failure depending on the type of policy and the context in which it is implemented.

In the past two chapters, we saw how difficult it is to create fiscal policy even if the government wasn't as dysfunctional as it is. Whether it is raising taxes or lowering them, how that is done, and the economic implications are frequently unknown even to those making the decisions. Worse, the differential effects of alternative policies may not even be a factor in many fiscal policy decisions since politics rather than economics usually drives taxation decisions.

When it comes to the expenditure side of the budget, be it cutting spending, funding massive stimulus projects, or implementing mindless sequestration, the government rarely has any idea what it is doing. There are even politicians who think it is possible to balance the budget. In other words, fiscal policy is more a matter of political dogma and expediency than any logical or rational approach to economic growth.

In the face of all that chaos, the members of the Federal Reserve have to determine what is the best course for monetary policy. Is this a job that even Superman would hesitate to take on? Probably. But someone has to do it, and it does get done—often better than anyone could imagine.

How Monetary Policy Works

The Federal Reserve came into being in 1914 largely because people basically didn't trust banks. And they had very good reason to worry. No, it wasn't just because Butch Cassidy and the Sundance Kid were riding around robbing banks and trains. Essentially, banks operate in a perpetual state of bankruptcy. They take in money and usually lend out more than they have on hand. That creates a small problem called *liquidity*. Financial institutions cannot give everyone back all the money they have on deposit if everyone shows up at the same. They are illiquid.

Facing a circumstance where there is not enough cash on hand is not typically a major problem for banks since normally not a whole lot of people ask for their money to be returned at any given time—unless, of course, there is a run on the bank.

How does a run on a bank start? Usually, through rumors or stories that a bank is in trouble. At that point, people panic and run to the bank to get their money. That is what happened to the Building and Loan Association in *It's a Wonderful Life*. George Bailey had only a limited amount of funds on hand, and when the rumors went out that the bank was in trouble, a flood of customers showed up. The only thing that saved George and Uncle Billy was that they had just enough to pay everyone who came in the door during business hours.

Unfortunately, during the latter portion of the nineteenth century and early parts of the twentieth century, a lot of banks didn't have enough cash on hand. During the normal ebb and flow of growth, what we call *business cycles*, some banks found themselves in trouble. That led to bank panics, and the runs on banks reduced capital available for lending since so much was leaving the banking system. The loss of available funds and the resulting decline in confidence accelerated downturns. Recessions and bank problems went hand-in-hand and they fed on each other, creating wild swings in the economy.

Into the breach came the Federal Reserve. The Fed was supposed to stop, or at least limit, bank runs. Reserve requirements and other regulations provided a measure of confidence that banks would not fail. Indeed, one of the biggest reasons for the creation of the Federal Reserve System was to stabilize the banking system and limit financial firm collapses.

Of course, nothing could protect bankers from recessions, depressions, or their own stupidity, so failures continued. Indeed, we have had two major periods in the past 20 years of bank shutdowns. First there was the savings-and-loan crisis during the first half of the 1990s and then the financial market collapse toward the end of the 2000s.

What made things different was the ability of the Federal Reserve to stabilize the economy. Economic slowdowns still occurred, and we did have the Great Recession, which was long and steep in no small part because the financial system largely froze up. But the Fed was able to come up with policies to deal with the issues, so the problems were less severe than they would have been.

Given that so many decisions on the part of the Fed had to be made quickly and were often so challenging, it has been critical that we have had and will continue to have an independent Federal Reserve. Can you imagine politicians running monetary policy? They cannot run fiscal policy, which we know is in total disarray.

The Federal Reserve Act of 1913 was structured in a way to keep politics out of the Fed. The Federal Reserve Board of Governors, the overseers of the system, is made up of a seven members led by the chairman. These individuals are nominated by the president and confirmed by the Senate. That immediately puts them into the political arena, at least as far as the selection and confirmation processes go. The chair and co-chair are chosen from the board members by the president.

Once the Fed members have been confirmed, though, they are ostensibly insulated from political interference by giving them 14-year terms of office. That is longer than any president's term so the Fed members are not beholden to the politician who nominated them. Also, the terms are staggered so no more than one member's term ends within two years of another's. No president can appoint more than four members—or so the theory went.

But in reality, few members of the Board of Governors are appointed to a full term. The way the Fed terms of office works is if someone resigns from the Fed, the term of office for that position keeps running until the 14 years is over! It's the dates of the term that are fixed, not the person. Thus, people might be appointed to a slot with as few as two years or even less left. They would then have to be reappointed and reconfirmed, or they would no longer be part of the Fed.

With ample turnover, which happens quite a lot, a president can appoint a large number, if not every member, of the Federal Reserve Board. That doesn't mean the members will simply do the bidding of the president. But it is not unusual for a president to appoint someone whose views on the economy and monetary policy coincide with the president's.

By law and the nature of their responsibilities, Fed members cannot and do not involve themselves with politics. They really do view themselves as being independent of the political process. But they do come to the job with certain views about how the Fed should operate, and that places them along a spectrum of political attitudes. Nevertheless, as so many former members have commented, once you become a central banker, your preconceptions fall by the wayside, and what is best for the country becomes the guiding factor in making monetary policy.

The leader of the pack, so to speak, is the board chairman. This is the most powerful person and is the major spokesperson for the Fed. Many people know the name of the Fed chair but would be challenged to name another member of the board.

As is the case with any organization, the head, in this case the chairman, has operated in a style that suits the individual's purposes. In the past decade, due to the attitude of, first, Alan Greenspan, then especially under the guidance of Ben Bernanke, members have been much freer to speak their views, even if they don't fully agree with the chairman's. That said, when it comes to monetary policy, when the chairman of the Federal Reserve Board speaks, everyone listens.

The Board of Governors, which operate out of Washington, D.C., is just one of the two major groups of individuals who oversee monetary policy. The second is the presidents of the 12 regional banks. And that is a story unto itself.

After the particularly bad panic of 1907, it finally dawned on our elected officials that maybe some entity was needed to oversee the nation's banks. Initially, the idea was to create regional Federal Reserve banks that would be situated close to all the local banks so they could be easily reached and reviewed. That is when politics entered, of course.

Since the 12 regional banks that we now have (the initial proposal had 15) would have great power and possibly be a nice source of employment and patronage (shhh, don't tell people that), the political grab was on. The result was a hodgepodge of locations including two that are nearly next-door neighbors, Philadelphia and New York, and two that are in the same state, St. Louis and Kansas City. Meanwhile, San Francisco is the only bank west of Dallas, Texas. So much for geographic diversity and close proximity to your client base. Isn't politics great?

Now we have 12 regional banks, picked to satisfy both the economic/financial concentration needs and political necessities of the times. So that the huge distances between branches, especially west of the Mississippi, could be covered and the changes in business activity and population could be accounted for, there are now also 24 branches (it used to be 25, but the Buffalo, New York, branch was closed).

So, we have a central bank with 7 board members headed by a chairman, 12 district banks and bank presidents, as well as 24 branch offices. It is this organization that is supposed to manage monetary policy and oversee the safety and soundness of the banking system.

Actually, the Fed has two key roles in the economy. The first is to ensure the stability of the banking system, and the second is to help

maximize employment as long as inflation doesn't get out of hand—
the dual mandate. How well the members handle those responsibilities
will always be a subject of great debate. But they do try to do it as best
as they can.

Problems Facing the Fed

The major problem facing the Fed members is that economic and
financial conditions are always in flux. That can be due to business
cycles, congressional "fixes," or something as simple as changes in regulations. Take, for example, the savings-and-loan crisis. All it took was
congressional modifications of the limits on interest that financial
institutions could pay on their deposits and the whole world changed.
Ultimately, that one move led to the collapse of hundreds of banks.

Until the early 1980s, banks were limited to how much they could
pay their depositors. But starting in the late 1970s, banks in New
England discovered ways around the limits. Meanwhile, in Congress,
retirees, the so-called Gray Panthers, argued that capping interest rates
hurt depositors, especially the elderly, who depended on interest income
for their retirement.

Congress came to the rescue of this growing and powerful group,
and the rest was history. In one (or two or three) stroke of the pen,
the savings-and-loan (S&L) industry was essentially rendered bank-
rupt. Banks that had been making long-term, fixed-rate loans under
the expectation that they could fund them with lower-cost, short-term
deposits suddenly had to compete for money. And in this case, competition meant raising depositor interest rates to attract more funds.

The net result was that many S&Ls were getting income from
30-year mortgages that were made years earlier and under low-
rate environments but were paying higher rates to attract money. If
the mortgage rate that the bank was receiving was 5 percent and the
deposit payout rate was 6 percent, it became really hard to make up the
negative 1-percentage-point difference in volume. Banks started losing
money like crazy.

It may have taken almost 15 years to reach its logical conclusion, but the result of the congressional action, which was supported

by Federal Reserve regulation changes, was a financial mess known as the S&L crisis. This banking disaster required government intervention and bailouts. Some banks were closed while others were merged. And in the most lasting aspect of the resolution of the crisis, some banks received government funds to absorb insolvent S&Ls and were able to create some of the megabanks we worry about now. There are always winners and losers whenever the government or regulators do something, and the resolution of the S&L problem was no different.

For the Fed, congressional action and rule changes meant dealing with two huge issues: The first was the crisis in the financial sector and the need to stabilize the system. The second was the impact on economic activity when banks became extremely conservative and some stopped lending. The recession that ran from July 1990 to March 1991 was in no small part caused by the financial problems in the financial sector.

What did the Fed do? What the Fed always did, at least until recently—lower interest rates. The Fed's rate-setting group, the Federal Open Market Committee (FOMC), had already been cutting the federal funds rate even before the recession started. This is the rate that banks pay each other for money and is generally considered to be the benchmark for short-term rates.

When the recession started, the rate had already come down from 9.125 percent in May 1989 to 8.25 percent in early July 1990. The economy had already been slowing and the hope was that lower rates would prevent a recession. Obviously, it didn't. Over the next two years, the funds rate was cut consistently until it finally reached a low of 3.00 percent in September 1992, where it remained until February 1994.

During this period, the Fed acted in a totally normal way: In the face of a slowing economy, it started to add punch to the punchbowl. The monetary authorities basic tool is the interest rate, and by lowering it, it hoped to foster more borrowing and faster economic growth.

But there is a long lag between the reduction in an interest rate and its impact on the economy. Households and businesses don't go out and borrow money every day. They do it when they either need to or want to. That is where expectations come in, and we know from the previous chapters that the outlook for the future matters a lot. Thus, the Fed not only has to change the cost of money, but it has to change the frame of mind of borrowers before the policy can work.

And the extent of the change and the level of rates matter as well. When the funds rate was at 9 percent, a change to 7 percent still kept the rate high. But when you go from 4 percent to 2 percent, now you are talking about making the cost of money extraordinarily low and that could, potentially, have a major impact. In other words, the Fed has to determine not just whether to change rates but how much and how fast as well, and that means the context of the policy is critical.

Nothing shows that point more than the actions of Fed Chairman Paul Volcker and his fight against rapidly rising prices. Facing inflation in 1979 that returned to double-digit rates, which was truly scary, the Fed chairman had double trouble: he had to not only cut the inflation rate, but he also had to change the perception that inflation was going to go even higher. He had to lower what economists call inflation expectations.

Inflation and inflation expectations can take years to build, and once they become deeply embedded in the psyche of households and businesses, trouble can only follow. After two decades of growth with relatively limited inflation, conditions began to change at the end of the 1960s. It is never a good idea to fight a war without paying for it, and that is what the nation did with the Vietnam War, which was also being conducted while the War on Poverty was being instituted. The surge in government spending and resulting budget deficit led to a rise in inflation.

But the pressures on inflation were not limited to large budget deficits. Indeed, a slow ending to the Vietnam War allowed the inflation rate to decelerate. The biggest blow was the oil embargo in 1973, which led to skyrocketing energy prices that were translated into double-digit inflation and a recession that started at the end of 1973 and lasted until early 1975.

Then came the second oil crisis in 1979. Energy costs soared again, and so did inflation. Worse, inflation expectations became rooted in the system. If people thought inflation would rise, they acted accordingly. That only fed the inflation cycle as firms raised prices, workers demanded higher wages, and people consumed out of fear their money would be worth less in the future.

So, what was a good Fed chairman to do? Well, if you are Paul Volcker, you use what has come to be called the *nuclear option*. When he took over in August 1979, the inflation rate was above 11 percent and headed ultimately toward a peak of 14.6 percent in April 1980. This was a level that threatened the economic future of the nation.

In order to save the economy by ridding it of inflation, the Fed chairman decided to hike rates to levels never before seen. We are not talking about 10 percent or even 15 percent. At the end of 1980 and during the first half of 1980, Mr. Volcker set the fed funds rate at 20 percent, and that led to a prime rate of 21.5 percent, with mortgage that were also pushing 20 percent. Indeed, my first mortgage, taken out in the summer of 1981, was 17.5 percent. I was probably the only person in western Massachusetts to buy a house that August!

Was this a case of a central banker, Paul Volcker, going wild? No, there was a real method to his seeming madness. Not only did the economy need to be slowed, but the belief that inflation would continue at a high rate and even accelerate had to be completely wrung out of the public's mind-set. What better way to do that? By crushing growth, which is precisely what happened.

In July 1981, the economy entered a steep recession as borrowing and spending dried up. That slowed demand, making price and wage increases difficult. But that was not the only benefit of Mr. Volcker's extreme actions: By making clear that interest rates would remain high for as long as necessary, the belief that prices would continue to rise disappeared. Indeed, the University of Michigan's Inflation Expectation Index went from over 10 percent in early 1980 to 3 percent by January 1983. Mission accomplished.

Though Mr. Volcker ended the threat that double-digit inflation posed to the nation's economic future, the cost was high. There were back-to-back recessions in the early part of the 1980s, and many businesses went under. Farmers were so incensed that they drove their tractors into Washington, D.C., to protest. Still, with inflation wrung out of the system, the economy was poised for strong economic growth, and the Reagan expansion would never have occurred if Paul Volcker hadn't saved the nation's bacon, no matter what the pig farmers thought.

The key point here is that how you conduct monetary policy is totally dependent on a variety of economic factors. For most of its existence, the Fed was able to do what it had to do by either raising or lowering the fed funds rate, thereby discouraging or encouraging borrowing and spending by firms and households. At least that was the case until the great financial collapse of 2008 occurred.

Meltdown of the U.S. Financial System

The essentials of the near cataclysmic meltdown of the world financial system in 2007–2008 are known to just about everyone. A housing boom, which coupled strong sales with soaring prices, proved too enticing for some financial institutions. They made decisions that were not based on any logic but on hope and prayers.

Let's review: After the recession of 2001 ended, the economy began to shift gears. Housing, as usual, led the way. Sales spiked, and the real estate market became the place to be—the place to make tons of money. The key ingredient was sharp increases in home prices. As home purchases rose during the 2002–2005 period, prices followed. Using the S&P/Case Shiller 20-City Index, home prices were up 7.3 percent in 2002, 9.2 percent in 2003, and 13.0 percent in 2004, with the gains peaking at 13.4 percent in 2005.[1]

It seemed to everyone that prices could increase forever, and that was the trap. They couldn't. A bubble was forming that was unsustainable. But many in the housing and finance sectors wanted to see it go on and on and on. The problem was, in those four years, over 30 million units were sold, and there were not that many more people left who had decent credit and who also wanted to buy homes.

What do you do when qualified buyers become few and far between but there are lots of homes for sale and lots of firms, ranging from realtors to builders to mortgage companies to financial institutions, buying and packaging the mortgages who need the world to keep spinning? You lower the credit standards so more people can buy houses, which is precisely what happened.

By early 2007, as the no-longer-funny joke went, "if you could fog a mirror you could get a loan." And indeed, the lower credit requirements for buyers made sense, but only under one condition: prices had to keep rising! If that happened, even if a borrower defaulted, the house could be sold and the lender paid back. Unfortunately, bubbles do burst, and when prices started falling, as they did starting in 2007, a disaster was baked in the cake.

Could the Fed have prevented the inevitable housing collapse? That is something that will be argued for decades, but there were regulatory means available that might have limited the damage. The Fed could also have raised interest rates, making loans largely unaffordable, which Chairman Volcker did, though under somewhat different circumstances. What was different, however, was inflation. In the 1970s, the inflation was economy-wide. In the 2000s, it was largely in the housing sector, so the Fed was cautious about creating economic policy for just one part of the economy. That, it turns out, may have been a mistake.

Regardless, when the bubble burst, it not only took down the housing sector, but all those banks that had been playing musical chairs with housing assets discovered they had no place to sit. The world had changed, prices were falling, and losses were piling up. Ultimately, investment banks such as Lehman Brothers collapsed, while other huge financial institutions such a Countrywide Financial Corporation, Bear Stearns, Merrill Lynch, and Wachovia Bank all had to be merged.

The rout was on and the collapse of the economy was just around the corner. Indeed, the Great Recession had already begun by the time most of the financial institutions went belly up. The result was a massive economic slowdown, where firms were in survival mode and the first to go were employees. In the eight months from October 2008 to July 2009, nearly 5.5 million jobs were lost.

In the face of all this, the FOMC started cutting rates and then cutting rates more. Since this was the standard operating procedure for getting out of a recession, the Fed was simply following normal operating procedures. But this was no normal downturn, which the Fed and everyone found out soon enough.

The Fed's fear of the future was seen in its interest rate policy. In September 2007, the funds rate was 5.25 percent. By the end of 2008, when the world was collapsing, it had dropped to close to zero percent. Yet the worst was still to come.

With the economy shrinking at an enormous pace—the fourth quarter 2008 gross domestic product (GDP) drop was 8.3 percent annualized—it looked like the monetary authorities were out of bullets and all was lost. But that was not the case. Instead, extraordinary circumstances required extraordinary actions, and that is exactly what the Fed did. It abandoned simply targeting the fed funds rate, which it directly controlled, and started focusing on all other interest rates. It introduced the idea of quantitative easing, rather than interest rate easing.

It was nice and simple when all the Fed had to do to control inflation or economic growth was to raise or lower the fed funds rate. It made life easier for so many of us who were called "Fed Watchers" because we interpreted the Fed's actions and forecasted their moves. But the advent of quantitative easing changed everything, for both the Fed and the economy.

The Fed is different from just about any other part of the economy in that it has a balance sheet but it can basically do what it wants with the assets and liabilities. It can buy as many securities as it desires with a flick of the wrist or a click of the mouse. Nothing stops it from doing that. Indeed, before the financial crisis started, the Fed had about $700 billion in assets on its balance sheet. That total moved toward $4 trillion as the Fed kept buying more securities.[2]

Why did the Fed expand its budget sheet so much? First, it simply could not lower the funds rate any further—no one has figured out how to create negative interest rates so zero is as low as you can go. In addition, banks were not lending out money because they had lost so much money, and in any event, the weak economy made lending much too risky. Therefore, the Fed had to work its magic in different ways. One idea was to lower not just short-term rates but rates all along the yield curve. They did that by buying Treasury securities, and quantitative easing was born.

The monetary authorities knew that if they became the buyer of first and last resort for securities of any maturity, they would change the prices and rates on those assets. When the Fed buys securities, it increases the demand for those assets, causing prices to rise. When it comes to securities, higher prices mean lower interest rates. So the Fed set out to buy all types of securities. It paid for those assets by simply crediting banks with more reserves, and since it controls the computers, it could do as much of this as it wanted.

The Fed's massive asset purchase policy was a response to the changing conditions and the need to be imaginative when the circumstances demanded it. Here, it was the context of a long-lasting, weak economic recovery that required that not just short-term but all interest rates be reduced.

The success of the Fed's quantitative easing can be measured in two ways. The first is direct: how much did it lower interest rates? When you consider that just about all rates, ranging from 3-month Treasury bills to 30-year Treasury bonds, hit record lows, you can conclude that on this measure the Fed was truly successful.

But the second measure is more problematic. Did the lower rates cause the economy to grow faster than it would have if the Fed had done nothing and rates were significantly higher? This is what amounts to proving a negative and is one of the most difficult aspects of evaluating any government policy. A similar issue arose when the 2009 stimulus plan was discussed. Did it work or was it a failure? Those who look only at the lackluster rate of growth that resulted from the stimulus think it was a failure. But that doesn't account for the fact that without the massive government spending, growth may have been different.

The Correct Way to Evaluate the Policies

The correct way of evaluating fiscal or monetary is in comparison to what the economy would have been like in absence of the policy. Firms do that all the time. They say, if we did nothing, this is what our profits would have been. After we invested in the marketing program, our profits are this. They then compare the costs with the benefits and get the return on the investment.

Did the Fed's quantitative easing program work? To determine that, you have to consider what sectors of the economy are most interest sensitive, since it is interest rates that the Fed was changing. Housing construction and sales, motor vehicle demand, and business investment, what are called big-ticket purchases, are viewed by economists to be interest-sensitive sectors and should be the focus of any analysis.

It is difficult to see how the housing market recovery that started in 2011, picked up steam in 2012, and really accelerated in 2013 would have happened without mortgage rates hitting record lows. The huge increases in prices, sales, and construction were all powered in no small part by historically low interest rates.

Similarly, the motor vehicle sector recovered dramatically, especially between 2011 and 2013. During the housing boom years, 2003 to 2006, motor vehicle demand averaged 16.7 million units per year. When the economy collapsed in 2009, it fell to 10.4 million vehicles, a 35 percent drop.[3] By the end of 2013, the sales pace had almost completely retraced the decline as the monthly rate broke the 16 million level. Could that huge upswing in demand have occurred without the low vehicle loan rates? Doubtful.

Finally, there is business investment. Private, nonresidential business investment, adjusted for inflation, peaked in late 2007/early 2008 at nearly $2 trillion. By the end of 2009, it had plummeted to only $1.6 trillion, a 20 percent falloff. By the spring of 2013, that decline had been recovered. Businesses were faced with a lethargic economy, but one that had low interest rates. What did they decide to do? They invested in the future. Those low rates had to make a big difference.

So, Fed policy, which for the longest time had been simply linked to changes in the federal funds rate, a short-term rate, had morphed into a policy that could change all types of interest rates. That gave the Fed a whole new set of tools that it will have in its back pocket if another crisis hits.

As we have seen, low rates grow the economy, while high rates slow activity, but that doesn't mean the Fed should simply keep rates low. The Fed's dual mandate of strong growth with low inflation requires a trade-off. One of the biggest fears created by the aggressive quantitative easing program was that all the liquidity the Fed had created by buying assets would eventually be put to use. That would cause the economy to surge, but unfortunately, inflation would skyrocket as well. That would be really troublesome. Low rates are good but only as long as inflation is not a threat.

Similarly, while we fear high interest rates, it is not necessarily bad for the Fed to raise rates, even to very high levels. Paul Volcker may have been vilified for driving interest rates up to levels that were unimaginable, but his policy worked. He destroyed inflation and inflation expectations and set the stage for an extended period of strong economic growth. That he burned down the economy in order to save it is a topic for debate, but only whether he went a little too far.

Both Paul Volcker and Ben Bernanke moved interest rates into previously unheard-of levels. They used imaginative programs to deal with huge, potentially catastrophic challenges. And they did that knowing they had the power to make those changes. They did that without political interference.

Yes, both Mr. Bernanke and Mr. Volcker were attacked for their policies by members of Congress. Indeed, Mr. Volcker probably made it impossible for Jimmy Carter to be reelected as the economy was driven into recession during the first half of 1980, a presidential election year. That did not make a lot of Democrats happy. Similarly, Mr. Bernanke was attacked for keeping rates too low for too long by those in Congress who feared inflation. Many of those were Republicans.

In other words, Fed chairs have angered members of both parties, and they were able to do so because their only concern was doing what was best for the economy. The Fed's independence is critical to the workings of monetary policy. It is hard to see a politically sensitive Fed taking politically unpopular but economically necessary actions. In other words, the best thing about the Federal Reserve is that we don't have politicians running monetary policy.

But that puts pressure on the Fed to communicate its policies clearly. For the longest period of time, the Fed basically said nothing. Those of us who were Fed Watchers had to analyze the data to see if policy had changed. The FOMC didn't come out and tell us what they were doing.

The attitude that the Fed didn't have to say anything changed under Alan Greenspan. He began to explain more about Fed policy, and in 1994, the FOMC actually started issuing statements about their decisions. This was a major sea change from the closed-mouth approach that had previously been Fed policy.

While on the surface it appears that more information is better than less, when it comes to Federal Reserve policy, that may not necessarily be the best way to operate. The reason, as is always the case, is that conditions change and sometimes very rapidly.

During the Bernanke years, the FOMC not only issued statements about what their policy decisions were, but they started explaining them. Then they began releasing minutes of meetings just three weeks after the meetings ended. Those minutes got into further detail about the discussions that occurred and the views of the members.

But the move toward changing the FOMC into the Federal Open Mouth Committee really hit its stride in 2011. Not only were detailed statements and minutes released, but the Fed started to include economic forecasts made by the members. And, maybe most important, the Fed chairman started holding press conferences after four of the eight FOMC meetings, the meeting when the projections were also made public.

This sounds great, but too much of a good thing can be bad. We now know what the members are thinking, especially since they all like to give speeches around the country and the world. Indeed, Fed members, whether they are one of the 7 members of the Board of Governors or one of the 12 presidents of the regional banks, are seemingly out in the world all the time, giving us their views of where things are and where the economy may be going.

That creates a cacophony of policy noise. Frequently, members agree and view the economic situation somewhat similarly. But that is not always the case. For example, just before the economy started to collapse, there were members of the Fed who were against lowering interest rates because they were still worried about inflation. Similarly, the timing of the withdrawal of the quantitative easing, a program nicknamed "tapering," was heatedly debated. Some wanted to wait until the economy was strong, while others argued that the possibility of sharply rising inflation and the threat of damage to the financial system made an early reduction in bond purchases preferable.

With Fed members bickering in public, the value of more information about FOMC actions was destroyed. The purpose of providing information is for investors to be able to incorporate the material into their decisions and not be surprised. The more the debate, the less clear the future course of action and the less valuable the information.

Worse, the information can be provided badly. A classic example of that was when Chairman Bernanke stated in June 2013 that the FOMC could start reducing its asset purchases later in the year with the goal of ending the policy by mid-2014.[4] The economy was improving, and so was the outlook for the remainder of the year and 2014. The Fed chairman then proceeded to say that the decisions would be dependent on the economic data. That is, the economy had to continue to strengthen and the outlook had to remain positive for tapering to start.

Unfortunately, but not surprisingly, the markets heard only what they wanted to hear, which is a problem with any type of communication that has a number of parts to it. All that came through was "tapering starting later this year." That created anticipation that the process would begin at the September 2013 FOMC meeting. What failed to make any impact was the caveat concerning the economy. Basically, the Fed chair created expectations that a certain action was going to occur unless something terrible happened. What he intended to say was that no change in policy would be implemented unless something good happened.

The result was a communications disaster. As the September meeting approached, the economic data began to deteriorate. In addition, there were fears that Congress would shut down the government, which would harm the economy further. The FOMC punted, and the markets were not very happy. This is a classic case of conditions changing and the Fed's wishy-washy communications being made obsolete by the deteriorating circumstances.

Because economic conditions can sometimes change rapidly and dramatically, it is hard to see the value in having an open-mouth policy. Those members who worried about inflation in 2007 appeared to be largely clueless about the emerging economic crisis. Those who argued for a sooner rather than later tapering of quantitative easing also seemed to be out of touch with reality. Where inflation would come from was never made clear. In a world economy where foreign firms are quite willing to undercut U.S. company prices in order to steal market share, surging inflation required a long period of excessive growth. And no one had that in his or her forecast!

By providing so much information, the ability of the Fed members to accurately forecast the future is put on display. How showing that some members are bad economic analysts creates confidence in the markets or the public about the validity of monetary policy is anyone's guess. But the Fed seems to think that is the case.

When we talk about context, to the Fed it alludes to all sorts of economic, regulatory, and political factors. Circumstances change and often rapidly. Few foresaw the oil embargoes, the bursting of the dot-com bubble, or the collapse of the housing market and financial sector, but they happened. Monetary policy has to be conducted with a keen eye toward the context in which it is being made and how those circumstances will change.

One of the factors that can change is what happens outside of America's shores. In the next chapter, we look at some of the ways what happens in places such as Panama or China can affect the shop floor in Small Town, USA.

Notes

1. S&P/Case-Shiller Home Price Index data, analysis by Naroff Economic Advisors, Inc.
2. Federal Reserve Board of Governors, release H.4.1, January 9, 2014.
3. U.S. Department of Commerce, Bureau of Economic Analysis data, analysis by Naroff Economic Advisors, Inc.
4. Chairman Ben Bernanke, press conference, June 19, 2013.

Chapter 10

The Panama Canal Widens and the Middle Class Grows in China—How Does That Affect Indiana?

A top-selling computer starts as an idea that some genius dreams up in Anywhere, USA. An investor in New York may pay the nascent company's salaries. The research and development might take place in a campus-like series of buildings in California. A prototype may be tested in Germany. Then a factory in China or Mexico may start making the pieces, which are ultimately shipped back to the United States for final assembly.

What this illustrates is that companies are no longer tethered to their markets. As a result, business integration across borders is one of the keys to economic success. But, as corporations widen their supply chain, they need to keep a wary eye on what's happening—the context, if you will—in that global loop.

In this chapter, we show how events taking place outside of America's borders can affect us. China, with one of the strongest growth rates in the world, fights to keep its currency from rising too rapidly. Greece is unable to pay its pensioners or lenders. That causes a tightening of credit across Europe. The middle class grows in Brazil, increasing demand for products previously unaffordable.

Sometimes a global change can be physical. In this chapter, we also look at how the widening of the Panama Canal can affect trade, ports, and jobs from Bayonne, New Jersey, to Long Beach, California, and, yes, to Fort Wayne, Indiana.

Ports Get Ready for Change

On an overcast October day, the black-hulled *Genius Star XI* is slowly churning through the waters of Kill van Kull, the industrial waterway that separates Staten Island from New Jersey. Two tugs help to maneuver the vessel under the Bayonne Bridge, which connects the two states. The Panama-flagged boat, a bulk carrier, has about 20 feet to spare to fit under the span.

But the bridge, which resembles the iconic Sydney Harbor Bridge, is actually too low for the giant new vessels that may dock here in the future once a wider and deeper Panama Canal is expected to open in 2015.[1]

Once the Canal is made larger and deeper, ocean-going ships, which used to carry 5,000 containers, will be able to load approximately 12,500 to 13,000 containers. Vessels, which could not be beamer than 106 feet to fit through the canal's locks, can now have a beam of 180 feet.[2]

What that means for the Bayonne Bridge is a massive construction project. The Port Authority of New York and New Jersey, at a cost of $1.9 billion, is raising the roadbed of the bridge by 64 feet so larger vessels can get under it to dock at the terminals that line Newark Bay.[3]

The Bayonne Bridge project is far from unique. Ports around the East Coast are spending billions of dollars to get ready to service the larger class of boats that will move goods through the canal. Dredgers are digging deeper channels since the new boats will need more water under their hulls. Some ports have spent hundreds of millions of dollars on larger gantry systems to load and unload the containerships since the old systems are not high enough or wide enough. And ports on the West Coast, in an effort not to lose business, are trying to improve rail service to get containers to the east faster.

The ports are an example of how events taking place outside of America's borders can affect us. In the case of the Panama Canal, it's a physical event as opposed to a currency shift or a political event. But, what's at stake potentially is a boatload of money. According to some projections, the share of world trade that passes through the canal will increase significantly once larger ships that carry almost three times the number of containers can move across the isthmus. In theory, some of those larger ships will dock along East Coast ports, generating more jobs for truckers and revenues for the ports.[4]

It's not just the East Coast ports that may be winners. Try Northeast Indiana, which is over 700 miles away from the nearest deepwater East Coast port.

As of the fall of 2013, Norfolk Southern, a rail freight company, was mulling whether to expand its intermodal facility (rail and trucks) in Fort Wayne to accommodate an increased number of containers arriving from Asia.

"For a rail connection to be efficient in the Midwest, it has to be at least 700 miles [from a port] for a railroad to ship from the port to an inland location," explains John Sampson, the president and CEO of the Northeast Indiana Regional Partnership, an economic development group. "It turns out that Fort Wayne is 720, 730 miles from Norfolk."

The railroad already uses the Indiana yard as a transfer point for its Triple Crown subsidiary. Triple Crown uses an unusual system that puts railroad wheels on tractor trailers. "They turn trucks into trains," explains Sampson.

This Triple Crown system cuts down on the cost of fuel and eliminates the problem of needing long distance truck drivers, who are getting harder and harder to find. Once the trailers get to Fort Wayne, the drivers make only day trips. "That Triple Crown location would be the receiving location for these containers from Asia," says Sampson.

For the region, the Triple Crown expansion would be beneficial. Currently, many of the shipping containers coming into Northeast Indiana originate from the West Coast. The metal boxes then get transferred to railcars to get them to Chicago. From Chicago, trucks transport them to other Midwest cities.

"We've always been trying to work around Chicago because of the delays, the congestion," says Sampson. Moving containers from the East Coast to Fort Wayne, "will change the whole dynamic," he says.

And, it's not just huge container ships that will benefit from the canal's expansion. Many of the bulk carriers, which used to have to travel around Africa's Cape of Good Hope, will be able to fit through the expanded canal.

"This expanded Canal will be able to handle Cape-size vessels," says Rex Sherman, the research director at the American Association of Port Authorities in Alexandria, Virginia.

The passage through the canal could shave as much as 10 days off a trip to Asia for a bulk carrier.[5] For example, the Port of Corpus Christi, Texas, views the expansion of the canal as a way to increase its shipment of U.S. agricultural products, coal, and liquefied natural gas (LNG).

"In today's world (2013), only 20 percent of the LNG fleet can get through the canal," says John LaRue, executive director of the Port of Corpus Christi Authority. "Once the canal is expanded, 80 percent will get through, so it's a major change."

Moving more natural gas will provide Texas natural gas producers with the potential to make lots of money because the resource companies are extracting large volumes of gas from the Eagle Ford Shale formation, which covers a huge swath of South Central Texas.

"Because of the Eagle Ford Shale formation in Texas, we have a tremendous volume of gas that is available and will be for years to come," says LaRue. "So that leads to the potential for the U.S. to export gas to Europe, some of the islands in the Caribbean, and a great deal principally to Asia."

The economics appear favorable. In February 2014, the price of natural gas on the New York Mercantile Exchange, a commodity exchange, was about $6.06 per million cubic feet. In Asia, the price at about the same time was about $16 per million Btu.

LNG exporters are keen to take advantage of this price differential and the ability to ship the fuel through the Panama Canal. "We have one LNG terminal going through permitting," says LaRue during an interview in the fall of 2013. In the future, there could be a lot more since several companies are trying to win approval to export LNG.[6]

U.S. coal exports to Asia from the Powder River Basin in eastern Wyoming and part of Montana could also benefit from the expanded canal. According to the Bureau of Land Management, as of mid-2013 there were 13 active coal mines in the region.[7] Although most of the coal is used by domestic power plants, the coal companies are trying to increase exports since many U.S. utilities are shifting to natural gas.

The economics of moving large volumes of commodities is relatively simple, says LaRue. "You can get more cargo on the same ship and since most of the ships are on charter, you are paying the same amount no matter how much you put on the vessel."

But the expanded canal also means that Asian companies can ship goods to Europe more quickly. "Westbound traffic means that Indonesian coal will be able to compete more directly with American coal in Europe, so it works both ways," says Sherman.

Sherman says the expansion of the Panama Canal does not necessarily mean that trade will expand—it may just go to different places. "It may shift the direction trade is going; it may favor ports in one part of the world over ports in another part of the world," says Sherman. "We are talking about transportation, and the demand for transportation is derived from the demand for goods, and that's impacted by a lot of things."

One of the factors that may affect whether East Coast ports make any money off the expanded canal is how the West Coast ports react.

The View from the West Coast

The West Coast ports have a lot at stake. About 68 percent of containers from Asia landed in such ports as Los Angeles, Long Beach, Seattle–Tacoma, and Oakland.[8] But to a certain extent the West Coast ports are not worried because of the economics of moving containers and because of the natural advantage they have.

Moving a container from Asia to the West Coast of the United States usually takes about 12 days and costs about $2,000 per container, according to Dr. Noel Hacegaba, the acting deputy executive director and chief operating officer of the Port of Long Beach. From the ports, the containers are usually loaded on railcars to head east. He estimates the rail journey adds another five to seven days. Thus, the total time to move the container is about 17 to 19 days.

By way of comparison, Dr. Hacegaba estimates it generally costs shippers hundreds of dollars more to move a container through the Panama Canal and then on to the East Coast. He says the trip is also four to six days longer.

Once the expanded canal opens, Dr. Hacegaba expects that the cost of shipping through the canal will rise as well since the Panamanian government is borrowing billions of dollars to pay for it. "In order for the Panamanian government to recoup its investment, we anticipate that the fees to transit the canal are going to go up, not down," he says.

Another reason why the West Coast ports are not concerned is that the shipping industry keeps building larger and larger vessels. "In the next four to six years, nearly half of the new ships that are currently being manufactured will be 10,000 TEUs or larger," he says.[9] A significant portion of the vessels will be 14,000 TEUs to 18,000 TEUs. None of those larger vessels will fit through the expanded canal. "So that will eliminate [from using the canal] what we believe will be the norm over the next 5 to 10 years," he says.

A third factor that may prevent shippers from using the expanded Panama Canal is the additional draft of the larger ships. The new Panamax-size vessels (Panamax stands for the maximum size that can transit the canal) will have a draft (a depth) of almost 50 feet, which is about 9 feet deeper than the vessels that transited the canal before the expansion. Many ports on the East Coast are scrambling to increase the depth of their channels for the larger vessels.

"They need funding to get the dredging done, and dredging not only takes funding but it also takes time," says Dr. Hacegaba, whose port has deep water.

The Port of Long Beach is also in the process of a \$4.5 billion expansion that will be completed in 2019. One of the major projects in that expansion is Middle Harbor, which combines two aging terminals into one mega-terminal with a capacity of 3 million TEUs. "To put that into perspective, when it's completed, this terminal by itself will rank as the fourth largest port in the U.S.," says Dr. Hacegaba.

Dr. Hacegaba thinks the greater threat to West Coast ports is the Port of Prince Rupert in British Columbia, Canada, which takes three fewer days to reach from Asia. After transferring to rail, a container can arrive in Chicago in four days.

In the future, there may also be competition from the Mexican Port of Lazaro Cardenas, on Mexico's west coast. Until recently, it was not worth using the port because of a \$100,000 fee for each container passing through Mexican territory. That fee has now been reduced to a single \$55,000 bond for as many containers as a shipper is moving.[10]

In addition, the Mexican government has given a concession at the port to Hong Kong–based Hutchison Port Holdings to develop a new terminal capable of handling the largest containerships.[11]

Once a container lands in Mexico, it can travel to the United States via a rail connection to Laredo, Texas. "From there, the railroad can move freight right into the Midwest and East Coast," says Dr. Hacegaba. "So, it's my opinion that for the U.S. West Coast, Mexico and Canada present more of a threat than the Panama Canal."

Trade beyond the Canal

The canal itself is far from the only global factor affecting U.S. trade patterns. For example, as India, China, and Brazil continue to increase the size of their middle class, there could be hundreds of millions of potential new consumers of American products. The accounting and consulting firm Ernst & Young, working with Oxford Economics, estimates the consumer spending in such "rapidly growing markets" (RGMs) will grow from \$21 trillion in 2013 to \$56 trillion in 2030.[12]

Exports from such countries as China and India, as a percentage of world gross domestic product (GDP), will grow from 10 percent of world total to close to 20 percent in 20 years, predicts the Ernst & Young report. "RGMs will become an increasingly dominant force in global trade over the coming decade," says the report.

This shift is not lost on many American companies that have established manufacturing operations in countries such as China, not to export back to the United States but to sell to Chinese companies.

Sampson, on a trip to China to try to introduce Chinese companies to Northeast Indiana, recalls a presentation he received from the U.S. Commercial Service, the trade promotion arm of the U.S. Department of Commerce.

"It was pretty eye-opening for me because there is so much discussion in the U.S. about offshoring jobs and reshoring to the U.S. commercial market, and the U.S. person made it very clear that better than 60 percent of U.S. companies doing work in China are actually doing it for the Chinese market, the growth in the domestic market," says Sampson.

Even some Midwest companies that are not exporting directly to Asia may stand to benefit, even if indirectly. For example, C&A Tool Engineering, Inc. in Churubusco, Indiana, does a lot of work on diesel fuel injection systems for such companies as Cummings, Caterpillar, and Siemens, explains Rob Marr, vice president of the company.

The way that works to C&A's advantage is that the engine companies may decide to do the engineering work and make their prototypes in the United States. As they design the new engines, they go to a company such as C&A.

"So we'll sit down with them and say 'this works and that doesn't,'" says Marr. Then, the company may come back to C&A and ask the Churubusco firm to build 10 engines with 5 different options for testing purposes. "Then they may come back and say, 'Hey, we made some changes and now we want you to build 25 engines,'" he says. "So you go through these various stages so the next round they may want you to build 150 of them that they actually put on trucks and put on the road."

After the 150 trucks are driving with the new engines, the companies may start production, although it may not involve C&A. "There is no guarantee, and a lot of times that is not an option because they do want to do the work wherever their market is," says Marr.

C&A also does a lot of precision machine work for medical technology firms that are developing replacement parts for hips, knees, and other joints. As far as Marr can tell, the demand for those products has not yet hit some of the developing nations, probably because they are expensive.

"The medical people over there are no different than anybody else," he says. "You have to have someone who can fund what you're doing and someone who can afford your product," he says. But, he adds, if the Chinese market is only 10 percent of the American market for new hips and knees, "it's still an enormous market."

C&A has international trade as part of its history. The majority of the machines it buys are built in Switzerland or Germany. In fact, anyone visiting the company might well think they are no longer in Indiana. When the company erected its first new building 20 years ago, C&A put a Swiss motif on it. The architecture looks more like Andermatt in the Alps than Indiana in the Midwest.

The company did not design its buildings to resemble an Indiana version of a theme park. Instead, the architecture is symbolic of the company's aspirations.

"We use it as an Old World craftsmanship kind of theme," he explains. "So we create a culture of precision and respect, and our goal is to elevate our trade."

That culture continues to the shop floor, he says. "Everyone wants to look at manufacturing and say, 'You are a dirty old factory,'" says Marr. "But our facility is clean, it's organized. How can I expect you to take pride in what you do if you work in an environment that is not conducive to that culture?"

History: The Moat around Fortress America Has Dried Up

Once upon a time, there was Fortress America. The country was isolated and protected by oceans. After World War II, the only industrialized nation left standing was the United States. With the rest of the nations of the world trying to rebuild after having their cities and factories bombed into rubble, the American manufacturing and agricultural sectors became the one and only source of materials to feed, clothe, and equip businesses and households.

Many credit World War II for dragging the nation out of the Great Depression. Clearly, the war changed everything, as underutilized factories were pushed into supplying the war effort. From 1941 through 1944, GDP grew nearly 15.5 percent per year, the strongest expansion in the 83 years the government has been publishing the data.[13]

The end of the war, however, led to shrinking military production, and the returning veterans hit the unemployment lines. The nation went back into recession in February 1945, before the war was even over. While that downturn lasted just eight months, the subsequent recovery petered out after only three years. By October 1948, the U.S. economy had slipped into recession once again.

What really revitalized the U.S. economy and allowed it to become the economic engine of growth for the world? All the markets in the United States and the rest of the globe were open for our goods without the worries of foreign competition.

It was a heady time for the corporate sector. U.S. firms were essentially monopolists in what was a very limited global economy. They didn't have to worry about competition from anywhere else. Profits were easy, demand was constantly growing, and as long as the American public accepted the products, sales were strong.

That "sole survivor" position, however, had not just enormous positive impacts on the United States but ultimately negative consequences as well for the nation's manufacturing sector. In the 1950s, the economy began to pick up steam, and by the 1960s, U.S. companies had expanded and grown dramatically. The second-longest expansion on record occurred during the entire decade of the 1960s, lasting nearly nine years.[14]

As the rest of the world constructed new and technologically advanced productive capacity, the United States remained fat and happy. But the dark clouds were gathering as the American market stood out as the best and biggest place to sell goods. What did foreign companies do? They took their goods, created in those new, efficient, and low-cost plants that were run with relatively low wage labor and shipped as much as possible to the United States.

To get an idea of how imports went from largely irrelevant to a major factor for consumers and business, all you have to do is look at the ratio of imports to GDP, adjusted for inflation. This shows the relative importance of imports to the entire economy. In 1947, that ratio was 2.7 percent, which is pretty small. With little productive capacity around the world, there was little available to send to the United States. Thirty years later, that percentage more than doubled, to 6.1 percent.[15] By 2008, it had more than doubled again, increasing to 15.8 percent. The United States is now extremely dependent on foreign products, and the competition between domestic and foreign companies has ramped up dramatically.

Why did the United States lose its position so rapidly? Simple: The context in which domestic firms were operating changed, and for many corporate executives those trends were simply not recognized or taken seriously.

The impact of not recognizing that the context of producing and selling goods had been altered dramatically and permanently was devastating. Consider the vehicle sector, which dominated not only U.S. sales but also world demand. In 1976, 84 percent of U.S. vehicle sales were domestic vehicles. At the end of 2013, General Motors, Ford, and Chrysler—which is now owned by the Italian firm Fiat—had only a 45 percent share of all sales.[16]

What happened is that the world has come to the United States. And that trend is not only continuing but accelerating. As productive capacity has increased around the world, firms are looking for markets to sell their wares outside their own countries. What better place to do that than the biggest market in the world—the United States.

At the same time, U.S. companies had been largely selling only to the U.S. markets. Indeed, exports were not seen as the way to grow. That may have made total sense in the 1950s and 1960s as the rest of the world was still digging out from the rubble of World War II and had little income to spend. But by the 1970s, with wealth rising across the world, that business model made absolutely no sense at all.

To see what happened when the view that the global economy mattered entered into the planning models of businesses, consider the same measure for the importance of exports as we did for the importance of imports. Comparing the level of exports (adjusted for inflation) to total economic activity (GDP), you see that until about 1970, exports ranged from about 2.5 percent to maybe 4 percent—not a whole lot. But then things started changing quickly. Within 25 years, the importance of exports had jumped to 9 percent of the economy and rose to 13 percent in 2013. The light had gone on: the rest of the world really did matter!

Finally, the United States has started trying to catch up with the rest of the world's obsession with selling to anyone and everywhere in the global economy. Unfortunately, the gap remains extremely wide.

Why is it so difficult for American firms to sell as much to the rest of the world as the rest of the world sells here? Simply put, the United States is considered to be the "market of last resort" for firms around the world. The attitude is that if you cannot make it here, you cannot make it anywhere, so they do everything to make it here.

That said, U.S. exports have been soaring. However, so have imports, and during the decade of the 2000s, exports were less than 70 percent of the size of our imports. Amazingly, that had been higher, about 80 percent, over the previous three decades. When world growth slows, as it did in the second half of the 2000s, the way out for foreign firms has been to sell everything possible to U.S. consumer, and they did that. Only when the global economy started to improve did the importance of exports move up closer to imports again.

Can the United States catch up? Business executives clearly understand that their competitors can exist down the block or 12,000 miles away, but many still don't actually recognize that their markets are where their competitors are: everywhere.

The flattening of competition has occurred because of the communications revolution. Basically, the Internet has made the world what economists call a "featureless plain." The Internet has changed the effective physical location of the world's manufacturers. The world may be flat when it comes to economic theory, but it is not flat when it comes to consumers and producers.

What begins in one country ultimately ends up in that country, but the process of going from idea to production to sales goes around the world. In a featureless plain, or what others call a *flat world*, you can keep going, but you wind up falling off the edge. That is not how it really happens.

Instead, the world is now really a "Möbius Economy," a strip or band or twisted cylinder, named after the German mathematician August Ferdinand Möbius, who, along with Johann Listing, discovered the properties of this magical strip back in the late 1850s. Basically, the

Möbius Economy is a world where there are no barriers and no ends. If you start in one place and continue on, you ultimately end up back where you began.

That interrelatedness of world production and sales is what is driving all firms in the global economy. The Internet and its unlimited, relatively costless means of information distribution allows consumers and producers to be everywhere while they don't go anywhere. Sit at the computer and the world is in front of you.

And that integration has enormous implications. We are all in this together, and with apologies to the people who put together the advertising campaign for Las Vegas, what happens there doesn't stay there. What happens anywhere happens everywhere.

Even Small Countries Can Crash the World Economy

Nothing shows that we depend on everyone else, no matter how big or small we are, than the chaos created by the Greek debt crisis. In 2010, according to the World Bank, Greece had an economy that was about $292 billion.[17] That was 0.4 percent of the world economy, maybe 2 percent the size of the U.S. economy and less than 2 percent of the European Union's economy. Yet when Greece was facing default, the world financial markets shuddered.

How is it possible that a country as small as Greece could create fears of a worldwide financial meltdown? It is because we are all in this together. Greece had a debt of about $413 billion, about 35 percent larger than its economy, and it could not pay even the interest on the debt.

If the Greeks had defaulted, the losses would be felt first in the European nations, which held much of the debt. Those losses could have collapsed banks, triggering a crisis not unlike the 2007–2009 housing/financial sector meltdown in the United States. Since U.S. and other world banks did business with European financial institutions, they, too, could have been at risk. And that would have meant losses at financial institutions around the world and a possible global crisis.

In other words, what happened in Greece didn't stay in Greece. That is a whole lot different than in the past, when European nations were not part of one currency/monetary union. The world changed, and those who have to deal with financial crises now must consider the context in which even a small nation's problems exist.

Free Trade Is a Goal, but Fair Trade Is a Necessity

The integration of the world's financial sector and the potential for chaos has changed perspectives. What the Internet has done is make the movement of goods and services one of the most important factors in any economy's growth. And that brings up the issue of fair versus free trade.

For the global economy to work smoothly, goods and services must move freely and easily between nations. Economists have argued for about 100 years that if countries concentrate on what they do best and trade with other countries that have their own special ways of producing goods and services, the world will be better off. That is the idea of "comparative advantage," and it is a concept that has underpinned the drive for free trade.

Free trade also means that artificial barriers cannot be created. While countries love to sell their goods to everyone else, they are rarely happy when foreign firms take away sales from domestic companies. To stop that, they sometimes put up barriers to entry.

There are two major barriers to entry when it comes to trade: tariffs and currency manipulation. Every country has tariffs, which are just a form of tax placed on imported products in order to raise their prices. The higher costs of imported goods lowers demand for those products. That allows for less efficient companies in the country to compete with foreign firms and even survive. Consumers and businesses, which pay higher prices for their goods, lose.

While there have been a number of major tariff-lowering agreements negotiated through the World Trade Organization, every country retains tariffs of one form or another. That is because there is a view, often correctly so, that countries subsidize their domestic firms, giving them an unfair competitive advantage. Supporting domestic firms that are less competitive in the world market enables these companies to sell their products outside their home countries (their exports) at lower prices than they can get at home. Essentially, they like to dump goods on foreign markets.

Tariffs and dumping are just two forms of unfair competition that restrict free trade. The most devious and problematic form of unfair trade is currency manipulation. Most countries have their own currency, and to buy and sell goods around the world, they have to trade their currency for others. That is where the value of a currency—the exchange rate—comes into play.

Countries manipulate trade and competitiveness by managing the value of their currency. A simple example makes that clear. Let's say a Chinese manufacturer produces a washing machine for 2,000 yuan. If the yuan is worth 16 cents, then that washing machine would sell for $320 in the United States (2,000 × $0.16 = $320).

Now, consider what happens if the Chinese government decides to weaken the exchange value of the yuan so that one yuan is now worth only 14 cents. That would mean the washing machine produced in China for 2,000 yuan would cost only $280 in the United States (2000 × $0.14 = $280). By lowering the exchange rate of the yuan, the Chinese government has reduced the potential price of Chinese products in the United States, and those lower prices would increase demand for Chinese products.

In the United States, countries certified as currency manipulators might have "countervailing duties" placed on them. That identification, though, comes with political and economic risks of similar actions being taken by the manipulator. We're talking politics here, not just economics, and tit for tat is common practice.

The problem, though, with tariffs, dumping, government subsidies, and currency manipulation is that it raises questions about free trade. Is it really occurring? That has driven a major discussion about the difference between free trade, which is the ultimate goal, and fair trade, where companies actually compete on a relatively even playing field.

To the extent that free trade doesn't exist, it is not clear that even fair trade makes sense. The advantages of free trade are readily seen in all the economic models, but it is not clear that if one country has fewer barriers than others, that country actually benefits. Indeed, a country with limited trade restrictions could lose out to those that don't reciprocate. That is why the fair trade argument has gained so much credence: if you cannot have free trade, make it as fair as possible for the companies in your country. That can be accomplished by either getting other countries to lower their barriers, the preferred method, or by taking action against those that retain restrictions.

Currency Manipulation Has Negative Implications beyond the Obvious

There are other major problems that trade barriers, especially currency manipulation, create. Take the situation with China, which has clearly managed downward the value of its currency with respect to the dollar. It is not clear how much more U.S. exports would have grown if the yuan were closer to its freely floating value. However, there have been estimates that the currency is as much as 50 percent undervalued, so a doubling of the yuan would cut the cost of U.S. goods potentially in half, and that could have led to a major rise in sales to China.

Even if a freely floating yuan would not have meant a whole lot more in exports to China from the United States, that does not mean there are not real worries about the currency's being manipulated. By keeping Chinese products artificially low in the United States, China is not only creating unfair competition with America firms, but firms in every other country around the world that cannot match the reduced currency value and lower artificial prices. Firms in nations other than China that would like to export similar products to the United States may not be able to find a market because they would have to sell those goods at prices above the Chinese.

In essence, by keeping their currency value down and their export prices low, the Chinese can keep competitors out of U.S. markets. That allows them to monopolize the supply chain into American markets. Since we are dealing with a global economy and domestic firms want to buy goods, materials, and services at the lowest cost, China has effectively shut its competition out of the market, slowing other countries' exports and growth.

Should we be concerned that we have low prices in the United States but few suppliers? Of course. What firms would want to have their supply chain controlled by someone they know is manipulating the market? Currency manipulation is something that should concern everyone since, in the long run, it makes sense for there to be as many companies in as many countries as possible competing for sales in the United States. Only through that competitive environment can we be sure that we wind up with the lowest prices, not just now but over time.

The issue of Chinese currency manipulation also dovetails into the concerns about budget deficits. China owns nearly $1.3 trillion, or about 10 percent of the outstanding U.S Treasury securities.[18] That greatly troubles some, but is it really something to worry about? The answer, as always, is that it depends on the circumstances.

Why does China hold so much U.S. debt? One thing for certain, it is hardly because of the great rates of return the Chinese are getting. U.S. securities are viewed as the safest in the world and are therefore deemed to be riskless. That may mean lower returns for those who hold the securities, but at least they know they will be getting their entire investment back. That is not the case with other nations' debt.

With the dollar being the world's reserve currency, having a large holding in dollar-denominated assets provides China with a lot of liquidity. It can sell those assets whenever it wants to. If a crisis arises, the funds will be there.

But the real reason the Chinese hold Treasury securities is that they need to keep the Chinese currency down versus the dollar. Currency is like any other market where supply and demand set the price. If the Chinese use yuans to buy dollars two things happen: First, the supply of yuans goes up, lowering their price, and when they are used to buy dollars, the demand for dollars goes up, raising the dollar's price versus the yuan.

The Chinese are buying Treasury securities to keep the value of the yuan low versus the dollar, not because it is a good investment. As a consequence, the Chinese are the ones facing a dilemma: they can keep buying more dollar-denominated assets, thereby keeping the yuan low, Chinese product prices in the U.S. down, exports to the U.S. growing, and the Chinese economy expanding; or they can slow their purchases of Treasury securities or even sell them. But that would raise the value of the yuan, raise the prices of Chinese goods in the United States, reduce exports, and thereby slow Chinese growth.

That really is not a dilemma. As long as China needs to sell to the United States large amounts of goods in order to keep its economy going, it will have to keep buying Treasury securities. But once that changes, for example, when Chinese domestic demand rises to a level where exports are not as crucial to growth, then the need to manipulate the currency will fade, and their demand for Treasuries will dissipate as well.

Clearly, whether the United States needs China to fund its budget deficit or the Chinese need U.S. securities to manipulate their currency depends on the context of the economies. And that is an obvious example of not only how the world is integrated in both financial and economic ways, but also how context determines the type of relationships that exist.

As we have seen in this chapter, there are lots of global events that can change the economic future. In the next chapter, we look at how some key changes in technology, energy, demographics, and the aging of the Baby Boomers might affect us.

Notes

1. There have been delays in the projected opening of the canal, which was supposed to open in mid-2014 but now is delayed. As of the beginning of 2014, Panama was squabbling with its European contractors over who should pay for cost overruns. A good account was written on July 17, 2013, by Kevin Gale, editor-in-chief of the *South Florida Business Journal:* "When Will the Panama Canal Expansion Really Be Done?" www.bizjournals .com/southflorida/blog/2013/07/when-will-the-panama-canal-expansion .html?page=all.
2. There are many descriptions of the new sizes of the ships that will move cargo through the canal, including one from Maritime Connector, which matches seafarers with ships. http://maritime-connector.com/wiki/panamax/.
3. The Port Authority of New York and New Jersey, Bayonne Bridge Navigational Clearance Program. www.panynj.gov/bayonnebridge/?tabnum= 6#faqsBayonneBridgeClearQu02.
4. Forecasts about how much the expansion will increase world trade are controversial since some forecasters think shipping companies will look for less expensive alternatives such as the Suez Canal, while others think shipping companies will utilize the new canal even if tariffs are higher.

5. GlobalSecurity.org, an online informational site on national security. May 7, 2011. www.globalsecurity.org/military/facility/panama-canal.htm.

6. Reuters, "US Approves Additional Natgas Exports from Freeport LNG" November 13, 2013. www.reuters.com/article/2013/11/15/usa-lng-freeport-id USL2N0J01P520131115.

7. Bureau of Land Management information on Powder River Basin Coal. November 26, 2013. www.blm.gov/wy/st/en/programs/energy/Coal_Resources/PRB_Coal.html.

8. The total volume for Trans-Pacific trade is estimated at 22 million TEUs in 2012, according to Drewry Maritime Research's "Container Market Review and Forecaster" 2Q, 2013 edition, p. 59. American Association of Port Authorities estimates the total volume of containers coming to the U.S. West Coast was 15 million TEUs in 2012. This comes to 68 percent of Trans-Pacific container trade.

9. TEU stands for 20-foot equivalent unit, which describes the volume of a metal 20-foot standard shipping container. Thus, a 10,000-TEU vessel would be capable of carrying the equivalent of 10,000 twenty-foot shipping containers.

10. KC Smartport, "America's Inland Port Solution." October 20, 2013. www.kcsmartport.com/pdf/SmtPrtOneRoute.pdf.

11. Ibid.

12. Ernst & Young, "Rapid-Growth Markets Forecast," April 2013. www.ey.com.

13. Bureau of Economic Analysis, GDP data, Naroff Economic Advisors analysis.

14. National Bureau of Economic Research, "Business Cycle Expansions and Contractions."

15. Bureau of Economic Analysis data and Naroff Economic Advisors, Inc.

16. Market Intelligence data as reported by the Wall Street Journal on January 13, 2014. http://online.wsj.com/mdc/public/page/2_3022-autosales.html.

17. World Bank, World DataBank, World Development Indicators, Greece.

18. U.S. Department of Treasury, Treasury International Capital (TIC) System, Major Foreign Holders of U.S. Treasury Securities, monthly report, January 16, 2014.

Chapter 11

What Do We Do Now?

The saying goes that economists have been put on this earth to make weather forecasters look brilliant. That may be true, but economics does provide the framework for looking into the future, even if the future is foggy. While you would never want to bet the bank on an economist's forecast, you would never want to bet the bank without one. Of course, it is probably never good to bet the bank on anything, but households and businesses do it every day, though maybe in a smaller way. They make retirement plans, put into motion long-term business plans, or make major capital investments—be it a house or a new plant—that depend on certain circumstances holding true. The simple fact, though, is that conditions change and recognizing they can and do change is the key to success. In this chapter, we discuss some of those potential trends.

"The Future Ain't What It Used to Be"

It is hard to believe that one of the most important economists of the twentieth century was former New York Yankees star and Hall of Famer Yogi Berra. Of course, like every famous quote, there is a question about who first said it. Regardless, Yogi made the comment "the future ain't what it used to be" famous, and that sentence completely sums up the whole concept of looking at the world and the economy through the lens of context.

Context makes us consider whether the current "common knowledge" makes any sense. It requires us to factor in not just what has happened but what may happen in the near and often distant future. Conditions change. The world evolves. Economic relationships are not constant. That is what understanding economics in context means. Essentially, the answer to any economic question is, very simply, it depends!

Of course, forecasting the future is dangerous. Fifty years ago, the Internet was nonexistent, and personal computers and mobile phones were goods that were at best only a glimmer in some scientists' minds. Thus, any forecast of the future has to recognize that it is being made in the context of what we know now. Context determines our forecasts.

There are several major trends that we have identified. The global economic integration, emerging developing countries' middle classes, energy supply restructuring, demographics, and technology will be key drivers of future economic activity and income distribution across the world. They will alter, potentially dramatically, the way we look at private investment, consumer spending, government budgets, trade, and political relationships. The changes of the past 50 years will likely look like baby steps compared to the next 50 years. That is the one thing we do know about factors that drive the economy: in each decade, the rate of change accelerates.

Here are some ideas about the future of the U.S. economy and its place in the world order.

Flying Robots, 3D Printers, and the Future

On a late October evening, twilight is starting to engulf Manhattan. City lights are twinkling on, and New Jersey is backlit in fuchsia. There is no place better to watch the show than the 44th floor of the Hearst

Tower, with its unobstructed views of Central Park and the Hudson River. Or a visitor can ignore what's going on outside and instead look at the future.

No, Hearst, the venerable publisher, has not invented a time machine. But one of its publications, *Popular Mechanics*, is exhibiting the winners of the ninth annual Breakthrough Awards, which in some ways is a crystal ball into the future, perhaps showcasing technologies and products that may help drive future economic growth.

Walking around the aerie are 20-something innovators in T-shirts as well as corporate-types from companies like General Motors who were working on the cars of the future and drones that land on aircraft carriers. Some of the brainy types are showing off their ideas on laptops, in floor-model demonstrations, or, in at least one case, literally levitating in one part of the room.

The hovering part came from Vijay Kumar's flying robots— YouTube sensations—that can fly, dart, and interact with their surroundings without anyone guiding them with a joystick.[1] In the fall of 2013, the tiny drones didn't have FAA approval for commercial applications yet, but Kumar, a professor at the University of Pennsylvania's School of Engineering, believes that ban will eventually be lifted. Once the FAA relents, how could these agile helicopter-like flyers help society? He envisions farmers using them to monitor plants in their fields. The bots might check out which plants need additional care, a shot of fertilizer, or extra water. He thinks it could lead to a breakthrough in non-labor-intensive "precision farming."

He can also envision his swarms of flying robots helping first responders. If a building is on fire, as happened after the World Trade Center was attacked, he says his swarms could fly up stairwells to discover if there is anything that can be done before firemen risk their lives.

Not far from Kumar is 23-year-old Stephen Lake, the cofounder and CEO of ThalmicLabs, who was demonstrating an armband, called "Myo" that allows him to control electronic devices through gestures.[2] Sensors detect even relatively minor finger and arm muscle activity. What will this do? He envisions people being able to control computers, smartphones, and other digital devices by simply slipping on a Myo. He thinks he's on the forefront of "wearable computers," that will change society.

"It really is one of the first wearable interfaces out there," he says. "You can control video games and entertainment, but if you are in an office on the productivity side, you could be giving a presentation and actually pull up information on the screen and annotate it by just pointing. It is a blurring of the line between us and computers."

As of the fall of 2013 he said his company had presold over 40,000 of the gesture control armbands in more than 145 countries. The devices were expected to ship in mid-2014.

In another nook at Hearst is a large 50-inch television set marketed by Seiki, a Chinese company.[3] But the big set is not just any television: the display has four times the resolution of high-definition sets sold off the shelf in 2013. These 4K, super-high-definition sets, have been available for some time. But they cost $5,000 to $10,000 apiece. This Seiki set retails for under $1,500.

Why is that important? Because in 2011, according to the *New York Times*, the Nielsen Company estimated 96.7 percent of American households owned a set.[4] And why would they want to buy a new one?

"4K Ultra HD is the newest resolution standard in TV, and it has the potential to change the face of digital entertainment," says Sung Choi, the vice president of marketing for the Chinese company Tongfang Global and the Seiki Digital brand. "4K Ultra HD offers visual clarity and realism that is second to none."

The Seiki sets have more than 8 million pixels on a 50-inch panel, four times as many pixels as standard HD. "It will look as if you can step right inside the screen," says Frank Kendzora, executive vice president at Tongfang Global and Seiki.

And it may not just change entertainment. The pair from Seiki thinks there are many other applications for the high-resolution sets, such as health care imaging to provide more detailed images of the human body or to provide a much sharper screen on mobile devices.

Another one of the Breakthrough Awards went to MakerBot's Digitizer 3D scanner, which can scan any real-world object and make a computer file from it.[5] Combine the computer file with a 3D printer, which melts biodegradable plastic filament into a very thin layer that on a layer-by-layer basis makes a solid object, and you have a copying machine for real objects.

NASA plans to send a 3D printer into space in 2014 so it can make spare parts for objects that get lost or break. "3D printing provides us the ability to do our own *Star Trek* replication right there on the spot," says NASA astronaut Timothy "TJ" Creamer.[6]

Jerry Beilinson, the deputy editor of *Popular Mechanics*, thinks the printer has the potential to make a future impact on the economy because the machine, which is the size of a small copier, allows backyard inventors to make inexpensive models of their ideas. "You can scan any small object on a turntable that creates a 3D file, then you go and print out a copy of that object. It's not quick and seamless, but that whole loop now exists," he says.

The 3D printers also won't produce instant chocolate cake and pork chops like the versions on *Star Trek*. But in a few years, who knows?

Beilinson knows a good idea when he sees it. He founded the *Popular Mechanics* awards program in 2005. However, he alone does not make the decision over who wins. The magazine has a complex process that includes lower level editors, past winners, Beilinson, and the editor-in-chief, Jim Meigs. In addition, the publication contacts 250 research institutions, national labs, and funding agencies such as the National Science Foundation to scope out potential ideas.

"I must say we've been pretty good at crystal-balling," he says. "As I look back, there are few things that I say 'why did we do that, that was off base.'" His involvement with the awards often takes him into contact with some of America's great inventors, such as Dean Kamen, who is best known for creating the Segway but also has made dozens of other inventions such as the first wearable insulin pump for diabetics and the first home dialysis machine.

"One of the things Dean said is that innovation these days is exponentially faster than when he was starting out in the 1970s," says Beilinson. "Because when he was starting out every time you needed a simple circuit, or any piece of electronics, you started out by building or designing that piece of electronics just so you could get to the invention you were trying to create. Now most inventors are sourcing components that already exist and combining them in new ways. Say you are making an unmanned aerial vehicle, and you need accelerometers and GPS chips to help it navigate; you don't design and build those instruments—you just buy the parts you need."

"We are in a period that is substantially different than any other period we were in during the twentieth century," says Beilinson. *Popular Mechanics* calls the era the "New Innovation Economy."

In the past, a lot of research and inventions came from large corporations such as AT&T's Bell Laboratories, which invented the transistor, the solar cell, and the laser.[7] Of course, many of those companies are still around (Bell Labs is part of Alcatel-Lucent). But Beilinson says what has changed is the huge growth of small start-up companies. "We're seeing it in Silicon Valley, and we're seeing it in New York," he says.

The editor says one of the reasons for the growth is the development of a kind of ecosystem to support the creative types. The inventor may no longer require the equipment that only a big company can afford. Instead, the inventor can join a place such as TechShop, which has sophisticated machines and tools that members can use for a relatively low monthly membership.

In addition, inventors no longer need to operate in a vacuum. Many rent space in old offices or manufacturing facilities, where they can ask other inventors in the next cubicle for advice. Or, Beilinson says, individuals can post an idea on a cloud-based forum where information is traded back and forth. Instead of relying on a corporate engineering staff, which may be busy with multiple projects, there is this kind of broad world of people sharing information, he says.

Raising funds is not as difficult as it used to be either. In the past, an inventor might have to max out a credit card or borrow money from parents and friends in order to fund an obsession. At the 2013 Breakthrough Awards, three of the winners funded their start-up on Kickstarter, which calls itself the world's largest funding platform for creative projects.[8] On Kickstarter.com on a day in late October 2013, some engineering students were trying to raise money to build a small satellite, someone else was trying to raise money to make a smartphone into a bike key, and yet someone else was trying to raise money for a device that will help people remember their dreams.

Beilinson points out that even retailing has changed. In the past, an innovator might have had a great idea but couldn't find a way to sell it. Now, he points out, there is Amazon, eBay, and other companies. The transfer of money and the security and the process is all taken care of for you by the e-tailer. "You don't need to have that infrastructure, and you don't need to get yourself into a brick-and-mortar store at all if you have a product," he says.

What does all this mean for the economy and the future? Beilinson thinks there will be more opportunities for entrepreneurs and technically minded people to start their own companies. And some of those companies will be in manufacturing, which some pundits once declared was dead.

"There are an increasing number of people we've talked to who get a premium price for small-batch manufacturing. They are able to survive and thrive with relatively small volumes partially because they are selling high-value, high-price products, and partially because they don't have a lot of overhead," he says.

And maybe a few of those companies will manufacture a product or invent some new object that will change the context surrounding the economy. Who knows, the next technological wonder may be featured in a Breakthrough Award in the future.

Will the Consumer Continue to Reign? Maybe, Maybe Not

For the past 50 years, U.S. economic growth was all about the consumer. Even today, consumption makes up nearly 70 percent of economic activity. But will that be the case 25 years from now? More important, should it be the case?

One of the major points made about household spending was that income distribution and income growth are the driving factors behind the economy. In the United States, there is a winnowing out of the middle class. That may be disconcerting to most of us, but it should have been expected.

When the global economy became the Möbius World Economy, downward pressure on worker compensation became inevitable. Industrial wages, long protected by Fortress America, was opened to the reality that workers could be anywhere, and therefore the supply of employees available to manufacturing firms became limited only by the ability to train the workers.

Technology also changed the need for large segments of the business workforce. Middle management, the bastion of middle-class America, was doomed long before anyone realized it. It wasn't just manufacturing-floor workers who were being displaced by industrial innovations and the globalization of manufacturing, but information technology also reduced the demand for managers. Thus, the United States will have to restructure its economy to take into account the inevitable movement to a more concentrated distribution of income.

But the "regressing" of U.S. wages toward world levels is not simply an American phenomenon. While worker compensation in the United States may be going nowhere, that is hardly the case in many other countries.

Consider the situation in China. Manufacturing wages have quadrupled over the past decade and are expected to rise by double digits for possibly the next decade. Incomes of managers and directors are beginning to match U.S. salaries for similar positions, according to a Hays Asia Salary Guide.

That surge in income is already having huge implications for Chinese, U.S., and world economic activity. In China, the middle class is burgeoning. Economic activity is beginning to shift toward domestic consumption, not just exporting. But there is also a downside to rising wages: as manufacturing wages rise, foreign manufacturers' drive to locate industrial plants in China is waning.

It is likely that outsourcing manufacturing activities by U.S. firms to China for importation back to the United States is a trend that is nearing its end. Over the next decade, it may actually be more expensive to produce in China and ship to the United States than produce many of those same products in the United States.

While outsourcing or offshoring, or whatever people want to call it, may be waning, that does not mean that manufacturing will return to the United States en masse. The decision by a manufacturing firm to locate a production site depends not just on the wages in the United States or China but the costs of doing business in other countries. While we may see our imports from China slow, other even lower wage nations such as Vietnam could become the location of choice for manufacturers.

In other words, planning where to locate a firm is not as simple as looking at costs look, but planners will have to make assumptions about what they will look like in 5 and 10 years. Fifteen years ago, the decision was easy to build a plant in China and ship the output to the United States. We even shipped plants to China to start the process. But if a company made the same decision two years ago, they may have found that the cost structure has changed dramatically enough to make the assessment questionable. The no-brainer may have become a really bad choice.

In the 1990s, no CFO or CEO could get fired for deciding to move production to China. That is not the case now and will be less the case in the future. Making the decision where to locate must take into account the workings of economics and that growing demand for labor means rising wages. The context can and does change.

Similarly, the perception that China is a place where we get goods from but not a place where we sell goods is also succumbing to changing context. Twenty years ago, that was the situation because the Chinese middle class largely didn't exist. Now, it is growing rapidly and a McKinsey and Company study estimated that by 2022 there will be about 300 million Chinese in urban areas with salaries that would place them in middle- to upper-income class levels.[9]

The Chinese consumer market, which was relatively small 20 years ago, will be massive in 20 years. That makes it an ideal place to sell goods. In essence, China could or more likely will become the United States as far as being the world's market of last resort. For U.S. companies, the opportunities for sales will only rise. That is especially true since the Chinese currency is likely to appreciate versus the dollar, making U.S. goods cheaper in China. The very existence of this market will require the United States to become a major export nation if it is to keep up its growth rate.

Thus, the idea that exports don't matter made sense once upon a time, but as conditions and the context of world economic incomes changed, the whole approach to trade has to change dramatically. The same thing happened with Japan. First, the Japanese competed by exporting cheap products. Then, as incomes rose, they developed a first-class manufacturing sector, followed by a fully developed financial sector. The result was that within 30 years after being defeated in World War II, Japan was once again a major economic force in the world. China only followed that proven blueprint.

Fracking: Controversial but Changing the Future

Van driver Fidel is tanking up a shuttle bus at the Gulf Oil gas station that is in shadow of Newark Airport. All day he will drive from parking lots in Newark to the terminals and back. He worries about traffic, and he worries about the weather. But the one thing he does not need to worry about is the price of gasoline.

That's because his red and white polka-dot-covered bus does not use gasoline. He's filling it up with compressed natural gas (CNG). And while other drivers at the conventional gas pumps are paying $3.53 cents a gallon for regular unleaded that day, his company, Haynes, is paying the equivalent of $2.30 per gallon. "It's way cheaper," he says. "I wish I could use it for my own car."

Why is Fidel's fuel so much cheaper than conventional gasoline? In a word: supply.

In the fall of 2013, one storage field in Pennsylvania had enough natural gas stored up to supply the entire Northeast for six months.[10] So much gas was being produced in places such as West Virginia, Pennsylvania, Texas, Oklahoma, and Louisiana that companies that have large fleets of delivery trucks such as United Parcel Service and Federal Express or shuttle buses like Fidel's were converting them to run on the less expensive and cleaner fuel.

The main reason for the ample supply of natural gas is an extraction technique called hydraulic fracturing, better known as *fracking*. After a well is drilled, the company hoping to produce oil or gas injects fluid—such as water and acids—as well as solids—such as sand—to create tiny fractures in shale formations that contain hydrocarbons. Many groups are opposed to the technique because of environmental concerns. But fracking has become a game changer for the economy.

Larger supplies of natural gas means companies operating in the United States have a reliable, plentiful supply of relatively low cost energy. At the same time, utilities are shifting over from coal and oil to natural gas, a shift that could help consumers with more stable electric bills and potentially clean up power plant emissions. Potentially lower energy bills helps consumers better manage their finances in the future without being worried over the impact of flare-ups in the Middle East.

The shift to natural gas is a trend that is expected to continue for some time because the energy industry is just beginning to tap the resource. The Energy Information Administration (EIA) estimates that daily natural gas production in the United States will grow from 24 trillion cubic feet to 33 trillion cubic feet by 2040, an increase of 37.5 percent. By 2040, shale gas will represent about half of U.S. output.[11]

This shift to shale gas is all relatively recent. In 2004, Range Resources, an energy exploration and development company, drilled a well called Renz 1 in Mt. Pleasant Township, Pennsylvania. Range began testing a hydraulic fracture technique. The initial test was so successful that Range started buying properties for future drilling.[12]

Range had drilled into a huge shale formation that dated back 390 million years. At that time a huge inland sea covered the region. On one side of the sea were tall mountains, which resulted in a lot of run-off of sediment and nutrients pouring into the sea.

"It was semi-isolated, so ultimately there was a deficiency of oxygen in the deeper part of the sea, which was still probably only a couple of hundred meters deep at the most," says geologist and professor of Geosciences Michael Arthur of Penn State University's Marcellus Center. "And the lack of oxygen helped exclude organisms that would have otherwise consumed the organic matter that was produced and raining down. The result was a kind of rich, organic shale that is up to as much 20 percent organic carbon, which is phenomenal," says Arthur, who has spent years studying the origin and nature of "black shales."

The discovery of the Marcellus gas came at just the right time. U.S. natural gas production had been declining, and the United States was using up its reserves. Without shale gas and gas found in tight formations that need stimulation to get it out, the EIA estimates U.S. production of gas would have been about 11 trillion cubic feet of gas per day. As of 2013, the United States was consuming about 25 trillion cubic feet of gas per day.[13]

Production will begin to outstrip demand relatively soon.[14] The growing supply is one of the reasons why the EIA estimates the United States will become a net exporter of natural gas, with most of it going by pipeline to Mexico and Canada. But the United States will also be exporting liquefied natural gas (LNG), with the bulk of it being loaded on tankers and shipped to Europe and Asia.

The United States is not the only place where there are large shale gas and tight gas deposits. They can also be found in Mexico, Argentina, Canada, India, Australia, Russia, and China.[15] But the United States leads the world in fracking technology.

Fracking is also helping the energy industry expand U.S. oil supplies. The EIA estimates that since 2009 domestic production of "tight oil," that is, oil from fields that required some kind of hydraulic fracturing, has grown from 500,000 barrels per day to 2.5 million per day in 2013. The EIA expects production from fields in places such as Texas and North Dakota will continue to grow until 2020 before the fields start to slowly decline, depending on the industry's ability to coax more oil out of the formations.[16]

Can We Squeeze More Out of the Ground?

Obtaining more production from the shale formations is a big question mark.

"Here's the real kicker, the efficiency of the extraction process is really low so we are talking that we might get 10 to 15 percent of what's in the ground," Arthur explains. "It's called technically recoverable reserves." But he says the energy extraction industry has people trying to improve this efficiency. "What if we become really, really good at taking this out of the ground?" he asks. "Let's say we can take three times as much gas out over time. With innovation and all kinds of improvements in 20 years, we could be much more efficient at this."

By way of contrast, in the Permian Basin in Texas, the Texas Railroad Commission, which regulates the state oil and gas industry, estimates the oil industry has recovered almost 30 percent of the 100 billion barrels of oil in the ground there. And the wells are still pumping out the petroleum.[17]

Here's an idea of what greater efficiency might mean for just one giant shale formation—the Marcellus, which sits under West Virginia, Pennsylvania, and New York (which did not allow fracking as of early 2014.)

One of Arthur's colleagues, Terry Engelder, has estimated that the Marcellus formation holds about 500 trillion cubic feet of extractable gas. At current rates of usage, that would supply the entire United States for 20 years. "Something more conservative would be 230 to 250 trillion cubic feet, but it looks to be large, and there is no evidence Terry's estimate is wrong," says Arthur. Even the more conservative estimate would mean the Marcellus could supply the entire United States for 10 years—at the relatively low efficiency rates. If the efficiency increases, add more years to the life of the field.

The availability of significant amounts of natural gas in Texas has attracted the attention of foreign investors, who have announced plans to build new factories and a chemical plant in Corpus Christi.

"The steady, reliable, and reasonable cost of energy is important to them," says John LaRue, the executive director of the Port of Corpus Christi, whom we met in the last chapter. "Plus the access to the U.S. and the NAFTA markets, Mexico and Canada."

According to LaRue, one of the companies is a Chinese steel pipe manufacturer who plans to spend $1.3 billion and will employ 600 to 700 people. Another new company is an Austrian company that will produce high-quality iron briquettes that are used in making steel for the European auto industry. The $750 million investment will employ 250 workers in the first phase. Yet another new investor is a large Italian company that is planning to erect a $1.1 billion polyethylene terephthalate (PET) plant, a base material for plastic that will employ 200 to 250 employees.

Fleet operators, such as the people who own the van operated by Fidel, are also starting to shift to natural gas. According to the *Wall Street Journal*, citing industry projections, about 5 percent of heavy-duty trucks will run on CNG in 2014, up from 1 percent in 2013. As the *Journal* notes, one heavy truck consumes as much fuel as 40 sedans in a year, and such vehicles gobble up 20 percent of U.S. fuel.[18]

The availability of the fuel is also starting to affect the products companies supply to consumers. For example, on July 31, 2013, Ford Motor Company said it would offer buyers of its popular F-150 pickup truck the option of running on compressed natural gas. Shifting to CNG will cost a buyer an additional $7,500 to $9,000, says Ford on its web site. But the company estimates that since CNG sells for at least $1 a gallon less than gasoline, buyers will get a return on their investment in between 24 and 36 months.[19]

According to Ford, the Environmental Protection Agency (EPA) estimates that shifting to CNG cuts greenhouse gas emissions by 30 percent. That prospect appeals to Fidel, the shuttle bus driver. "We have to use conservation if we want to be here for another million years," he says. "This fuel is good if it helps the environment."

However, Arthur is worried because even though the use of the fuel cuts down on greenhouse gas emissions in vehicles, natural gas is still a hydrocarbon. In the fall of 2013, he was working on a paper on the implications of shale gas for carbon dioxide and methane gas concentrations in the atmosphere. "Part of the analysis kind of assumes that if you make this really cheap resource available globally, there will be a disincentive to adopt renewables, which are at least at this point more costly," he says. "And we will have this energy fossil fuel energy economy for a lot longer, and that's going to have even greater repercussions for global warming, for sea level rise, so it could end up costing us dearly in that regard."

The Economics of More Energy

The new dynamics of energy is likely to be one of the biggest game changers for the future economy. Since the oil boycotts in the 1970s, energy supply and the cost of energy have driven everything from economic policy to monetary policy to foreign policy. Securing sources of energy supplies has been a major factor in wars and threats of military intervention. Fears of disruptions have roiled the energy markets and created the concept of "geopolitical risk" that gets priced into energy costs anytime global problems, especially in the Middle East, heat up. That is all changing.

We don't know what the structure of energy usage will look like in 25 years, but one thing we do know: it is not going to be the same. In the 1970s, forecasts were for the world to run out of oil by now. However, technology has revolutionized energy production, especially in the United States.

Since energy costs have driven so much of the economy over the past 50 years, there is little reason to think that they will not do so over the next 50 years. But this time it will be different. Instead of shipping

so much of our income out of the country to pay for foreign products, the money will remain largely in the United States. That will allow for greater domestic purchasing power. Remember, imports are just an out-flow of potential domestic spending, and the less we import (or the more we export), the more money there is for spending in the United States.

The availability and usage of natural gas because of the fracking technology will alter our manufacturing plants, our motor vehicles, and our outlook for inflation. It will also change the way we pay for the repair of roads, which get paid for by taxes on each gallon of fuel we use.

Declining gasoline demand, whether it comes from rising mileage standards, electric vehicles, or the changeover from gasoline to natural gas–fueled vehicles, means the end of the gasoline tax as the primary source of funding road infrastructure. The context in which we pay for our roads has been altered forever, and the charges for usage have to change accordingly. Amazingly, that simple and obvious conclusion has not yet hit the public mind-set. All we know is that there is less and less money for roads.

The likelihood that the United States could become energy inde-pendent has also yet to hit the energy markets. There, daily concerns outweigh long-term thinking. Every time something happens that could potentially affect oil supplies, the price of oil surges. However, except for Iraq's invasion of Kuwait and the aftermath of the first Iraq War, there has been no "crisis" that has led to a significant reduction in supplies. Thus, the whole concept of geopolitical risk makes no sense to energy supply even now. If "crises" don't do anything to supply, markets should price the minimal risk accordingly.

Going forward, geopolitical risk largely disappears from oil pricing. That leads to lower energy prices both from growing supplies and the backing out of the political risk premium. How much is that premium? The estimates vary all over the map, but it doesn't matter. Whether it is $5 per barrel or $25, it will move toward zero and that lowers prices.

Lower energy costs obviously will help the U.S. and world econo mies, not just because demand rises but inflation expectations fall well. People will have more money to spend after they have paid the heating, cooling, and transportation bills. But also, without risks energy supplies and growing availability, energy's impact on inflati will wane.

During the past 25 years, on an annual basis, energy costs have increased by as much as 57 percent and fallen by as much as 38 percent.[20] That volatility has whipsawed the economy, consumers, and businesses, and made planning for the future extremely difficult. It has also made monetary policy decisions more complex. While the Federal Reserve may look at inflation measures that exclude energy, there is also a realization that energy cost increases greatly change consumer spending power. Thus, energy's impact on inflation, both positive and negative, is problematic.

To the extent that the growing supply of more reasonably priced, secure, domestically produced energy will stabilize energy inflation and therefore overall inflation, only good things can come from it. Interest rates, which reflect inflation, will be lower with the expected reduction in energy costs. Consumer spending will be stronger as households have more money to spend on non-energy-related products. Businesses that are energy dependent will be attracted to the lower-cost American economy. And all that adds up to a better economy. Thus, anyone who looks at energy or inflation or interest rates has to look at the changing context of energy production if their business decision is to make any sense.

The Aging of Boomers Will Change the Economy Once Again

All things must pass, and that is the case with Baby Boomers. When they were young, businesses looked at the market for children's clothing, sporting goods, and baby food and salivated. When they became young adults, they drove the sales of jeans, vehicles, and fast food restaurants. When they became middle-aged, they drove the suburbanization of America and altered the landscape of cities and regions. And now, as they are approaching retirement, they are changing the face of demand once again.

That businesses have followed the aging of the Baby Boomers only made total economic sense. They were the bulge in the snake. Feeding the beast, though, is the classic example of businesses designing new and better products and marketing campaigns to account for the changing context of demand.

What does the aging of the Baby Boomers mean? Obviously, it starts with health care. Boomers will require more of it and at a growing pace. They will also be moving onto Medicare, which means they will be spending tax dollars, not just private dollars for health care. The projections of expanding financial strains on the health care system and public finances are a direct result of the growing demand of the elderly Boomers.

But that, too, will change. The greatest challenge facing the United States over the next 50 years is likely to be paying for aging Boomers without bankrupting the economy or, and this is rarely discussed, creating a system that will be overbuilt and excessively costly. Boomers will age and get sick. But they will also eventually pass from the scene.

In 40 years, the youngest Boomers will be 90 years old while the leading-edge Boomers, if they made it that far, will be over 105 years old. Not surprisingly their ranks will be shrinking precipitously. The context in which health care is being provided will be changing rapidly once again. The extensive infrastructure needed to care for the very old will have to be redeployed. That can either be extremely costly or relatively seamless. Managing health care not just for today's demand but for future demand is critical.

But it isn't just all about health care. When Boomers became young adults, they led the trend toward gentrification, which started the revitalization of cities. When they started having children, they led the movement not just to suburban locations but to exurban settings as well. The metropolitan areas were broken wide open.

As Boomers move out of full-time work, their locational decisions will once again change urban form. Baby Boomers are "retiring," maybe not all at once, but at a growing pace. About 10,000 turn 65 every day, and they are looking to throttle back. This group has led the changes in the economy and household location for 60 years, and once again they will create a major rethinking about where people want to live and work.

Boomers are reevaluating what they want most in a housing location. Instead of large homes and suburban lifestyles, they are looking for "high-density, amenity-rich" locations. That usually includes cultural, sports, and entertainment facilities as well as nearby retailers and restaurants.

The impacts of the change in Boomer locations will affect how metropolitan areas evolve and change the growth expectations for states. For most Boomers, the selling of the McMansion brings them to the same location decision that businesses face: Do they stay in place or do they move to a different setting? If they move, do they stay in the region or do they go somewhere else.

The "Greatest Generation," those who fought in World War II and the Korean War, looked to the South and then the Southwest. Sun and fun was the calling card, and places such as Florida and Arizona saw their populations soar. But the idea that all you need is warm weather to attract retirees is being retired. Boomers need more.

Over the next 25 years, Baby Boomers and other retirees will have a variety of choices. Central cities that have all the amenities that the new generation of retirees is looking for will become magnets for growth. As the cities grow, businesses that service this newly growing portion of the population will expand as well. Just as the outflow of households led to an outward migration of companies from the cities to the suburbs, a return to downtown will create a similar inflow of firms that see this group as their prime market.

Thus, within metropolitan areas, there will be a rising supply of suburban housing as Boomers sell their homes, coupled with a rising demand for areas within cities and near other places such as universities, that also support a large number of desired amenities. That will mean a massive change in housing construction, and home prices will rise and fall according to the changes in where people want to live.

But the impacts are not just within regions. While some retirees will want to reside relatively near where they had been living, especially if they continue to work in a scaled-down manner, others will still follow the sun. But while 20 years ago you could put up a retiree community in Florida and sell out quickly, going forward, a home and a golf course just will not cut it.

For many retirees looking for those places where they can do lots of things, smaller residences in their home communities as well as warmer locations will likely be how they decide to spend their "golden years." Multifamily dwellings rather than single-family homes may be the residences of choice. Those warmer places will also have to contain the same types of amenities that the home communities offer. Thus, cities

About the Authors

Joel L. Naroff is the president and founder of Naroff Economic Advisors, a strategic economic consulting firm. He advises companies across the country on the risks and opportunities that economic developments may have on the organization's operating environment. Joel has been the chief economist for a number of large financial institutions, and prior to moving into banking, he was a tenured professor in the Isenberg School of Management at the University of Massachusetts at Amherst. Joel received bachelors' degrees in economics and chemistry from Stony Brook University and a Ph.D. in economics from Brown University.

An accomplished public speaker, Joel's humor and unique ability to make economics understandable have brought him a wide following. His presentations on national, international, regional, and industry topics show how evolving economic trends can impact businesses, governments, educational institutions, and not-for-profits. It was from these speeches that the book was born.

A nationally recognized economic forecasting expert, Joel has received numerous honors, including the Lawrence Klein Award for Blue Chip forecasting excellence. He has twice received the National

Association for Business Economics Outlook Award as the top economic forecaster as well as the Bloomberg Business News top economic forecaster award. He is often quoted in the national press, appears frequently on television, writes a column called "Random Economics" for *The Philadelphia Inquirer*, and does business commentary for KYW Newsradio in Philadelphia.

Since all work and no play makes economists even more boring, Joel spends his spare time at his second home in Margate, New Jersey, where he rides his bike as much as possible. He is married to Cindy, an English teacher, and has one son, Adam, who is a music teacher.

Ron Scherer is a veteran journalist who lives and works in New York City. His distinctive writing style has appeared on the pages of *The Christian Science Monitor* for 37 years. He has written major series for the *Monitor*, covered breaking news such as 9/11, and written about the economy on a daily basis.

A graduate of Principia College in Elsah, Illinois, Ron has worked for United Press International and *U.S. News & World Report*, where he led the New York bureau.

The bulk of his journalistic endeavors have been at the *Monitor*, where he worked on the financial pages and covered economic policy in the Reagan White House. In Washington, Ron's horizons broadened beyond business and finance to trade, energy, the budget, and taxes. After four years, Ron moved to Sydney, Australia, to cover the South Pacific region.

After moving back to New York, Ron has focused on breaking news for the *Monitor*'s online publication and longer trend pieces for *The Christian Science Monitor Weekly*, such as the 2013 cover story, "Ride On!" about the surge in cycling in American cities. After 37 years at the *Monitor*, he retired in July 2013.

Ron has written freelance articles for *Global Finance* magazine and *New York* magazine. He has appeared as a guest host on *CNN Financial* and has been interviewed by radio stations around the nation.

Ron, an avid sailor, can be found on Long Island Sound in the summer trimming the sails on *SeaKap*, while his wife, Kathy Simmons, pilots the yacht.

Index